WOMEN
AGAINST HITLER

WOMEN AGAINST HITLER

Christian Resistance
in the Third Reich

Theodore N. Thomas

PRAEGER

Westport, Connecticut
London

Library of Congress Cataloging-in-Publication Data

Thomas, Theodore N.
    Women against Hitler : Christian resistance in the Third Reich /
Theodore N. Thomas.
        p. cm.
    Includes bibliographical references and index.
    ISBN 0–275–94619–3 (alk. paper)
    1. Protestant women—Germany—History—20th century.
2. Bekennende Kirche—History. 3. Church and state—Germany—
History—1933–1945. 4. Germany—Church history—1933–1945.
5. Persecution—Germany—History—20th century. 6. Church and
state—Bekennende Kirche—History. I. Title.
BX4844.55.A4T46   1995
280′.4′094309043—dc20   94–8564

British Library Cataloguing in Publication Data is available.

Library of Congress Catalog Card Number: 94–8564
ISBN: 0–275–94619–3

First published in 1995

Praeger Publishers, 88 Post Road West, Westport, CT 06881
An imprint of Greenwood Publishing Group, Inc.

Printed in the United States of America

The paper used in this book complies with the
Permanent Paper Standard issued by the National
Information Standards Organization (Z39.48–1984).

10 9 8 7 6 5 4 3 2 1

For Jane-Anne

Contents

A photographic essay follows chapter 3

Illustrations

PHOTOGRAPHS

Pastors, Wives, and Families:

Ruth Bockemühl and her husband, Pastor Peter Bockemühl
Pastor Peter and Ruth Bockemühl and sons

Theologinnen:

Acknowledgments

I gratefully acknowledge unpayable debts of gratitude to a number of people who contributed substantially to letting the world know about the contributions of women to the Protestant Church Struggle of 1934-1945.

Chief among them is Pastorin Ilse Härter of Goch, Germany, whose name features prominently in this book. Pastorin Härter was a participant in the Church Struggle, and she has contributed substantially to helping scholars write an objective history. In addition to providing primary documents and the published and still-unpublished results of her many years of research, she has, since 1989, been a faithful correspondent who has encouraged, corrected, and challenged some of my positions.

Pastorin Leni Immer of Wuppertal was one of my first contacts with an eyewitness of the roles that women played in the Church Struggle. More than once she has proved herself a gracious hostess, tour guide, and intermediary for interviews that would otherwise have been impossible.

Frau Dr. Rita Scheller's invitation to participate in the Convention of Protestant Churches of Pomerania in February 1990 allowed me to meet several eyewitnesses who have subsequently written and provided valuable information. Dr. Scheller has continued to keep me appraised of newly emerging auto-biographical material.

While plundering archives and interviewing eyewitnesses in Germany, I enjoyed reunions with old friends who hospitably provided lodging and other kindnesses. Among them were Andreas and Janet Reinhardt in Berlin; Christian and Danielle Reinhardt in Ahlten; Craig and Margaret Farmer in Augsburg; Käthe and Reinhold Haag in Frankfurt am Main; Maria Illing in Heidelberg; Barbara and Dale Mallory in Berlin; Frau Irmgard Reger in Lorch (Wurttemberg); Bill and Deanna Wilson and their family in Köln; and Pastor Egbert Zieger and Frau Gerda Zieger in Winsen/Aller. I also enjoyed shorter but equally gracious visits (and meals) with Pfarrer Ulrich Wolf-Barnett and his wife Victoria Wolf-Barnett in Bielefeld; Frau Ruth Bockemühl in Wuppertal;

Oberkirchenrat Alfred Fendler and Lieselotte Fendler in Oldenburg; Pastorin Ilse Härter and her sister Edith Feldmann in Goch; Lydia Heiermann in Wuppertal; Pastorin Leni Immer in Wuppertal; Ingeborg von Mackensen in Iserlohn; Dr. Ilse Meseberg-Haubold and her family in Oldenburg; Dora von Öttingen in Frankfurt; Louise Tecklenburg in Berlin; Felicitas Vedder in Oldenburg; Evamarie Vorster and her family in Liederbach; and Pastor Martin Wistinghausen and his wife in Hildesheim.

I was repeatedly amazed and thankful for the scope of gracious help that research librarians in the United States and Germany knew how to extend. This includes the staff at the Library of Congress in Washington, D.C.; the staff at the Kartäuser Church Library in Köln; and the archivists in the German church archives: Drs. Michael Wischnath and Christa Stache of the Evangelisches Zentralarchiv in Berlin; Dr. Bernd Hey in Bielefeld; Frau Elisabeth Gradl of the Evangelische Frauenhilfe im Rheinland, e.V. in Bonn; Pastor Alexander Semmelrock in Darmstadt; Dr. Dietrich Meyer in Düsseldorf; Dr. Hans Otte in Hannover; Frau Stadtkirchenbuchführerin F. Ebeling in Hildesheim; Dr. Christine Peter in Heidelberg/Wieblingen; and Dr. Hermann Ehmer in Stuttgart.

Good friends and colleagues have made helpful contributions in reading and rereading the text: Dennis Grow, Gay Gullickson, James Harris, Katharina von Kellenbach, Patrick Kelley, George Kent, Michael Phayer, Alan Philips, Gary Selby, Michael Sheridan, Mary Sheridan, Martha Solomon, and Earle West.

The Silver Spring Church of Christ in Silver Spring, Maryland, granted a six-week sabbatical for a study trip in 1990; moreover, research among eyewitnesses in Germany was only possible with the help of the Hearst Award from the History Department of the University of Maryland and generous grants from Walter and Juanita Strosnider.

Jane-Anne, Todd, and Terry offered years of encouragement, kind curiosity, and patient understanding. Suffering frequent and extended impositions because of this project, they lived with me and loved me through it—thanks to my wonderful wife and two fine young adult sons.

Glossary

Abitur—A school-leaving certificate awarded to students who have prepared for university study.

ADFV—Allgemeiner Deutscher Frauenverein, General German Women's Association.

ADLV—Allgemeiner Deutscher Lehrerinnenverein, General German Female Teachers' Association.

APU—Altpreussische Union, The Old Prussian Union.

Ariernachweis—Statement attesting to one's Aryan purity.

BDFV—Bund Deutscher Frauenvereine, Union of German Women's Clubs.

BDM—Bund Deutscher Mädel, League of German Maidens, the female branch of the Hitler Youth.

BK—Bekennende Kirche, the Confessing Church.

BRD—Bundesrepublik Deutschland, "West Germany" between 1945 and 1990.

Bruderrat—Council of Brethren, an administrative, policy-making, and advisory unit of the Confessing Church.

Cuius regio eius religio—The formula proceeding from the Peace of Augsburg (1555): "The religion of a region is to be that of its ruler."

DC—Deutsche Christen, "German Christians." The words, always given in quotation marks here, do not refer to "Christians in Germany" but to a theopolitical party whose aim was to wed Christianity and German nationalism in the Nazi mold.

DDR—Deutsche Demokratische Republik, "East Germany" between 1945 and 1990.

DEFB—Deutsch-Evangelischer Frauenbund, German Protestant Women's Union.

EKD—Evangelische Kirche in Deutschland, the Protestant Church in Germany, which was organized and named in 1945.

Evangelischer Kirchenbund—The Protestant Church League.

Frauenschaft—The Nazi party women's organization.

Führerprinzip—The Nazi "Leadership Principle," which maintained that efficient administration results from the authority of every leader extending downward and unquestioning obedience from every subordinate moving upward.

Gemeindehelferin—Female parish assistant, equivalent to Pfarrgehilfin.

Gestapo—An abbreviation of Geheime Staatspolizei, the Nazi secret state police.

Gleichschaltung, gleichgeschaltet—"Coordination," meaning the co-option of social institutions by the Nazi party, whereby every social organization had to have a Nazi party member as its head; also variously translated as "assimilation," and "synchronization."

Gutachten—An expert's written judgment on a given issue.

JRB—Jungreformatorische Bewegung, The Young Reformers' Movement, a church-political party formed during the Church election campaigns of the summer of 1933. The JRB opposed the candidacies supported by the "German Christian" party.

KA—Kirchenausschuss, the "Church Committee" established by Hans Kerrl, headed by Wilhelm Zoellner.

Kirchenkampf—The Church Struggle.

Landeskirche—The established Protestant Church within each state of Germany. The combined Landeskirchen (plural) constituted the German Protestant Church.

See Table 1.1 and Map 1.1.

Lic.—A theological degree, licentiate in theology, which is equivalent to a doctorate.

Mittlere Reife—A school certificate awarded after approximately ten years of public education.

NSDAP—Nazionalsozialistische Deutsche Arbeiter Partei, the National Socialist German Workers party, or the Nazi party.

Ortsgruppenleiter—The Nazi party member in charge of coordinating the activities of all Party groups within a municipality.

Pastor, Pfarrer—a roughly equivalent term for the English "pastor." In some Landeskirchen, a distinction is made between a Pastor, who is simply an ordained clergyman, and a Pfarrer, an ordained clergyman who works with a parish.

Pastorin, Pfarrerin—Feminine forms of Pastor and Pfarrer.

Pfarrfrau—A pastor's wife.

Pfarrgehilfin—A female parish assistant, equivalent to Gemeindehelferin.

PNB—Pfarrernotbund, Pastors' Emergency League.

Präses—The presiding officer of a synod in the Reformed and Union churches.

Reichbruderrat—The Reich Council of Brethren, the highest council of leader-advisers of the Confessing Church.

RM—Reichmark, the basic unit of currency in the Third Reich.

SA—Sturm-Abteilung, or Storm Troops, the paramilitary force that served as the enforcer of Nazi party policies.

Sippenhaft—Literally, "tribe-custody"; the Gestapo practice of arresting the kin of primary suspects.

SPD—Sozial-Demokratische Partei Deutschlands, the Social Democratic party of Germany.

SS—Schutzstaffel, or Security Staff, a military corps d'elite of the Nazis, which was sworn to absolute obedience and personal allegiance to Adolf Hitler (an allegiance that was independent of the usual military chain of command).

Superintendent—An ecclesiastical title; a pastor who has oversight of other pastors of other churches in his diocese.

Theologe, Theologin—Male theologian, female theologian.

VETD—Verband Evangelischer Theologinnen Deutschlands, the Union of Protestant Female Theologians of Germany.

Vikar—A male theologian with a university degree who is in a two-year program of practical training under an ordained pastor. Typically, a Vikar's two years would end with the "Second Theological Examination," leading to ordination.

Vikarin—The word is the feminine form of Vikar, but the expectations and opportunities were different for women. A female theologian took this title after university graduation when she trained under an experienced pastor; until 1943 a Vikarin could not expect full ordination. Even when the German Protestant churches began to ordain women, Vikarin remained the woman's title until 1963, when the Landeskirchen began to award the titles Pfarrerin or Pastorin.

VKL—Vorläufige Kirchenleitung, or Provisional Church Administration, the leadership of the Confessing Church.

Volk—The people; specifically, in the Third Reich, the German people.

Völkisch—Literally, the word means "folk-ish," or having to do with the people (das Volk); however, völkisch carried a specific connotation during the Third Reich, when it denoted racist pride of things German—as opposed to things Jewish, Polish, Gypsy, or other nationalities.

Three Stories: A Narrative Introduction to the Church Struggle

FELICITAS VEDDER

On Saturday morning, 24 February 1934, Gestapo agents from Belgard appeared at Pastor Martin Vedder's parsonage door in Gross Poplow, Pomerania, with a document for the pastor to sign. It was a statement whereby he would agree not to read a certain pulpit declaration that was circulating among dissident Protestant congregations throughout Germany. The pulpit declaration, which had originated in the far-off Rhineland and had by now made its way across Germany to Pomerania, urged pastors and church elders to disobey conscientiously any directives from the newly re-organized German Protestant Church, which was headed by Nazi Reich-Bishop Ludwig Müller.[1] Vedder and thousands of other pastors like him had branded the official leaders of the German Protestant Church as heretics.

"We trust, Herr Pastor," the Gestapo agents said, "that you will give us as little trouble as your colleagues, all of whom have already signed this statement."[2] Pastor Vedder demurred, insisting that such a decision was not his alone to make, and that he would have to confer with the elders of his church. He personally doubted that the other pastors in his region had already signed, and the police naturally showed him no evidence. The agents promised that at eight o'clock the following morning, Sunday, they would return for his signature. They then disconnected the pastor's telephone so that he could not confer with colleagues elsewhere.

As Pastor Vedder continued to work on his sermon and the choir gathered at the parsonage for a last rehearsal, the local chief of police, himself a member of Pastor Vedder's congregation, called on the pastor's wife, Felicitas Vedder, to ask whether she could please persuade her husband to sign the document. What, asked the police chief, would become of her and their one-year-old Lieselotte if something should happen to the pastor? "This friendly and concerned approach was far more difficult to withstand," confessed Felicitas Vedder later, "than the threats from the policemen from out of town."

When Pastor Vedder conferred with his board of elders, they adamantly agreed that the Church must not bow to the state's dictates, and so, when the police arrived the next morning, he refused to sign their document. One officer placed the pastor under house arrest and remained with him in the parsonage, while the other took up his post at the front door of the Gross Poplow church.

About twenty minutes before the Sunday service was to begin, an automobile pulled up to the parsonage. A young Vikar, who had been endorsed by Church headquarters in Belgard, announced that he was there to conduct the church services (naturally with no intention of reading the pulpit declaration). Frau Vedder ran immediately to the local tavern, where the town's leading citizens, who were aware of what had happened the previous day, were waiting. When she reported what was transpiring, a small crowd of church members, who were somewhat anxious about the posted policeman on guard, streamed into the church, which was soon filled beyond capacity. The congregational elders told the Vikar that the congregation did not need his services. An elder would lead the worship that Sunday. So, while the worship service got underway in Gross Poplow, Felicitas Vedder traveled to the neighboring town of Kollatz, where she arranged for a similar service to be held there in the pastor's absence. The Gross Poplow parsonage remained under police quarantine until Tuesday, when the Gestapo withdrew its officers. Pastor Martin Vedder soon learned that he had not stood alone. Throughout Germany, so many pastors had refused to sign the document that the government feared a popular uprising if it imprisoned them all.[3]

For Felicitas Vedder, that February weekend in 1934 was the beginning of what would later be known as the "Church Struggle." From 1934 through 1945, her husband's churches in Gross Poplow, Kollatz, and the surrounding villages identified themselves with other congregations throughout Germany as the "Confessing Church," a Christian body which insisted that not even Hitler's totalitarian state had the right to dictate what the Church could and could not preach. The Church Struggle became Felicitas Vedder's own, intensified personal battle when, in August 1939, the government drafted her husband into military service, a Nazi ploy that was intended to eliminate the leadership of the Confessing Church. When the army reported Pastor Vedder as missing in action in Crimea in 1944, his widow stepped into his place to minister to the Gross Poplow churches. There she preached, buried, married, taught, consoled, healed, inspired, protected, and led her people so well that the Polish authorities who annexed Pomerania at the end of the war feared her influence. They arrested her, separated her from her two children, and kept her in a Belgard prison until shortly before Christmas of 1945.

So it was that in extreme northeastern Germany, from a post-war orphanage on an island in the Baltic Sea, twelve-year-old Lieselotte Vedder put pencil to paper:

In Camp, 26 November 1945

Dearest Aunties:

I must write the sad news that on November 9, as we have heard, our dear, dear Mommy was dragged away by the Polish police, taken to Polzin, and later to Belgard. . . .

Early on November 9 at 8:00 we were dressed and had breakfasted when the Polish mayor swept us out of the room. We were not allowed to take anything with us, only what we were wearing. Then he ordered Mommy to stay at Aunt Schwante's until the official from Jagertow came. Sure enough, in the afternoon a car full of Polish policemen inspected all our things, gave us bedding with pillows, and then closed and locked the door, taking Mommy away with them. We stayed a few days with Aunt Schwante. Then one night the mayor came and drove nearly the whole village out. In Polzin we all had to undress down to our underwear, laying out matches, money, gloves, gold, photographs and letters. Then we got on a train. We rode until we came to where some barns were, where it was so terrible, I can't describe it.

Dear Aunties, write and tell us what we should do! We have enough to eat, but what about school? If we are supposed to be with you, then come get us.

We greet you heartily:

Your Lieselotte and Hellmut[4]

The story does have a happy ending, however. Released from the Belgard jail, Frau Vedder made her way by foot and streetcar (and even with the aid of some drunken Russian truck drivers) to Potsdam, where her sister worked in a home for the elderly. When both her sisters reported that they had heard nothing from or about the children, she collapsed. Two days later, however, Lieselotte's letter arrived. With renewed strength, Felicitas Vedder made her way to the orphans' camp on Rügen and brought the children back to Potsdam in time for a Christmas celebration. Out of the scraps of what was left of their bombed and burned city, the aged residents of the home, who eagerly anticipated the children's arrival, scraped together a Christmas tree complete with candles and crèche, a doll with a wardrobe for Lieselotte, and a pair of boxing gloves for Hellmut.[5]

TABEA IMMER

The familiar car with the uniformed policemen pulls up in front of the home of Karl and Tabea Immer as it has done several times before.[6] As has become almost customary since September 1933, Pastor Immer calls to his family: "Children, these men are here to do their duty. You must be as friendly to them as you can be. And helpful." With that, the pastor opens the door to the parsonage so that the police of Barmen, a Wuppertal suburb in Germany's Rhineland, can enter the home and search it.

"Guten Tag, Herr Pfarrer," an officer greets the pastor. "Guten Tag," Pastor Immer returns, calling each official by name. He knows them and their families from their attendance at his Reformed Church in the Gemarke neighborhood. His children play with and go to school with their children. The officers and the pastor understand that orders are orders and that, embarrassed as they are, the police are there to carry out their assignment: to search the parsonage for any evidence of the Church's criticisms of Adolf Hitler's Third Reich.

The children hop to their assignments. The eldest, eighteen-year-old Leni, opens drawers for inspection. Karl Jr. points out file cabinets. Waltraut pulls away cushions from chairs, and Alida, Friederike, Adalbert, and even seven-year-old Udo help in similar ways.

On the occasion of one of these first house searches, after the police had looked in vain in every imaginable corner and nook, the officer in charge approached Pastor Immer: "Herr Pastor, could you please just give us something that would not be too dangerous for you, so that we don't go back to headquarters empty-handed?" In response to such a request, the good pastor, with a smile and a willing nod, pulled a church bulletin out of a file and handed it to the officer. The absence of a government swastika stamp made it technically illegal, but its contents would prove otherwise relatively harmless.

Thus rewarded for both their industry and friendliness, the officers drive back to headquarters in Wuppertal, while the Immer family breathes a collective sigh of relief. However, their relief does not last long. There will be further visits from the police, and with the passage of time, the home town policemen will be replaced by officers from further corners of Germany who, being neither familiar nor friendly, will be unwilling to accommodate the pastor of Barmen-Gemarke. In fact, from 1933 to 1945 the German government regarded Karl and Tabea Immer and the circle of Christians around them as traitorous subversives.

What was their offense? Often in the evenings in the attic of the Immer parsonage, members of the Barmen-Gemarke church would join the family to mimeograph the newsletter of the Coetus of Reformed Preachers, a club that Pfarrer Immer had established in the autumn of 1933.[7] The Coetus stood in opposition to the official, government-sanctioned leadership of the Protestant Church of the Rhineland, which had fallen into the hands of a theopolitical party known as the "German Christians": it was nationalistic, anti-Semitic, and intimately affiliated with the Nazi Party.[8] Pastor Immer's closest associates, including his wife and children, worked on an antiquated mimeograph machine to print the periodical. Then the children joined the adults in a risky game of hide and seek to distribute the journal. They slipped the periodicals into envelopes that Pastor Immer had imprinted with a logo of a jumping deer so that the mailing would appear to be from a rod and gun club. The stuffed and sealed envelopes then had to be mailed. To confound the postal authorities, who cooperated with the Gestapo in seeking out such subversive activity, the conspirators dared not put more than two envelopes in any single mailbox. Instead, they hiked from street corner to street corner throughout the city, and, as time wore on and the game became even more dangerous, they freighted the Coetus letters out of Wuppertal in trucks and tossed them into mailboxes in other towns.

By June 1934, the Coetus pastors and tens of thousands of active lay people in churches throughout the Rhineland were literally card-carrying members of a new church, the "Confessing Church," which openly opposed the ecclesiastical policies of the government of the Third Reich. The Confessing Church, which was created during a conference in Pastor Immer's Barmen-Gemarke sanctuary in May 1934, denied the legitimacy of the official Protestant Church, whose supreme Reich-Bishop was a hand-picked Nazi sycophant of Adolf Hitler and a pawn of the "German Christians."

With the passage of time, the Immer family's dangerous activities escalated. Tabea Immer poured endless cups of coffee and spread uncountable sandwiches for a stream of visitors who conferred—and conspired—with her husband: Karl Barth, Martin Niemöller, Martin Albertz and Hans Asmussen among them. Tabea Immer harbored a non-Aryan child in her home who was termed a nephew, protecting him throughout the Nazi reign of terror. Moreover, the Immers cooperated in illegally collecting money to support the widow and orphans of Pastor Paul Schneider, whom the Nazis murdered in Buchenwald. During one Gestapo search of their home, Tabea Immer's heart raced anxiously as a Gestapo agent fanned through the pages of the bank book in which the transactions for the purchase of a home for the Schneider family were recorded. When the family resolved not to participate in the rigged elections of 1936, Hitler Youth broke all the windows in the parsonage and painted "Here lives Immer, traitor to the people!" on the side of the house. Pastor Immer walked to the cemetery for a funeral the next Monday morning to the shouts of "Judas!" Arrests followed. Pastor Karl Immer went to jail in August 1937, where he suffered a stroke from which he never recovered.[9]

EMMI HOF

South of the Rhineland city where the Immers lived, in Weidelbach, Nassau, lived young Emmi Hof.[10] Emmi's father, Wilhelm Hof, the mayor of Weidelbach, supported his family with a general store that supplied the town with everything from pencils to herring. Wilhelm Hof was among the relatively few Germans who actually read Hitler's *Mein Kampf* when it appeared. "Now, I've just got to read this to you!" he would call to his wife and children with alarm when he found especially disturbing passages. Few other families were as well prepared for the coming of the Third Reich and its persecution of Christianity as the Hofs.

Emmi Hof grew up in a religiously active family. When the Nazi-supported "German Christians" threatened to take over the German Protestant Church of Nassau, the Hof family took its stand. They were among the first members of the opposition Confessing Church. Although Emmi's two brothers joined the Hitler Youth for a while, she and her two sisters stayed out of the girls' equivalent, the Union of German Maidens *(BDM)*.[11] Instead, Emmi organized and maintained a separate Protestant girls club, which defiantly continued to wear its illegal green uniforms. One day while leaving the church, the girls met a gang of Hitler Youth who attacked them with catcalls of *"Kreuzotter!"* and hurled stones and manure balls at them.[12] The local leader of the Hitler Youth addressed an official letter to Emmi Hof on 7 September 1934:

> On Monday evening at 7:30 in the school building there will be a discussion on the subject: "Protestant Youth Groups and the Hitler Youth." All members of the Protestant Youth Group under eighteen years of age, together with their leaders, are required to attend. Should I determine that you people did not attend, I will find myself forced to deal with you by other means. As you are well aware, certain events have transpired recently that simply will not be countenanced any more. . . .
>
> Heil Hitler
> G.S.
> Local Leader of the Hitler Youth[13]

Such measures did not dissuade Emmi Hof. She persisted in her Protestant Youth group and spent six months in the Immers' home in Wuppertal, where she was intimately involved in all of that family's clandestine activities on behalf of the Confessing movement. In 1938 she fell in love with Theo Groh, a young, not-yet-ordained, Confessing preacher. When in September 1939 Theo Groh received a call to work with a confessing congregation in Biedenkopf, the couple announced their engagement. While they were looking for an apartment in Biedenkopf, the draft called Groh into military service, so Emmi Hof and Theo Groh married immediately, four days before the groom had to move into military barracks. In October the Gestapo arrested Groh and questioned him about his activities in the Confessing Church, but they released him soon afterwards with no consequences. Emmi and Theo Groh were united briefly for a Christmas vacation in Munich in 1939, and again just before Easter 1940. Emmi wrote, "On April 1, 1940 I travelled to Berlin. We never saw each other again, as he died on June 6, 1940 near Amiens, France."[14]

RESISTANCE, PERSECUTION, AND EMERGENCE

Aging German Protestants can tell thousands of stories like these three: stories about how adults and children living in the period of 1933-1945 experienced Adolf Hitler's persecution of their faith and their churches. What follows here is an introduction to the "German Church Struggle" and four chapters that offer an expanded treatment of women who were involved in it. Although many books tell the story of the Church Struggle in great detail, most suffer from a major omission: they fail to recognize that women as well as men were involved in the Protestant Church's resistance to Nazism.[15]

The women we meet in the following pages participated in the Protestant Church's dissent against Hitler's ecclesiastical policies. They resisted the *Führer*'s attempts to take over the churches, his ultimate goal being the eradication of Christianity in Germany. Because of their involvement in the resistance, the women suffered with their church in the persecution; but by a delicious irony, the very Nazi misogyny and persecution which would have discouraged professional development for Christian women unwittingly contributed to the emergence of women as recognized, official leaders within the Protestant Church.

Resistance, persecution, and emergence—the story of women against Hitler in the German Protestant Church.

NOTES

1. The Free Evangelical Synod of the Rhineland had originally issued the statement. See Paul F. Douglas, *God among the Germans* (Philadelphia: University of Pennsylvania Press, 1935), p. 240.

2. The quotation and details of the event are from Felicitas Vedder, "Der Sonntag Reminiscere 1935" (unpublished, undated) in the author's files; and from an interview with Frau Felicitas Vedder, Oldenburg, 27-28 January 1990.

3. This would have followed on the heels of the unpopular arrest of hundreds of Confessing Church pastors the previous month. See chapter 1.

4. A copy of the letter, supplied by Felicitas Vedder, is in the author's files.

5. Felicitas Vedder, "Begegnung in Potsdam," *Die Schwester* (Oldenburg: Elisabethstift), Freundesbrief 4 (Weihnachten 1989); 7-8.

6. The account here is from Leni Immer's "Ein Pfarrhaus im Kirchenkampf," written and published in mimeographed format by the eldest daughter of Karl and Tabea Immer.

7. Coetus is Latin for assembly, club, or union.

8. The term "German Christans" appears here consistently in quotation marks. These individuals were Germans, but Immer and thousands of his pastor-colleagues denied that they were Christians.

9. For more on Karl Immer, see Bertold Klappert and Günther van Norden,

eds., *Tut um Gottes willen etwas Tapferes! Karl Immer im Kirchenkampf* (Neukirchen-Vluyn: Neukirchener Verlag, 1989).

10. The narrative on the Hof family is taken from the interview with Frau Emmi Blöcher (née Hof) at her home in Sinn-Dill on 19 February 1990, and from her subsequent correspondence with the author.

11. This was the Bund Deutscher Mädel or BDM.

12. A fair translation of *"Kreuzotter"* would be simply "vipers," but the literal translation, "cross adders," was a blasphemous reference to the girls' religious orientation.

13. From the letter supplied by Emmi Blöcher, a copy of which is in the author's files.

14. Blöcher interviews.

15. Four major works in English provide detailed accounts of the Church Struggle: Victoria Barnett, *For the Soul of the People* (New York: Oxford University Press, 1992), which does indeed report on Protestant women; John Conway, *The Nazi Persecution of the Churches 1933-1945* (New York: Basic Books, 1968); Ernst Christian Helmreich, *The German Churches under Hitler—Background, Struggle and Epilogue* (Detroit, Mich.: Wayne State University Press, 1979); and Klaus Scholder, *The Churches and the Third Reich*, Volume 1, 1918-1934; Volume 2, The Year of Disillusionment, 1934 (Philadelphia: Fortress Press, 1988). The two volumes cover background up to 1934. Conway, Helmreich, and Scholder deal with both the Catholic and the Protestant churches, while Barnett limits herself to the Protestant Church Struggle.

Chapter 1

The Church Struggle in Nazi Germany

The Protestants haven't the faintest conception of a church. You can do anything you like to them. They will submit.

—Adolf Hitler[1]

The Confessing Church was the only social institution in the Third Reich that successfully resisted domination by the Nazis. The Nazi goal was to control the activities of every club, union, school, professional association, institution, university, and church so that the entire social infrastructure of the country would function in synergy with the National Socialist machine; however, the Confessing Church successfully escaped *Gleichschaltung*, refusing to be co-opted. The Confessing Church survived the Nazi years.[2] While individual scientists, professors, physicians, and lawyers did indeed protest against Nazism's crimes, the professional organizations—the universities, the bar association, and the medical association—became cogs in the Nazi machinery. Most religious organizations fared even less well. The efficient state police dissolved numerous churches, sects, and faith fellowships so that they could neither mount nor maintain any opposition to Nazism.[3] The Confessing Church was the exception, as it generated organized opposition to the attempts of the Nazi government to exercise total control over Protestantism.

THE WAR AGAINST PROTESTANTISM

The Confessing Church formed in Germany in 1934 to oppose Adolf Hitler's designs to eradicate Christianity and the churches. Hitler, who was convinced that the Roman Catholic Church was too strong for him to change immediately, arranged instead for a concordat with Rome on 20 July 1933 by which the government of Germany agreed not to interfere with Rome's spiritual concerns if the Church, in turn, would respect Berlin's hegemony in the secular sphere.[4]

Hitler's respect for Protestantism was not nearly as profound. "[Protestants] have neither a religion that they can take seriously nor a great position to defend like Rome," he commented early in 1933.[5] He saw there a weak, divided institution that he believed he could dominate, change, and ultimately, eradicate. The chancellor and his party envisioned that after a victorious war, the German state would replace Christianity itself—the Protestant as well as the Catholic faiths—with a *völkisch* religion that worshipped the elements of Germanism: Blood, Soil, and the State.[6]

Hitler's anti-Christian bias was not at all evident to his early supporters. Indeed, the Protestant clergy as a class was solidly behind the man who promised to restore law and order, employment, and German national pride. Hitler pleased them when, in his speeches, he asked for God's blessings on his administration.[7] When he denounced "godless Bolshevism," should not every Christian have taken heart? When he said, "God created me a German[;] Germanism is a gift of God," who could have thought that he meant anything other than the God in whom Christians believed?[8] Hitler's National Socialist German Worker's Party was, after all, the party that explicitly pledged in 1928 to uphold a "positive Christianity." The words were there to read in the party platform:

> We demand the freedom of all religious confessions in the state, insofar as they do not jeopardize its existence or conflict with the manners and moral sentiments of the Germanic race. The party as such upholds the point of view of a positive Christianity without tying itself confessionally to any one confession.[9]

The Nazi party was the only one to make such an explicit claim of alliance with Christian faith, an alliance restated in Hitler's speech before the Reichstag, the German parliament, on 23 March 1933:

> The National Government sees in [Protestantism and Catholicism] most vital factors in the survival of our nationality. Their rights will not be touched. The National Government will accord and secure to the Christian Confessions the influence that is due them in schools and education.[10]

Privately, Hitler was a different man with a different faith. Claiming himself to be "heathen to the core," he maintained that it was impossible to be simultaneously a German and a Christian. "One cannot be both."[11] He regarded Christianity as a form of Bolshevism, a Jewish peril that was Germany's historic duty and destiny to destroy.[12] Although Hitler made no public statements to this effect, within his first year as chancellor he and his party made three major declarations of war against the Protestant Church: the law of 7 April 1933, the promotion of a Nazi bishop to oversee the German Protestant Church, and the appointment of Alfred Rosenberg as chief Nazi Party ideologist. The result of these measures was the Church Struggle, a contest that from 1933 until the fall of Nazism in 1945, pitted Adolf Hitler, his party, and the "German Christians" (DC), on one side, against a small, partly illegal, body known as the Confessing Church (BK), on the other.

THE ARYAN PARAGRAPH

In the first attack on Protestantism, on 7 April 1933, the government issued the "Law for the Restoration of the Professional Bureaucracy," legislation that demanded the retirement of German bureaucrats who were not of certifiable Aryan heritage. The law defined as bureaucrats officials of all bodies recognized by public law, a legal concept that included Protestant pastors. Paragraph 4 of the law demanded the retirement of any bureaucrat—and hence any pastor—who could not prove his unconditional support of the Nazi state. Specifically, the law threatened the positions of those Protestant pastors who had one Jewish grandparent or were married to Jewish women.[13] In all, this affected only a handful of men. Of the approximately 18,000 Protestant pastors in Germany in 1933, thirty-seven were non-Aryans. Of these few, eight were already retired and another eleven who had been in pastoral service before 1 August 1914, were exempt from the law.[14] Thus, the "Aryan Paragraph" would have forced eighteen men into retirement, a negligible manpower loss for the Church but a tremendous violation of the Church's independence. The secular government was assuming the power to decide who might and who might not be shepherds of the Church's flocks.

CHURCH ELECTIONS AND "GERMAN CHRISTIANS"

The second Nazi attack on the Church came in July 1933 when German Protestants held a plebiscite on a new church constitution, a move that was part of a plan for streamlining German Protestantism into a more efficient organization. Before 1933, the words "German Protestant Church" described not one institution but a colorful collection of Protestant churches, all members of a weak central alliance, the Protestant Church League, which itself was not a church, but rather an organization through which the provincial churches communicated with each other and by which they cooperated in a few common objectives (see Table 1.1).[15] The ecclesiastical map of 1933 (Map 1.1) reflected the political circumstances of Germany as it emerged from the Napoleonic Wars, a legacy of both the Peace of Augsburg of 1555 and the Vienna Congress of 1815. According to the Augsburg formula of *cuius regio, eius religio*, the magistrate of a political territory decided on the officially sanctioned faith of his land. The eventual result was that the Protestant territories defined in 1815

Table 1.1

Member Churches of the Protestant Church League in 1933

United Churches

1. Protestant Provincial Church of Anhalt *(Evangelische Landeskirche Anhalts)*

2. United Protestant-Evangelical Provincial Church of Baden *(Vereinigte evangelisch-protestantische Landeskirche Badens)*

3. Bremen Protestant Church *(Bremische Evangelische Kirche)*

4. Protestant Provincial Church of Electoral Hessia and Waldeck *(Evangelische Landeskirche Kurhessen-Waldeck)*

5. Protestant Provincial Church of Nassau-Hessia *(Evangelische Landeskirche Nassau-Hessen)*

6. Protestant Church of the Old Prussian Union *(Evangelische Kirche der altpreussischen Union)*:

   6a. Church Province Mark Brandenburg
   6b. Church Province East Prussia *(Ostpreussen)*
   6c. Church Province Border Mark, Posen, West Prussia *(Grenzmark, Posen, Westpreussen)*
   6d. Church Province Pomerania *(Pommern)*
   6e. Church Province of the Rhineland *(Rheinland)*
   6f. Church Province Saxony *(Sachsen)*
   6g. Church Province Silesia *(Schlesien)*
   6h. Church Province Westphalia *(Westfalen)*

7. United Protestant-Evangelical-Christian Church of the Palatinate *(Vereinigte protestantisch-evangelisch-christliche Kirche der Pfalz)*

Lutheran Churches

8. Protestant-Lutheran Church in Bavaria Right of the Rhine *(Evangelisch-lutherische Kirche in Bayern rechts des Rheins)*

Table 1.1 continued

Lutheran Churches continued

9. Brunswickian Protestant-Lutheran Provincial Church *(Braunschweigische evangelisch-lutherische Landeskirche)*

10. Protestant-Lutheran Church in the State of Hamburg *(Evangelisch-Lutherische Kirche im Hamburgischen Staate)*

11. Protestant-Lutheran Provincial Church of Hanover *(Evangelisch-lutherische Landeskirche Hannovers)*

12. Protestant-Lutheran Provincial Church of the Territory Lübeck in the Free State of Oldenburg *(Evangelisch-lutherische Landeskirche des Landesteils Lübeck im Freistaat Oldenburg)*

13. Protestant-Lutheran Church in Lübeck State *(Evangelisch-lutherische Kirche im Lübeckischen Staate)*

14. Protestant-Lutheran Provincial Church of Mecklenburg *(Evangelisch-lutherische Landeskirche Mecklenburgs)*

15. Protestant-Lutheran Church of the Territory Oldenburg *(Evangelisch-lutherische Kirche des Landesteils Oldenburg)*

16. Protestant Lutheran Provincial Church of the Free State of Saxony *(Evangelisch-lutherische Landeskirche des Freistaats Sachsen)*

17. Protestant-Lutheran Church of Schaumburg-Lippe *(Evangelisch-lutherische Kirche von Schaumburg-Lippe)*

18. Protestant-Lutheran Provincial Church of Schleswig-Holstein *(Evangelisch-Lutherische Landeskirche Schleswig-Holsteins)*

19. Thuringian Protestant Church *(Thüringer evangelische Kirche)*

20. Protestant-Lutheran Provincial Church in Wurttemburg *(Evangelisch-lutherische Landeskirche in Württemburg)*

Table 1.1 continued

Reformed (Calvinist) Churches

21. Protestant-Reformed Provincial Church of the Province Hanover
    (*Evangelisch-reformierte Landeskirche der Provinz Hannover*)

22. Lippean Provincial Church (*Lippische Landeskirche*)

---

differed from each other in terms of being either Lutheran or Calvinist. In 1817 Friedrich Wilhelm III of Prussia complicated matters further when he created a third church by forcibly unifying the two Protestant confessions in his realms into a "United Church," the United Protestant Church of the Prussian Union, while still allowing for congregational differences in theology and liturgy. Six other German states eventually developed additional "united" churches.

By 1933 the member churches of the Protestant Church League differed from each other theologically, geographically, and organizationally. The Protestant Church of the Old Prussian Union was the largest by far of the churches, with a 1925 membership of nearly 19 million, slightly under 30 per cent of all Germans.[16] A distant second place was held by the Protestant Church of Saxony (Lutheran) with 4.5 million members.[17] This was followed by the Protestant Churches of Hanover (Lutheran) with 2.5 million, Wurttemberg (Lutheran) with 1.7 million, Bavaria (Lutheran) with 1.6 million, and Schleswig-Holstein and Thuringia, both Lutheran, each with 1.4 million members.[18] These seven churches comprised 80 percent of the Protestant population of Germany in 1933. The balance included much smaller Lutheran churches in Brunswick, Hamburg, Lübeck, Mecklenburg, and Oldenburg; Union churches in Anhalt, Baden, Bremen, Hessia, Nassau, the Palatinate, and Waldeck; and Reformed (Calvinist) churches in Lippe and Province Hanover. Each regional church, even those that had been absorbed into the Protestant Union during the Bismarck era, had its own independent government, its own distinctive curial nomenclature, and its own set of ecclesiastical laws. The dysfunction within German Protestantism was so great that Reformed Protestants would not celebrate Holy Communion with Lutherans.

Still another factor points up the complex nature of German Protestantism. Membership in a given church was not so much a matter of theology as of geography. When Protestants from Hanover moved to Berlin, they automatically became United after having been Lutheran, a phenomenon referred to cynically

Map 1.1
Member Churches of the Protestant Church League, 1933

Numbers correspond to those on Table 1.1.

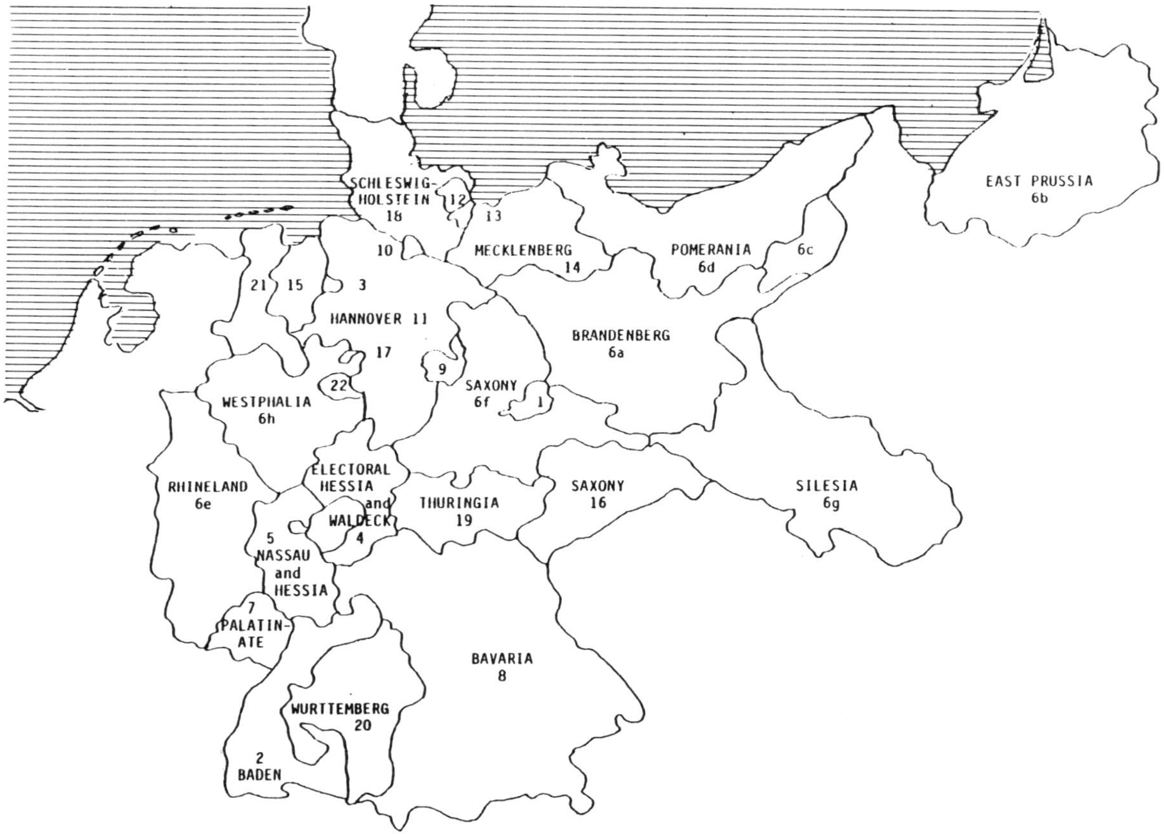

as "moving-van conversion."[19] There was, in the minds of most Germans, little other choice.[20] The desire to create administrative order out of this ecclesiastical chaos fit perfectly with the Nazi penchant for organization, streamlining, and application of the *Führerprinzip* (the Nazi "Leadership Principle") to every aspect of life in the new Germany. Hitler did not initiate the unification of German Protestantism, but he created a national atmosphere that encouraged it and he understood that he himself would profit from it.

On 17 April 1933, Hitler, meeting in Berchtesgaden with his personal adviser in church affairs, Army Chaplain Ludwig Müller, expressed his interest in a united "Protestant Reich Church," provided that the Church would recognize the Nazi Party's political leadership.[21] To that end, on 25 April he made official the appointment of Müller to the post of "Authorized Representative for Protestant Church Affairs," giving him the explicit assignment of encouraging Protestant unification. The chaplain conveyed the Führer's concerns to an assembled body of Protestant leaders: "The existing . . . fragmentation into twenty-eight provincial churches is incomprehensible to the Chancellor. He wants a bloc that will serve as a counter-balance against the uniform organization of Catholicism."[22] Hitler's Protestant allies who supported the unification efforts were the so-called "German Christians," a theopolitical party established by Berlin pastor Joachim Hossenfelder in June 1932. Three thousand DC pastors, representing a significant percentage of German churchgoers, pledged themselves to give Hitler what he wanted: "one Protestant German Reich-Church" to go with his matched set of one Volk, one Reich, and one Führer.[23] The "German Christians" claimed to be both Nazis and Christians, disciples of Hitler as well as of Jesus. Their concept of a German Protestant Church laid the heaviest emphasis on the word German. Non-Aryans would be excluded: a German Protestant Church under DC control would deny baptism to sincere Africans, Gypsies, Jews, or Slavs who had developed a faith in Jesus.

Even academically trained theologians among the ranks of the "German Christians" spouted preposterous stuff. For example, Dietrich Eckart was pleased to be able to cite Friedrich Delitzsch, the renowned Assyriologist, whose fantastic *Die grosse Täuschung* (The Great Delusion) insisted that Jesus, who had lived in "Galilee of the Gentiles," was no Jew: "Jesus' parents and ancestors were, as Galileans, according to Old Testament and cuneiform documentation, certainly not of Jewish blood; they belonged instead to that large number of Galilean Jewish proselytes."[24] Eckart also claimed to know that the penitent thief on the cross next to Jesus was a Gentile, while the second crucified thief, who reviled Jesus, was indeed Jewish.[25] Eckart's view was that Jesus' Jewishness was a fabrication by St. Paul and other early Christian missionaries who dragged Jewish elements into their proclamation of the Gospel.[26] Although DC theologians averred that the Bible—properly edited—was a revelation from God, they also believed that God was revealing His will through Adolf Hitler and the national awakening in Germany.[27] This radical departure from traditional Protestantism welded together political and theological convictions and made the

Reformation Confessions subject to radically new reinterpretation. Thus Hitler superseded Luther. These were the "German Christians."

On 25 April 1933, Pastor Hermann Kapler, chairman of the Supreme Church Council of the Old Prussian Union, proposed that a group of respected theologians be commissioned to draft a new constitution for a united Protestant Church. The ensuing Kapler Commission, consisting of Kapler, Dr. August Marahrens (Lutheran bishop of Hanover), and Dr. Hermann Hesse (director of a Calvinist seminary in the Rhineland), worked out details under the watchful eye of Ludwig Müller, who indicated what would and would not be acceptable to the state.[28]

Müller was particularly concerned that the governance of the Church should reflect the dominant management style of the new Germany: not congregation-alism (democracy), nor presbyterianism (representative democracy), but the Führerprinzip, meaning autocracy from the top down. The Kapler Commission complied: the new church constitution provided for a Lutheran Reich-Bishop, at whose side would function a cabinet of advisers and the "German Protestant National Synod," something of a consultative and legislative body.[29] The Church agreed to adopt the Führerprinzip, albeit with a wisely worded proviso that protected the Church against becoming a mere reflection of the state. One paragraph proved crucial in ensuing years:

> The inviolable foundation of the German Protestant Church is the Gospel of Jesus Christ, [both] as it was revealed to us in the Holy Scriptures and as it came to light again in the Confessions of the Reformation. This determines and limits the powers the Church needs to fulfill her mission.[30]

The Council of the Protestant Church Union unanimously approved the constitution on 26-27 May 1933 and acting on the Kapler Commission's suggestion, offered the bishop's chair to Pastor Friederich von Bodelschwingh, a man widely respected and highly regarded for his work with the Bethel sanitaria in Bielefeld and Lobethal. Since the "German Christians," however, had previously decided that Ludwig Müller would be a more fitting bishop, they opposed the von Bodelschwingh nomination. On 27 May, Müller nominated himself as the man who, because of his close personal standing with the Führer, could bring peace instead of strife into the Church. Von Bodelschwingh, Müller said, was "a man for deaconesses, not for SA men."[31] The Council, in spite of—or more precisely, because of—Müller's self-aggrandizing speech, elected Pastor von Bodelschwingh.

The DC were not pleased, nor was Hitler, maintaining that the Church had acted precipitously: "My will was that the constitution should first be formulated. Then the congregations should decide on it, and then the Reich-Bishop should be named. They did not do this, but simply named the Reich-Bishop." And then the Führer added, in words of presumptuous arrogance, "The church should not have gone over my head."[32]

On 23 June 1933, with Hermann Kapler's resignation from his chair of the
Supreme Church Council of the Old Prussian Union (allegedly because of "ill
health"), Hitler and Müller saw a way to manipulate Church affairs to their own
liking. Hitler replaced Kapler with a lawyer, August Jäger, who was neither a
churchman nor a theologian. As state commissioner for the Protestant Church of
Prussia, he held the power to take all necessary measures for its governance.
Although von Bodelschwingh was bishop of the German Protestant Church,
Jäger, operating on the proven principle that whoever rules Prussia rules
Germany, took charge of the Protestant Church of the Old Prussian Union.[33]

The Jäger appointment was a disaster for church unity. In Jäger, who was
"narrow, presumptuous, arrogant, and mean without equal,"[34] a man who
"could maintain, with apparent conviction, that five was an even number, and
issue false reports without turning a hair,"[35] Hitler had a sycophant whose
interest was not in serving the Church, but in imposing the Führer's will on
Germany's largest institution. Jäger immediately put the Protestant Church of
the Old Prussian Union under police supervision and set about filling all church
offices with "German Christians," which required him to retire administrators
who were of any other persuasion.[36]

Bishop Von Bodelschwingh, who in the meantime had been received by
neither Chancellor Hitler nor President Paul von Hindenburg, watched while
Jäger undermined his new office by appointing DC lieutenants all around him.
Reich-Bishop von Bodelschwingh resigned on 24 June 1933 after less than thirty
days in office.[37]

Now Hitler, through Jäger, could carry out his designs. On 14 July 1933, the
Nazi government promulgated a Reich Law which set 23 July as the date for
church elections, a plebiscite in which the rank-and-file members of the Church
could ratify the new constitution and elect members to the National Protestant
Synod which would, in turn, elect a Reich-Bishop. Legally, the state was not
empowered to call a Church election, but neither was the state qualified to
confirm a Church constitution. The German Protestant Church had already
slipped into the Nazi machinery.

The "German Christians" campaigned to assure that the new Reich-Bishop
would be someone who could work well with the Nazi chancellor. In the weeks
leading up to the Church election, an amazing thing happened: party members
re-activated their Church memberships. Nazi couples who had been content with
civil marriage ceremonies went to the churches to have their unions sanctified.
Members of the *Sturmabteilung* (SA), men who were not generally known for
their piety, became regular in their church attendance. Brownshirt uniforms
filled the pews. Many a pastor approved of the apparent positive spiritual impact
that the Führer was having on his people. The "German Christians" dubbed
themselves "the SA of Jesus Christ."[38] However, this ostensible renewed interest
in church life was nothing more than a cynical move to put DC elements in key
positions in the emerging government of the Protestant Church. By 23 July the
DC were in tactical position to take control.[39]

To secure what was probably already certain, Hitler, a nominal Roman Catholic, went on the radio on the evening of 22 July 1933 to urge German Protestants to elect delegates from the "German Christian" lists.[40] The result was that the DC won two thirds of the seats in the National Protestant Synod. The Nazis then consummated the takeover of the Church on 27 September 1933 when, at the National Synod in Wittenberg, the "German Christians" manipulated the unanimous election of Nazi Field Chaplain Ludwig Müller as the Reich-Bishop of the German Protestant Church. In his acceptance speech, Reich-Bishop Müller ominously declared, "The struggle for the soul of the *Volk* is beginning."[41]

ROSENBERG AND *THE MYTH OF THE 20TH CENTURY*

The third declaration of war against traditional Protestantism came in January 1934, when Hitler appointed Alfred Rosenberg to be the "Führer's Delegate for the Entire Intellectual and Philosophical Education and Instruction for the National Socialist Party."[42] Rosenberg was the author of *The Myth of the 20th Century*, a virulently anti-Semitic and anti-Christian work which proposed to replace Christianity with neopaganism in the new German state.[43] According to *The Myth*, the only way for the German state to deal with the Churches was to transform them, changing them and expunging them of everything Jewish.

Rosenberg's ideology had its impact, especially on German youth. By 1935 boys in Hitler Youth camps were hearing statements such as this from their Nazi instructors:

We must refuse both the Old and the New Testaments. If we accept either one of these texts, then we accept the Jews as God's chosen people, because they received this revelation . . . . For us the only valid example is Adolf Hitler. Otherwise no one.[44]

One teacher drew comparisons between Jesus and Hitler:

Christ is a nordic, Aryan person. . . . Christ is God-Man. Hitler is God-Man. Both are tools for godly purposes. Christ went into the wilderness, Hitler seeks strength and regeneration in the mountains. . . Christ was the greatest anti-Semite of all times.

High school youth in Kiel published the Rosenberg theses in their school newspaper in 1935, boasting: "We regard the word heathen as an honorable term, not as a reproach. We are proud of our German faith, our Northern Heathenism."[45]

Within twelve months of becoming chancellor, Adolf Hitler had appeased the Catholic Church with a concordat and through extortion and political chicanery, had begun to retrofit the Protestant Church into his fascist machine. By January 1934 he had put a blatant, neopagan anti-Christian in charge of the education and ideology of the only legal political party, the government had passed legislation that would allow the state to determine who the spiritual leaders of the Church might be, August Jäger had forced numerous influential non-DC church leaders into early retirement, and the bishop of the German Protestant Church was a Nazi army officer.

GROWING DISSENT WITHIN THE CHURCH

In the meantime, a handful of Protestant leaders, recognizing the gravity of these moves against the historical independence of the Church and its teachings, sounded the alarm. Pastor Martin Niemöller, preaching from his Berlin-Dahlem pulpit in the spring of 1933, railed against the imposition of the "Aryan Paragraph" on the Church. As Jäger continued to force church leaders into retirement, and as Müller put together an administration that consisted almost entirely of "German Christians", and tacitly—though not formally—adopted the "Aryan Paragraph" as Church policy, Niemöller and others organized an opposition within the Church in the form of the Pastors' Emergency League (PNB). On 21 September 1933 the league sent out a letter to all of Germany's pastors asking them to mutually support each other against the emerging "German Christian" domination of the Church. Members of the league were asked to sign the following statement:

1. I pledge myself to fulfill my office as a servant of the Word, bound only by the Holy Scriptures and by the confessions of the Reformation as the correct exposition of Holy Scripture.

2. I pledge myself to protest unreservedly against every infringement upon such a confessional position.

3. I realize that I share responsibility to the extent of my power together with those who are persecuted on account of such a confessional position.

4. In making this pledge I bear witness that the application of the Aryan Paragraph in the area of the Church of Christ is an infringement upon such a confessional position.[46]

The response to the league's letter was dramatic. Within days, thousands of pastors had pledged their purses and their careers to support one another against intrusions by the DC-dominated church government. By October 1933, there were 2,500 members.[47] Still, the march of the "German Christian" regiment did not falter. Jäger threatened PNB pastors in provincial churches with suspension and forced their retirement if they protested the brutal tactics of the "German Christian" administration.

A speech by DC spokesman Dr. Reinhold Krause precipitated a crisis on 13 November 1933 when he addressed 20,000 Protestants in the Berlin Sports Arena. Krause's address renounced the Hebrew Scriptures, St. Paul, and the historic form of the Church. "What we need," he said, "is one mighty, new, all-embracing German People's Church," which would "get rid of the Old Testament" with its "Jewish moral teaching and its stories of cattle dealers and pimps." The Church should remove all "perverted and superstitious passages" from the New Testament and anything tainted with the theology of "Rabbi Paul," and should adopt "a teaching which conforms perfectly to the demands of National Socialism."[48] At the close of the speech the assembly overwhelmingly pledged its support of a two-pronged resolution: to apply the Aryan Paragraph even to laymen in the church—thus no Jewish believers could be members of the German Protestant Church; and to cleanse the New Testament of everything that was "un-German."[49]

The Sports Arena speech alarmed many Protestant clergymen who had not yet perceived any danger in "German Christianity." The ranks of the Pastors' Emergency League grew accordingly. In addition, the Sports Arena scandal activated millions of lay people, whose general indignation made Reich-Bishop Müller recognize a ground swell of sentiment against the "German Christian" party. Müller quickly disassociated himself from Krause's speech and dismissed both Krause and DC party leader Joachim Hossenfelder from their Church positions. Under pressure from the Pastor's Emergency League, Müller retreated from formal implementation of the "Aryan Paragraph."[50]

Müller took another fateful step when he agreed, on 19 December 1933 to allow Nazi Youth Minister Baldur von Schirach to absorb the entire Protestant Youth Organization—numbering 700,000 youngsters—into the Hitler Youth. That maneuver to unite Church and state alarmed still more Protestant lay people and helped crystallize a growing resistance against Müller and the few "German Christians" left in his administration. By Christmas the Pastors' Emergency League had 5,500 members: Lutheran, Calvinist, and United pastors from all over Germany, amounting to approximately one third of the German Protestant ministerial brotherhood.[51]

Nazi Reich-Bishop Müller continued to foment unrest within the German Protestant Church. On 4 January 1934 he issued the so-called Muzzle Law which forbade Protestant pastors to criticize the Church government, and announced that the "Aryan Paragraph" would be reinforced in the Prussian Landeskirche.[52] Niemöller and the PNB reacted immediately to this last development, issuing a declaration that attacked Müller's high-handed, illegal measures. They called for civil disobedience, based on a tenet of the Confession of Augsburg: "When bishops teach something contrary to the Gospel, Christians are obligated to protest."

The Pastors' Emergency League requested all its members to read that declaration from their pulpits on 7 or 14 January 1934. When some 3,500 pastors cooperated, Bishop Müller suspended some and harassed others with coercive measures. His standing declined still more among the estimated 7,000 members of the league.[53]

The unity of the growing resistance movement was fragile, however, as became apparent on 25 January 1934, when Hitler agreed to hear Protestant leaders' complaints about Reich-Bishop Müller. Among those to be received by the chancellor were the bishops of the three largest Lutheran churches (August Marahrens of Hanover, Hans Meiser of Bavaria, and Theophil Wurm of Wurttemberg), Niemöller (as leader of the PNB), and a few others. The morning before the meeting, Walter Künneth, a friend who wanted to wish Niemöller well, interrupted the pastor's breakfast with a phone call. Niemöller jocularly reported to Künneth that the best of preparations had been made to work through President Hindenburg to have Hitler fire Müller. Dropping into navy jargon he reported that the PNB leaders had "laid their mines" by sending a memorandum to President Hindenburg. Niemöller knew that before Hitler saw the churchmen, the chancellor would have an audience with Hindenburg, who would administer, Niemöller said, "*letzte Ölung*"—a pun that implied both "greasing the wheels," and "extreme unction," that is, "last rites" for Müller.[54]

When the Protestant delegates finally stood before Hitler, the Führer immediately reproached them for trying to drive a wedge between himself and President Hindenburg, whereupon Hitler's second-in-command, General Hermann Göring, read verbatim a transcript of the telephone conversation between Niemöller and Künneth. Stepping forward from the group of churchmen, Pastor Niemöller admitted to the conversation and his unguarded language; but he continued to address the chancellor in vehement tones, charging Reich-Bishop Müller with malfeasance. Niemöller's spontaneous but unmistakable emergence as the de facto leader of the Church resistance frightened the other church representatives. The meeting did not go well. Hitler not only affirmed his support of Ludwig Müller, he dismissed the churchmen with the warning that if they could not agree to support the Reich-Bishop in unifying the Church, he would withdraw his protecting hand and state financial support.[55] The three Lutheran bishops were sufficiently intimidated that they the very next day issued a statement supportive of Müller.[56]

Significant numbers of league members throughout Germany were also alarmed at Niemöller's bold audacity and distanced themselves from him by resigning from the PNB. Twelve hundred Bavarian members withdrew, and 350 Hanoverians resigned. The Wurttemberg PNB dissolved itself completely. A significantly reduced Pastors' Emergency League membership of 5,256 remained relatively stable during the following years.[57]

The incident highlights the organic nature of what was soon to coalesce as the Confessing Church. Never a tightly organized institution, it would, after May 1934, remain a loose confederation of independent congregations and affiliated institutional churches (the Lutheran Churches of Bavaria, Hanover, and Wurttemberg, for example). Conversely, although the voluntary nature of the Confessing Church would make unanimous action impossible, its loose structure—more of a movement than a denomination—would render it flexible and adaptable, and thus able to survive the imprisonment of its most prominent leaders.

THE BARMEN DECLARATION

Throughout the winter and spring of 1934, small caucuses of distressed Protestant leaders, cooperating with the Pastors' Emergency League and similar organizations, met in Prussia, Westphalia, the Rhineland, Bavaria, Pomerania, and Wurttemberg.[58] Aggravated by a church government that was cutting salaries, removing men from office, imprisoning pastors, and administering the church with a violent and arbitrary hand, the people at these PNB-sponsored meetings emphasized their allegiance to the Reformation confessions of faith. They became informally known as "Confessors," and their meetings, as "Confessing Synods." After a series of regional meetings, Pastor Karl Immer invited representatives of Confessing groups from all the *Landeskirchen* to meet for a national synod in Barmen on 29-31 May 1934.[59] A total of 138 official delegates (and uncounted observers) from eighteen of the provincial churches met for three days to deliberate.[60] The result was that on 31 May, Lutheran, Calvinist and United Confessors signed a document drafted by the Swiss theologian Karl Barth. The declaration stated that Reich-Bishop Ludwig Müller's church administration had forfeited every justifiable claim to be legitimate because it had betrayed the principles of the Gospel by subordinating the Word of God to secular powers who were claiming to be the instruments of a new revelation. The Barmen Declaration excommunicated the "German Christians" as heretics, and in the place of the DC-dominated German Protestant Church, it established the Confessing Church, which promised to look to Jesus Christ alone as the final revelation of God, to consult only the Scriptures for spiritual instruction, and to hold to the historical confessions of the Reformation.[61]

The formal establishment of the Confessing Church clearly defined three camps in the Church Struggle. The Confessing Church and the "German Christians" represented the two extremes, while the majority of Protestant pastors occupied middle ground.[62] The "neutrals" in the middle ground inevitably strengthened Hitler's hand, as their refusal to protest meant that they in practice accepted the state's authority to intervene in Church affairs.[63]

THE FALL OF REICH-BISHOP LUDWIG MÜLLER, 1935

What the delegates signed in Barmen at the First Confessing Synod was theological and theoretical, only slightly addressing the practical implications of establishing a new church. At the Second Confessing Synod, in Berlin-Dahlem the following 19-20 October 1934, Confessing Church leaders met to organize the practical aspects of the new church.

Citing Article 1 of the 1933 Constitution, the BK's Dahlem synod declared an ecclesiastical emergency and called Protestants throughout Germany to refuse to obey orders that came from the "German Christian" administration of the German Protestant Church. They urged Confessing Christians who were still in provincial Churches under the domination of "German Christians" to elect a separate Brotherhood Council to administer their own Confessing Church. The Confessors, establishing a Provisional Church Administration (VKL), set themselves up as the sole legitimate Protestant Church of Germany. That claim was not lost on Hitler himself, who thus became aware of the depth of discontent with his Reich-Bishop.[64]

Reich-Bishop Müller had in the meantime taken strong measures to dissolve any resistance to his leadership. On 6 October 1934, he had placed the popular Wurttemberg Bishop Theophil Wurm under "protective custody," confining him to his own house under police "protection." On 11 October, August Jäger, accompanied by armed Gestapo officers, burst into the headquarters of the Lutheran Church of Bavaria in Munich, where he physically dismissed Bishop Hans Meiser from his office at gun point and placed him under house arrest.[65]

Jäger's extremism spelled defeat for both himself and his bishop. When news of the arrest of the Lutheran bishops spread beyond Germany, German Foreign Minister Konstantin von Neurath complained to Hitler about Jäger's imprudent actions. The Führer fired Jäger and freed the two bishops, but he did not dismiss Müller. Instead, he simply ignored the "*Reibi*," reducing him to a pitiful figure of failure and neglect.[66] Abandoned by the Führer, the party and the Confessing Church, Reich-Bishop Ludwig Müller was left bankrupt of all authority. He continued on officially as bishop of the Reich, but no longer could he influence policy matters. Hitler never received him again. To an April 1940 query whether the Führer intended to dissolve the office of Reich-Bishop, Müller received no reply.[67]

Müller's loss of influence did not mean that the Confessing Church would flourish. Müller at least had claimed to be a Christian. Christianity faced another foe in the avowedly anti-Christian, Alfred Rosenberg. On 4-5 March 1935 the Second Confessional Synod of the Church of the Old Prussian Union (in Dahlem) denounced Rosenberg and the "German Faith Movement" because of Rosenberg's latest publication, *On the Obscurantists of Our Time*, a scathing attack on Christianity which included a proposal for the implementation of a neopagan Germanic religion.[68] The Confessing Brotherhood Council drafted a pulpit declaration about Rosenberg and neopaganism to be read from all Confessing pulpits on Sunday, 17 March 1935. Interior Minister Wilhelm Frick, using the Gestapo as enforcers, forbade the reading of the pulpit declaration and arrested five hundred of the pastors who disobeyed. When these arrests became known, other Confessing preachers protested from their pulpits. The resulting arrests of an additional 215 pastors proved too much even for the Nazi Party, concerned as it was with reactions from Christian circles in the international community. Consequently, Frick released the pastors. The incident illustrates both the vulnerability of the Confessing Church and its growing moral strength.[69]

HANS KERRL, 1935-1941

Throughout 1935 the government continued to pass laws restricting the freedom and function of the Church, but the most significant was the Führer's decision to bypass Reich-Bishop Müller by establishing a Ministry for Ecclesiastical Affairs under attorney Hans Kerrl, who would control the German Protestant Church until his death in 1941. As Reich and Prussian Minister for Ecclesiastical Affairs, Kerrl was a capable administrator, a patriotic Nazi, and also a man who evidently was genuinely concerned for the welfare of the German Protestant Church.[70] His goal, which he announced on 23 August 1935, was to unite Church and state amicably. To the satisfaction of both the Confessing Church and "German Christian" elements, he denounced the neopaganism of Rosenberg and promised to protect the Christian confessions.[71]

Still, Kerrl, who was a party man, ruled like a Nazi. On 5 September 1935 he announced that he would control all police matters involving the Church. All arrests, deportations, and restraining orders were to be submitted to him for approval. On 24 September Kerrl changed the wording of his charge from "to restore constitutional conditions" in the German Protestant Church to "to restore order" in the Church, with no mention of the constitution which, like the Reich-Bishop, he simply ignored.[72]

On 3 October 1935, Kerrl tried to appease both the DCs and the Confessing Church by creating a National Church Committee (KA) to oversee affairs of the German Protestant Church throughout the Reich. Kerrl's idea was to call on moderate leaders from both the "German Christians" and the Confessing Church to serve together on the Church Committee in the interest of Christian unity. He received the cooperation of Superintendent Wilhelm Zoellner, a respected Westphalian Confessing Church leader, who agreed to serve as chairman. Kerrl, who thought he had now rendered the Confessing Church's VKL redundant, asked that body to dissolve itself.

In December 1935 Kerrl took from local congregations any autonomy in matters of ordination and fund-raising, an order that a few Confessing congregations promptly and pointedly disobeyed.[73] Though there were strong elements within the Confessing Church that thought they could live with the Church Committee arrangements, the Niemöller wing of the Confessing Movement, the "Dahlemites," prevailed over other opinions and led the national Confessing Synod at Bad Oeynhausen on 17-22 February 1936 in formally denouncing the National Church Committee on the grounds that, by cooperating with even moderate elements of the "German Christians," it demonstrated that it was not bound by the Reformation confessions of faith. In refusing Kerrl's order to dissolve, the VKL maintained that as an elected body it constituted the only legitimate leadership of the Protestant Church.[74]

Kerrl's response to the Bad Oeynhausen rejoinder was to tighten his grip around the Confessing Church. He formed a Finance Committee to oversee the fiscal arrangements of every church and a Law Committee to take legal matters involving churches out of the regular courts. In the summer of 1936 the Gestapo forbade leading Confessing Church preachers to address student groups. Among those who suffered under such a restraining order in December 1936 was KA chairman Wilhelm Zoellner himself. Thus rebuffed, Zoellner resigned, and the entire Church Committee then resigned as well.[75] Kerrl's experiment to unite, under government auspices, "German Christian" and Confessing elements in a unified Church administration had failed.

THE VKL'S SECRET MEMORANDUM TO HITLER

Did Adolf Hitler, who was absorbed with matters of state, know what was going on in the struggle between state and Church? Did he personally approve of the persecution of the Confessing Church? Was he aware of the ineffectiveness of Müller and Kerrl? What exactly was his intention as far as Christianity in the Third Reich was concerned?

To answer such questions the Provisional Church Leadership on 28 May 1936 drafted a 4,000-word memorandum intended for Hitler's eyes only. The document, which asked the chancellor to clarify a number of questions, sought to set out the Confessing Church's position on developments within German Protestantism. The VKL outlined six concerns:

1. The efforts to de-Christianize Germany, led by "even high authorities within the state," prompted the question whether such was to become the government's official policy.

2. The comments by Rosenberg, which reduce "positive Christianity" to mere "humanitarian service" were disturbing; coupled with a "mystic doctrine of the [German] blood," he described Catholicism and Protestantism as "negative Christianity."

3. Government policy seemed bent on the "destruction of the ecclesiastical system." There were numerous instances in which "one interference . . . followed the other . . . since the elections forced on the church in July 1933."

4. Under the catch-phrase "deconfessionalization," the government was eradicating Christian observances from public life: Hitler Youth leaders denigrated church attendance and young people serving their year of national service were allowed neither contact with their pastors nor access to Christian literature.

5. National Socialist philosophy contradicted Christian values:

> When Blood, Race, Nation, and Honor . . . are raised to the
> rank of qualities that guarantee eternity, the Christian is bound
> by the first commandment ["Thou shalt have no other gods
> before me."] to reject the assumption. While the "Aryan" human
> being is glorified, God's Word bears witness to the sinfulness of
> all men. When, within the compass of the National Socialist
> view of life, anti-Semitism is forced upon the Christian . . . [it
> contradicts] the Christian injunction to love one's neighbor.

6. Government procedures undermined morality and justice. Unique
judicial proceedings forced on the church resulted in injustice; and in
the concentration camps, the Gestapo was exempt from any judicial
control at all. Furthermore, the chancellor was elevated to the role of
deity, "vested with the dignity of the national priest, and even the
mediator between God and the people."[76]

The VKL took pains to maintain the confidentiality of the memo, but
nonetheless disaster struck. Dr. Friedrich Weissler, administrative head of the
Confessing Church offices in Berlin, entrusted one of three extant copies to two
vicars, Ernst Tillich and Werner Koch. Tillich and Koch copied the memo and,
on their own initiative, passed it on to the international press.[77] The entire
memo appeared in the *Baseler Nachrichten* of 23 July 1936 before Hitler ever
saw it. The New York *Herald Tribune* published the memorandum in translation
on 28 July 1936 with a 20 July dateline. The lengthy headline ran fourteen lines
deep in one column on the front page:

Reich Clergy Warn Hitler
He Does Not Outrank God

Text of Confessional Protest
Reveals Bold Stand Against Drive
to "Ban Christianity" in Germany

"Blood, Race, Soil" Theory Assailed

4,000 Word Blast at Nazi Methods

Gets No Reply, but Repercussions
Are Regarded as Inevitable[78]

After publication in the foreign press, Pastor Ernst Hornig of the Confessing
Church of Silesia printed 100,000 copies of the memorandum, distributing 5,000
copies each to fifteen Confessing Brotherhood Councils throughout Germany.[79]
With the memorandum in the public domain (though most Germans remained
ignorant of it), the VKL decided to issue a formal version of it for the general

public. The new version, issued 23 August 1936 in the form of a pastoral letter, was milder than the original document. It protested the suppression of the Church as well as Rosenberg's neopagan ideology, but it no longer referred to the concentration camps, the deification of Hitler, or anti-Semitism.[80]

When Kerrl heard that the pastoral letter containing the revised memorandum was to be read from the Church pulpits, he considered banning the proclamations but feared that he would have thousands of arrested pastors on his hands, a risk he was not willing to take while Berlin was playing host to the Olympic Games. Kerrl therefore politely *requested* that the provincial church governments forbid the public reading of the letter. The three Lutheran bishops, Marahrens, Meiser, and Wurm, agreed; but elsewhere in Germany the pastors read the letter and churches printed an estimated million copies of it for hand-to-hand distribution.[81]

The Confessing Church's new public stance in defense of Jews—all Jews, whether baptized or not—redefined the issues of the Church Struggle. The Nazis had heretofore been able to dismiss the Church Struggle as mere internecine warfare, as a series of arcane disputes among theologians, but the Confessing Church drew a clear line in the sand when it boldly published its alarm at de-Christianization, the apotheosis of Adolf Hitler, Rosenberg's *Myth of the 20th Century*, harassment of the churches, anti-Semitism, and the injustices of the Gestapo. Somewhat later, Lutheran Bishop Theophil Wurm of Wurttemberg joined them with his forceful public letters against euthanasia and racism.[82] The demarcation became increasingly clear. On one side of a spiritual conflict were the Nazi government and its puppet, the sanctioned German Protestant Church, and on the other stood the Confessing Church.

With the publication in German of the secret memorandum of June 1936, the government measures against Christianity intensified.[83] In November 1936 Reich Minister of Education Bernhard Rust demanded the removal of crucifixes from all schoolrooms.[84] In June 1937 Interior Minister Wilhelm Frick prohibited churches from collecting contributions for any but officially sanctioned causes, thus making illegal collections for the support of Confessing Church personnel In the same month the Gestapo broke into a meeting of the Confessing Church's Reich Brotherhood Council in Berlin and arrested forty-eight prominent Confessing Church leaders. By the end of June 1937, the official prayer list within the Confessing Church of Prussia contained the names of forty-five imprisoned pastors and deacons and twenty-five more who were under temporary arrest.[85] The name of Germany's most conspicuous Confessing pastor appeared on the prayer lists when the Gestapo arrested Martin Niemöller on 1 July 1937. Tried and acquitted in March 1938, Gestapo agents immediately rearrested Niemöller as the Führer's personal prisoner, and held him without trial in concentration camps in Sachsenhausen and Dachau until the end of the war.[86]

Meanwhile, Gestapo head Heinrich Himmler and Security Service chief Reinhard Heydrich set up SS Group IV-B to deal with "political churches, sects,

Masons and Jews."[87] The number of arrested and imprisoned pastors grew accordingly.[88] By the end of December 1937, Nazi officials had arrested over seven hundred.[89]

Similarly difficult for the Confessing Church was the year 1938. On 8 May Kerrl demanded from all congregations the names of their non-Aryan pastors. The Confessing Church refused to accommodate him.[90] In October the SS newspaper *Schwarze Korps* publicly charged the Confessing Church with treason because of the Church's preparations for a liturgy of peace in the face of what was thought to be certain war over the Sudeten crisis.[91] Immediately thereafter, the central administration of the German Protestant Church suspended all the pastors who were members of the VKL and stripped them of their salaries.[92]

With the outbreak of war in 1939, the persecutions eased somewhat as the government discovered priorities that outranked harassing the churches. On 8 September 1939 Hitler ordered, "No further action should be taken against the Evangelical or Catholic Churches for the duration of the war."[93] Nevertheless, measures directly affecting the activity of the Confessing Church continued. On 27 October 1939 Kerrl forbade pastors to assemble mailing lists of soldiers from their parishes. Any religious material sent to the front had to be approved by government agents. The Bavarian Gestapo forbade the mailing of church bulletins to the front. In November 1939 the government introduced compulsory paramilitary youth service for 14 to 18-year-old boys. The groups' exercises occupied four Sundays per month, usually the morning hours, the time when the youths might otherwise be with their families in church.

Laws harassing the Churches multiplied. Consider the matter of church bells. During the war, regulations limited churches to one bell apiece, and the military confiscated additional bells to be melted down into cannon. An October 1941 law required churches to ring their remaining bell to honor a slain soldier at his funeral, regardless of the dead person's faith or status with the church. Then pastors received further orders not to ring their church bell on Sundays before 1:00 p.m. if there had been an air-raid the night before.[94] In dozens of ways, some consequential, others merely petty, the government pestered the churches through the end of the war.

In the end, of course, Nazism fell, and with it the "German Christian" leadership of the German Protestant Church died, having been ideologically prostituted, spiritually pauperized, and absolutely discredited. In the spring of 1945 leaders of the Confessing Church emerged from illegality to take the positions of leadership within German Protestantism. As opponents of Hitler who now had the admiration and support of the worldwide ecumenical community, the Confessors decided the direction of German Protestantism through the postwar years and beyond. With the demise of the "German Christians" there was no longer a need for the Confessing Church to exist as an opposition party within German Protestantism. Institutionally, the Confessing Church evaporated, but its erstwhile leaders constituted the new leadership of German Protestantism. The self-conscious title of the new reconstituted church was "The Protestant Church *in* Germany," (not "*of* Germany"). The change in preposition proclaimed the Church's putative independence from the state.

THE CONFESSING CHURCH'S LEGACY

We have an understandable need to find heroes during a period like the Third Reich, and the Confessing Church obliges us by providing stories of bravery, courage, and martyrdom. Some are certifiably true. Others belong in the category of legend, while they may be true, they are unverifiable. Still others are certainly unhistorical, albeit at times uplifting. The first wave of books published after the fall of the Nazi regime abounded in near-hagiography and martyriology, followed by a wave of revisionist writings.[95] Those who wrote immediately and honestly, and those who now are able to evaluate their involvement with the Confessing Church with some degree of objectivity, are quick to point out that no person acted nobly at every moment.

Even during the unfolding of events, Karl Barth castigated the Confessing Church for not taking a clearer stand on the crucial issues of anti-Semitism, on the treatment of political opponents, on the strangling of the press, "and on so much else against which the Old Testament prophets would certainly have spoken out."[96] Nonetheless, Barth expressed admiration for the "thin thread of evangelical clarity, loyalty and courage" which with time became even stronger, "but also even thinner," thinner because of losses of life, because of occasional apostacy.[97]

Those who held the thin, strong thread paid dearly. Fines, imprisonments, separation from their families, anxiety, despair, depression, and permanent loss of health: these were the common lots of hundreds of Confessing pastors. Dozens died in the prisons and camps. Nonetheless one hears critics who wish that the Confessing Church had spoken out still more strongly, more clearly, and more promptly. Some leaders of the Confessing Church wished the same. Niemöller, whose record of courage and sacrifice is unimpeachable, sought to speak for the Confessing Church in contrition when he confessed his own "most grievous fault."[98] He and Otto Dibelius collaborated in penning the Stuttgart Confession of 1945, purporting to speak for all the Christians of Germany, including those of the Confessing Church: "We accuse ourselves of not having confessed more courageously, prayed more faithfully, believed more joyfully and loved more ardently."[99]

Nonetheless against those confessions of failure one must counterpose that the Confessing Church constituted the only enduring institutional resistance to Adolf Hitler and Nazism during twelve murderous years. While the officially sanctioned brand of Christianity, the "German Christian Faith Movement," succumbed to the Nazi machinery, and while a majority of Protestants tried to occupy a neutral ground, the Confessing Church resisted evil. "The darkness did not overcome it."[100] The story of that resistance is instructive to later generations of people who will continue to wrestle with the intertwined relationships of Church and state.

EPILOGUE: WHAT ABOUT THE WOMEN?

This brief account of the Church Struggle presents the Confessing Church just as one finds it in most scholarly books: as a church of men. Where were the women? Did they contribute anything to the Church Struggle? Did they demonstrate the courage of their convictions? To what degree did they suffer? What legacies did the women leave?

Women, indeed, played crucial roles in the Confessing Church, although historians have ignored them. Confessing women participated in synodical meetings, sat as members of "brotherhood" councils, raised money, administered parishes, taught Bible classes, and published and distributed clandestine literature. They served as secretaries, teachers, and social workers, often at the risk of their lives. They experienced Gestapo interrogations, arrests, and loss of employment. They were part of a conspiracy for good that resisted the Nazi takeover of the Christian churches. In tens of thousands of cases, they were the ones left to conduct the Church Struggle at home while their men were in prison or at the front. Their stories, if we could discover them all, would provide expansive reading.

We turn our attention now to the women who bore much of the burden for the day to day operation of the Confessing Church. When the pastors were forbidden to preach, when they were imprisoned, drafted, or murdered, women stepped in to care for orphaned congregations, leaving a permanent legacy to German Protestantism after 1945.

NOTES

1. Quoted in Hermann Rauschning, *Voice of Destruction* (New York: G. P. Putnam's Sons, 1940), p. 54.

2. See Karl Barth's comment to this effect in Eberhard Busch, *Karl Barth: His Life from Letters and Autobiographical Texts* (Philadelphia: Fortress Press, 1976), p. 273.

3. John S. Conway, *The Nazi Persecution of the Churches 1933-1945*, (New York: Basic Books, 1968), Appendix 11, "List of Sects Prohibited by the Gestapo up to December 1938," pp. 370-374; Appendix 14, "A Directive by Heydrich Ordering the Immediate Suppression of Certain Secret and Religious Societies, and the Arrest and Internment in Concentration Camps of all Persons Connected Therewith," pp. 378-382.

4. The signatories were Franz von Papen for the German government and Cardinal Eugenio Pacelli, later known as Pope Pius XII, for the Church. L.

Volk, *Das Reichskonkordat vom 20. Juli 1933* (Mainz: Matthias Grünewald Verlag, 1972).

5. Quoted in Rauschning, *Voice*, p. 54; Alan Bullock, in *Hitler, a Study in Tyranny* (New York: Harper Torchbooks, 1962), pp. 388-389. The comment was made on 7 April 1933 according to Rauschning, *Hitler Speaks* (London, 1939), p. 62.

6. See the Bibliography, Eyewitness Interviews, for a brief discussion of "The Thirty Program Points of the National Reich Church of Germany," the document which the Gestapo found in Dora von Öttingen's posession, for which she was imprisoned eight months in Frankfurt. The document was supplied by Frau Dora von Öttingen during an interview in her home in Frankfurt am Main, 20 February 1990.

7. A teenage Christian in the Rheinland remarked to herself on 1 February 1933: "[Hitler] closed [his speech] with a petition to God, that He grant his administration His blessing. I have often doubted whether Hitler is a Christian. Now it is clear to me. He wants, with God's help, to help our people. I can see that God has called him to be the liberator of the German nation." From an unpublished source in the author's files.

8. Quoted in Hans Buchheim, *Glaubenskrise im Dritten Reich: Drei Kapitel nationalsozialistischer Religionspolitik* (Stuttgart: Deutsche Verlags-Anstalt, 1953), p. 84.

9. Article 24 of the 1920 Party Program, from Ernst Christian Helmreich, *The German Churches Under Hitler—Background, Struggle, and Epilogue* (Detroit, Mich.: Wayne State University Press, 1979), p. 123. Helmreich translates from Wolfgang Treue, *Deutsche Parteiprogramme 1861-1954* (Göttingen: Musterschmidt, 1955), p. 146.

10. Quoted in Arthur Stewart Duncan-Jones, *The Crooked Cross* (London: Macmillan and Co., 1940), p. 9.

11. Ibid., quoting Kurt Lüdecke, *I Knew Hitler*, p. 465; and Rauschning, *Voice*, p. 49.

12. Dietrich Eckart, *Der Bolschewismus von Moses bis Lenin: Zwiegespräch zwischen Adolf Hitler und mir* (München: Hoheneichen Verlag, 1925), in which Hitler raves that the Jew Paul had emasculated Christianity with appeals to love and brotherhood.

13. The full text of the Law for the Restoration of the Professional Bureaucracy, "Das Gesetz zur Wiederherstellung des Berufsbeamtentums" is available in Bruno Blau, *Das Ausnahmerecht für die Juden in Deutschland 1933-1945* (Düsseldorf: Verlag Allgemeine Wochenzeitung der Juden in Deutschland, 1965), pp. 13-15.

14. Helmreich, *German Churches Under Hitler*, p. 148. Pastor Heinrich Grüber estimated that by 1938, out of 18,000 Protestant pastors, 24 were subject to the law. See H. S. Brebeck, *Martin Niemöller: Bekenner, Politiker oder Demagoge?* (Henef: H. E. Schneider, [1959]), p. 9.

15. The league was called der evangelische Kirchenbund.

16. Only the Church of England was larger. Daniel R. Borg, *The Old Prussian Church and the Weimar Republic: A Study in Political Adjustment, 1917-1927* (Hanover, N.H.: University Press of New England, 1984), p. ix.

17. Klaus Scholder, *The Churches and the Third Reich*, 2 Vols. (Philadelphia: Fortress Press, 1988), 1:32.

18. Membership figures are from Scholder, *The Churches*, 1:32,33. The theological affiliation of each *Landeskirche* is from Heinz Brunotte, *Die Evangelische Kirche in Deutschland. Ihre Organe, Amststellen und Einrichtungen* (Hannover: Die Kirchenkanzlei der Evangelischen Kirche in Deutschland, 1969), p. 14.

19. Frederic Spotts, *The Churches and Politics in Germany* (Middletown, Conn: Wesleyan University Press, 1973), p. 12.

20. Of Germany's 45,000,000 Protestants, only 150,000 were members of "free churches"—Baptists, Methodists, Free Lutherans, and so forth. William L. Shirer, *The Rise and Fall of the Third Reich* (New York: Simon and Schuster, 1960), p. 235.

21. Conway, *Nazi Persecution*, p. 35.

22. Scholder, *The Churches*, 1:308-309.

23. Concerning the DC pastors, see Shirer, *Rise and Fall*, p. 236. "Das Ziel der Glaubensbewegung Deutsche Christen ist eine evangelische Deutsche Reichskirche." Max Geiger, *Der Deutsche Kirchenkampf 1933-1945* (Zürich: EVZ Verlag, 1965), p. 19.

24. Eckart, *Bolschewismus*, p. 18. Another Eckart work, *Das ist der Jude! Laienpredigt über Juden- und Christentum* (München: Hoheneichenverlag, n.d.), p. 59, cites Friedrich Delitzsch, *Die grosse Täuschung. Kritische Betrachtungen zu den alttestamentlichen Berichten über Israels Eindringen in Kanaan, die Gottesoffenbarung vom Sinai, und die Wirksamkeit der Propheten* (Stuttgart-Berlin: Deutsche Verlags-Anstalt, 1920), pp. 39, 94 to deny Jesus' Jewishness.

25. Eckart, *Das ist der Jude!* p. 52.

26. Ibid., 28.

27. DC theologian Emanuel Hirsch wrote, "[The political revolution of January 1933] is a *holy storm* that has come over us and grasped us. . . . Of course, only a German can understand that internally." Robert P. Ericksen, *Theologians under Hitler: Gerhard Kittel—Paul Althaus—Emanuel Hirsch* (New Haven, Conn.: Yale University Press, 1985), p. 152. See Karl Barth's review of Hirsch's *Die gegenwärtige geistige Lage im Spiegel philosophischer und theologischer Besinnung* (Göttingen: Vandenhoeck and Ruprecht, 1934) in Karl Barth, *The German Church Conflict* (Richmond, Va.: John Knox Press, 1965), pp. 41-42.

28. Scholder, *The Churches*, 1:320-323; Conway, *Nazi Persecution*, p. 35.

29. "Ein geistliches Ministerium," was the phrase used to describe the cabinet of advisers. See Geiger, *Der deutsche Kirchenkampf*, p. 20.

30. Ibid., p. 21.

31. Helmreich, *German Churches under Hitler*, p. 136.

32. Ibid., p. 138.

33. Concerning the principle, "Wer Preussen besitzt, besitzt Deutschland!" see Wolfgang Scherffig, *Junge Theologen im "Dritten Reich." Dokumente, Briefe, Erfahrungen. Band 1, 1933-1935. Es Begann mit einem Nein!* (Neukirchen-Vluyn: Neukirchener Verlag, 1989), p. 5.

34. Helmreich, *German Churches under Hitler*, p 137. See also Buchheim, *Glaubenskrise*, p. 117, where he describes Jäger as a shrewd lawyer whose motto was, "Whatever gets the job done is just."

35. Otto Dibelius, whom Jäger suspended from his office as *General-superintendent* in Brandenburg, wrote of Jäger that his iron will and relentless obstinancy incarnated the will of the Nazi state. "There was something almost impressive in his sheer malignity and in the energy and singleness of purpose with which he pursued his ends." Otto Dibelius, *In the Service of the Lord* (New York: Holt, Rhinehart & Winston, 1964), p. 143.

36. Scholder, *The Churches*, 1:357-361; Conway, *Nazi Persecution*, pp. 36-37.

37. Manfred Hellmann, *Friedrich von Bodelschwingh d.J.: Widerstand für das Kreuz Christi* (Wuppertal: Brockhaus, 1988), pp. 127-128.

38. Helmreich, *German Churches under Hitler*, p. 142, citing Joseph Gauger, *Gotthard Briefe: Chronik der Kirchenwirren* (Elberfeld, 1934-35), 1:93.

39. Scholder, *The Churches*, 1:442-445.

40. Hitler said, "I am a Catholic. I have no position on the Protestant Church." Duncan-Jones, *Crooked Cross*, p. 13. Hitler was never excommunicated from the Church. On the contrary, he paid his Church taxes and, to the very end, listed himself as a Catholic in the Nazi Party handbook. Helmreich, *German Churches under Hitler*, p. 123.

41. Scholder, *The Churches*, 1:492, citing J. Glenthøj, *Dokumente zur Bonhoeffer Forschung 1928-1945* (München, Christian Kaiser Verlag [1969], p. 50.

42. The English form of the title is from Shirer, *Rise and Fall*, p. 240.

43. Alfred Rosenberg, *Der Mythus des 20. Jahrhunderts* (München: Hoheneichen Verlag, 1930).

44. This quotation and the following one are from Party Member Hannes Schneide, when teaching Hitler Youth in a training camp in Bernau on 30 July 1935. (Captured German Documents, microfilm, T-81, Series 43, Roll 16, frames 86533-86534, 98697. National Archives, Washington, D.C.).

45. Quoted by Duncan-Jones, *Crooked Cross*, pp. 11-12.

46. Helmreich, *German Churches under Hitler*, pp. 146-147. See also Eberhard Bethge, *Dietrich Bonhoeffer: Man of Vision, Man of Courage* (New York: Harper & Row, 1970), p. 241.

47. See Helmreich, *German Churches under Hitler*, p. 149.

48. See Paul Banwell Means, *Things That Are Caesar's* (New York: Round Table Press, 1935), pp. 248-249 for a longer citation in English. Means's cita-

tion is augmented by further paragraphs in Helmreich, *German Churches under Hitler*, p. 150.

49. Conway, *Nazi Persecution*, p. 53.

50. Scholder, *The Churches*, 1:558.

51. Geiger, *Der deutsche Kirchenkampf*, p. 23.

52. Helmreich, *German Churches under Hitler*, p. 153.

53. Conway, *Nazi Persecution*, pp. 71-72.

54. Helmreich, *German Churches under Hitler*, p. 414. According to other accounts, Hitler was disturbed, not only at Niemöller's attempt to drive a wedge between himself and the president, but by both implications of the theological phrase "*letzte Ölung.*" Henry Picker's *Hitlers Tischgespräche im Führerhauptquartier 1941-1942* (Bonn: Athenäum-Verlag, 1951) p. 357, records Hitler's own rendition of Niemöller's words: "We gave the old man [Hindenburg] extreme unction. We oiled him so well, he [Hitler] will now fire that randy old goat [Müller]." For other accounts of the meeting see Theophil Wurm, *Erinnerungen aus Meinem Leben* (Stuttgart: Quell-Verlag, 1953), p. 92; Hugo Hahn, *Kämpfer wider Willen: Erinnerungen des Landesbischofs von Sachsen D. Hugo Hahn aus dem Kirchenkampf 1933-1945* (Hetzingen: Brunnquell Verlag, 1969), p. 50; and the diary entry for 9 January 1940 in Hans-Günther Seraphim, *Das politische Tagebuch Alfred Rosenbergs aus den Jahren 1934-35 und 1939/40* (Göttingen: Musterschmidt-Verlag, 1956), p. 97.

55. Helmreich, *German Churches under Hitler*, p. 155.

56. Reinhold Sautter, *Theophil Wurm: Sein Leben und Sein Kampf* (Stuttgart: Calwer Verlag, 1960), p. 28.

57. Helmreich, *German Churches under Hitler*, p. 156.

58. Other organizations included Pastor Karl Immer's *Coetus* of Reformed Preachers in Barmen; and the Rhineland Pastors' Brotherhood. On Immer see Bertold Klappert and Günther van Norden, *Tut um Gottes willen etwas Tapferes! Karl Immer im Kirchenkampf* (Neukirchen-Vluyn: Neukirchener Verlag, 1989), pp. 193ff; on The Rhineland Pastors' Brotherhood see Wolfgang Scherffig, *Junge Theologen im "Dritten Reich:" Dokumente, Briefe, Erfahrungen. Band I, 1933-1935. Es begann mit einem Nein!* (Neukirchen-Vluyn: Neukirchener Verlag, 1989), and Scholder, *The Churches*, 1:533.

59. The most important regional meetings were:
a. The meeting of Free Reformed churchmen in Barmen-Gemarke called by Pastor Karl Immer, 3-4 January 1934;
b. The Free Protestant synod of the Rhineland ("Protestant" because it consisted of representatives of all three denominations: Lutheran, Reformed, and United), also held in Barmen on 18-19 February 1934;
c. The First Westphalian Confessing Synod, which met on 16 March 1934 in Dortmund, also involving representatives of all three confessions;
d. A large meeting of 25,000 Confessing laypeople in Dortmund, 18 March 1934;
e. An 11 April 1934 meeting in Ulm featuring speeches by Bishops Theophil

Wurm (Wurttemburg) and Hans Meiser (Bavaria) protesting the brutal enforcement tactics of the church administration in Berlin;

f. The 29 May 1934 First Confessing Synod of the Protestant Church of the Old Prussian Union in Barmen one day prior to the more famous Reich Synod held the next two days in the same city.

Helmreich, *German Churches under Hitler*, pp. 160-162; and Joachim Beckman, ed., *Briefe zur Lage der Evangelischen Bekenntnissynode im Rheinland Dezember 1933 bis Februar 1939* (Neukirchen-Vluyn: Neukirchener Verlag, 1977), p. 54.

60. Scholder, *The Churches*, 2:140; and Helmreich, *German Churches under Hitler*, pp. 138, 162.

61. The complete text of the Barmen Declaration in English is available in Arthur C. Cochrane, *The Church's Confession under Hitler* (Pittsburgh: Pickwick Press, 1976). The original German text is available in Alfred Burgsmüller and Rudolf Weth, eds., *Die Barmer theologische Erklärung, Einführung und Dokumentation* (Neukirchen-Vluyn: Neukirchener Verlag, 1984).

62. According to the *"Lagebericht des Chefs des Sicherheitsamtes des Reichsführers SS"* from May-June 1934, 8,000 pastors held membership in the Pastors' Emergency League (precursor to the Confessing Church); 2,000 were "German Christians" and 9,000 were officially neutral, though the opinion of the SS was that "most of the neutrals could be considered to sympathize with the Pastors' Emergency League." Heinz Boberach, *Berichte des SD und der Gestapo über Kirchen und Kirchenvolk in Deutschland 1934-1944* (Mainz: Matthias Grünewald, 1971), p. 56.

63. Shirer, *Rise and Fall*, p. 236.

64. Scholder, *The Churches*, 2:265-276.

65. Ibid., 2:259-261.

66. *Reibi* stood for *Rei*[ch]-*Bi*[schof], a derisive term used for Müller.

67. Müller continued in an official residence with an episcopal salary to the end of the war when Russian forces arrested him on 31 July 1945. Released fourteen days later, after he convinced the Russians that he had befriended the Jews, Müller committed suicide.

Jäger lived until 1948 when the Polish government executed him. Helmreich, *German Churches under Hitler*, pp. 175, 304, 501.

68. Alfred Rosenberg, *An die Dunkelmänner unserer Zeit: Eine Antwort auf die Angriffe gegen den "Mythus des 20. Jahrhunderts"* (München: Hoheneichenverlag, 1935).

69. For details and figures on the arrests, see Conway, *Nazi Persecution*, p. 122; and Helmreich, *German Churches under Hitler*, p. 179.

70. Conway, *Nazi Persecution*, p. 130.

71. Hahn, *Kämpfer wider Willen*, pp. 110-112 offers a sympathetic portrait of Kerrl; see also Helmreich, *German Churches under Hitler*, p. 505.

72. Helmreich, *German Churches under Hitler*, p. 190.

73. Churches declared their independence from state control by ordaining

candidates without official approval. Dr. Karl Koch, of the Confessing Church of Westphalia, protested against Reich-Bishop Müller in this way on 21 October 1934 when he "illegally" ordained five candidates in Pastor Martin Niemöller's St. Anna Church in Berlin. Paul F. Douglass, *God among the Germans* (Philadelphia: University of Pennsylvania Press, 1935), pp. 261-262. The Confessing Church in Essen took this a step further on 8 December 1935 with the "ordination" of three women. See chapter 3 below.

74. Conway, *Nazi Persecution*, pp 137-138; and Beckmann, *Briefe zur Lage*, pp. 547-553.

75. Beckmann, *Briefe zur Lage*, pp. 1-8.

76. The memorandum was signed by the members of the Second Provisional Church Leadership: Fritz Müller, Martin Albertz, Hans Böhm, Bernard Forck, and Otto Fricke; and by the *Bruderrat* of the German Protestant Church: Hans Asmussen, Karl Lücking, Friedrich Middendorff, Martin Niemöller, and Reinold von Thadden.

The citations and names of the signatories are from the translation offered by the New York *Herald Tribune*, 28 July 1936, pp. 1, 4, and appear with permission from the New York *Herald Tribune*, 28 July, 1936; (c) 1936, New York Herald Tribune, Inc. All rights reserved. Reprinted by permission.

77. Weissler, who was arrested and murdered in a concentration camp, and who was the first martyr of the Confessing Church, was a non-Aryan—that is, Jewish—Christian. See Bethge, *Dietrich Bonhoeffer*, p. 606.

78. From *New York Herald Tribune*, 28 July, 1936; (c) 1936, New York Herald Tribune, Inc. All rights reserved. Reprinted by permission.

79. Ernst Hornig, *Die Bekennende Kirche in Schlesien 1933-1945: Geschichte und Dokumente* (Göttingen: Vandenhoeck and Ruprecht, 1977), pp. 42, 167, 168.

80. Conway, *Nazi Persecution*, p. 164. Conway is correct in saying the VKL did not give the congregations the complete text of the original memorandum; but Hornig's independent publication and distribution made the memorandum available to the churches.

81. Helmreich, *German Churches under Hitler*, p. 201.

82. Wurm wrote Interior Minister Wilhelm Frick on 19 July 1940 and 5 September 1940 protesting the euthanasia policy (Conway, *Nazi Persecution*, pp. 264-265 and Sautter, *Theophil Wurm*, pp. 63-66); on 20 December 1942 Wurm published a letter addressed to Hans Lammers, head of the Reich Chancellery, about the state's eradication of the Jews (Helmreich, *German Churches under Hitler*, p. 331). The letters enjoyed quick, broad dissemination (Sautter, *Theophil Wurm*, p. 65). On 3 March 1944 Lammers issued an injunction against any further public expression from Wurm. (Sautter, *Theophil Wurm*, p. 68).

83. Helmreich, *German Churches under Hitler*, p. 201.

84. Conway, *Nazi Persecution*, pp. 186-187.

85. Helmreich, *German Churches under Hitler*, p. 215.

86. James Bentley, *Martin Niemöller 1892-1984* (New York: Free Press,

1984), pp. 140-142.

87. Boberach, *Berichte des SD*, pp. xxxvi, xxxix, n. 4; p. 23, n. 2; 905-906.

88. Helmreich, *German Churches under Hitler*, p. 215. By August 1937 the prayer lists in Prussia contained the names of sixty-five imprisoned pastors, twenty-four others with restraining orders against public speaking, and an additional twenty-nine who had been dismissed from their offices.

89. Conway, *Nazi Persecution*, p. 209. Shirer, *Rise and Fall*, gives the figure as 807, p. 239.

90. Hornig, *Die Bekennende Kirche*, pp. 55, 221, 222.

91. With the possibility of war looming large, the Confessing Church had prepared a liturgy to be used on Sunday, 30 September 1938, beseeching God's forgiveness for the personal and national sins of the German people, and describing the imminent war as punishment. See Conway, *Nazi Persecution*, pp. 220-221, 230.

92. Because of the entrenched strength of the German bureaucracy, Confessing pastors who were ordained before May 1934 continued to draw their salaries, even from DC-dominated consistories. Pastors ordained in the Confessing Church after May 1934 were considered "illegal" and drew no salary from the consistories.

93. Conway, *Nazi Persecution*, p. 232, citing a circular from the Chief of Race and Settlement Headquarters, 8 September 1939, Unpublished Nuremberg Document NG-1392.

94. Conway, *Nazi Persecution*, p. 238; Helmreich, *German Churches under Hitler*, p. 321.

95. For examples of near hagiography, see bibliographical entries in the "Secondary Sources: Books" section under Bernhard Heinrich Forck, *"... und folget ihrem Glauben nach:" Gedenkbuch für die Blutzeugen der Bekennenden Kirche* (Stuttgart: Evangelisches Verlagswerk, 1949); Werner Öhme, *Märtyrer der evangelischen Christenheit 1933-1945: Neunundzwanzig Lebensbilder* (Berlin: Evangelisches Verlagsanstalt, 1980); Leo Stein, *I Was in Hell with Niemöller* (London: Stanley Paul, 1942); and the book probably written by Pastor Hermann Maas of Heidelberg, *Den Unvergessenen: Opfer des Wahns 1933 bis 1945* (Heidelberg: Verlag Lambert Schneider, 1952). See also the secondary source article by Gudrun Orlt, "Das Verbot eines bösen Menschen brachte erste Frau in die Gemeinde: Vor 50 Jahren wurde Pastorin Aenne Kaufmann ordiniert, *Der Weg* (Düsseldorf) 50, no. 85, (December 8, 1985).

For examples of revisionism see Friedrich Baumgärtel, *Wider die Kirchenkampf-Legenden* (Freimund: Verlag Neundettelsau Mfr., 1958) in which he specifically takes Wilhelm Niemöller to task for embroidering the facts; H. S. Brebeck, *Martin Niemöller: Bekenner, Politiker oder Demagoge?* (Henef: H. E. Schneider, [1959]); and Hans Prolingheuer, *Kleine politische Kirchengeschichte: 50 Jahre evangelischer Kirchenkampf von 1919 bis 1969* (Köln: Pahl-Rugenstein, 1984-85).

96. Barth, *The German Church Conflict*, p. 45. The passage was written

during the summer of 1935.

97. Ibid., p. 45.

98. Martin Niemöller, *Of Guilt and Hope* (New York: Philosophical Library and Book Corporation, [1946]), p. 15.

99. Dibelius, *Service*, p. 259. Many members of the Confessing Church were not at all pleased that Niemöller and Dibelius had presumed to speak thus for them.

100. Barth was acclaiming the Confessing Church with a citation from the Gospel According to St. John. Busch, *Karl Barth*, p. 273.

Chapter 2

Confessing Laywomen in the Church Struggle

Even if we know so little about her, we don't want to forget her.
—Werner Öhme on Inge Jacobsen[1]

If most histories of the Church Struggle convey the distinct impression that the Confessing Church consisted primarily of men, the church membership rolls tell a different tale. The Confessing Church counted among its members far more women than men. A popular proverb of the day had it right: "The Church is led by men, but borne by women."

A pastor making daily decisions about ministering to his parish relied in nearly every case on the women of his congregation to support his efforts and, indeed, to do much of the work: a secretary, a parish assistant, a hostess, a kindergarten teacher, a nurse, a patroness, the women of the Protestant Ladies' Auxiliary and, not the least, a female theological assistant (a *Theologin*) and the pastor's wife.[2] The women knew that Gestapo agents shadowed their work on behalf of the Church. Consciously risking security and freedom for the sake of religious conviction, they committed themselves to the cause, proving themselves indispensable to the life and survival of the Confessing Church.[3] "Without the women," Wolfgang See and Rudolf Weckerling reflected, "there would have been nothing."[4] Pastor Joachim Beckmann agreed: "The women supplied the courage to persist."[5]

THE CHURCH SECRETARIES

The pastors' secretaries, for example, guarded some of the most dangerous secrets of the Confessing Church. Senta Maria Klatt, who served as the personal secretary for both *Generalsuperintendent* Otto Dibelius and Pastor Kurt Scharf in Berlin, resorted to desperate measures in December 1933 when she saw a Gestapo car pull up in front of her church offices in Berlin. This is how the situation transpired. When Reich-Bishop Ludwig Müller and Nazi Youth Minister Baldur von Schirach agreed to turn over the entire Protestant youth organization to Shirach's Hitler Youth, the Pastors' Emergency League protested. Dibelius drew up a protest letter comparing this Nazi youth takeover to Herod's murder of the innocents. Klatt typed Dibelius' document, slipped it into the zipper lining of her muff, and prepared to carry it across town to a printer. Then she saw the Gestapo car. Knowing that the officers would certainly search her and find the zipper lining and the letter, Fräulein Klatt tore the document into pieces and literally ate it before the Gestapo agents could get to her. Years later, the octogenarian recounted: "You should try that sometime. You can barely get the thing down!"[6]

Senta Maria Klatt shared the distinction of being a Christian of Jewish lineage with a number of other women who served the Confessing Church as secretaries. Indeed, hiring non-Aryan Christian women was one way in which the Confessing Church tried to protect them, even if, as in Klatt's case, they could neither type nor take dictation, and spelled poorly. Among other Jewish secretaries in the church's service were Irene Breslauer,[7] Charlotte Friedenthal,[8] and Hildegard Jacoby.[9] Klatt endured scores of arrests and Gestapo inquisitions. Breslauer fled to Scotland and took a new name. Friedenthal, after serving with Superintendent Martin Albertz in Berlin, fled Germany with the help of Pastor Dietrich Bonhoeffer's "Operation 7," a conspiracy of anti-Hitler officers in the army's counter-intelligence agency, who smuggled Jews into Switzerland and plotted the assassination of the Führer. Hildegard Jacoby fell seriously ill in prison, and died on the day of her release.

Berlin church secretaries Dorothea Herrmann and Helene Jacobs went above and beyond the duties of mere secretarial work, and as a result saw the inside of a prison in 1943 for outfitting Jews with falsified identification papers and securing food coupons for them on the black market.[10]

Confessing secretaries who did not go to prison or suffer martyrdom still lived in constant tension, aware of their danger. Karl Immer's secretaries, Elisabeth Müller and Adele Menges[11] continued with him in spite of the danger attached to his *Coetus* publishing. So also Martha Goesser worked with Wuppertal pastors Peter Bockemühl and Hermann Klugkist-Hesse on the forbidden journal *Unter dem Wort* which the Gestapo later confiscated and banned.[12] Hermine Hermes served as the secretary for the Pastors' Emergency League, privy to many of that organization's dangerous secrets. She protected its leading personalities with her discretion.[13] Theologian Irene Atzerode found her ministry in serving as Superintendent Hugo Hahn's secretary in Dresden, an office from which "German Christian" elements expelled the Confessing bishop.[14]

TEACHERS

Women who served as teachers in church schools associated with Confessing congregations spent their professional and private hours under the watchful eyes of the Gestapo. Not only were Gestapo agents in the churches listening to the pastors' sermons, they even, on occasion, recorded the activities of the children's worship services.[15]

Kindergarten teacher Johanna Eckart defended herself in court in Neuruppin in 1939 because in her Bible classes with girls of the congregation she had included activities such as card games, billiards, and occasional rounds of hide-and-seek. In doing so, according to the indictment, she had violated the "Law for the Protection of the People and State of 28 February 1933" and disregarded the police order of 23 July 1935 regulating denominational youth groups. Paragraph 1 of the police order forbade church youth groups from enjoying any activity that was not explicitly religious. The law reserved the more obviously entertaining games and sports exclusively for the Hitler Youth and its feminine counterpart, the Union of German Maidens.[16]

High school teacher Maria Luise Helmbold in Eisenach worked as an active lay member of the tiny Confessing Church in Thüringia, supporting the leading pastor, Ernst Otto, whom she assisted with office work and in teaching Bible classes.[17] When the "German-Christian" Bishop Sasse drove Otto out of his pastoral office, Helmbold carried to the bishop a petition with two thousand signatures demanding Otto's reinstatement. For this courageous act, Nazi school authorities punished Helmbold with a transfer to a rural school district deep in the Thuringian Forest, where she continued undeterred in active work with small Confessing congregations. In addition to a full teaching load, Helmbold served as an elder in her congregations and preached in the villages of Hämmern and Steinach, traveling by foot, bicycle, or snowshoe from one village to the next.[18]

HOSTESSES AND PATRONESSES

Anna von Gierke, a recognized pioneer in educational reform for children, lost her school when she refused to dismiss the children of Jewish families. Von Gierke, however, did not stop being an innovative educator. Though deprived of her classrooms, she still had a home in Berlin. There, shifting to adult education, von Gierke hosted weekly salon evenings for Confessors, who on alternate weeks heard lecturers on literary and biblical topics.[19]

The role of the hostess was crucial in these years. The woman who could open her home and extend civil kindnesses to her guests, and at the same time bring influential Confessing leaders together in a relatively safe environment, did a great service for her church.

Helen von Nostitz-Wallwitz, who was widowed in World War I and left with eight children, still found time and energy for the Confessing Church of Saxony.

Confessing leaders met in her home and she accepted mail at her personal address to protect the deposed Confessing Superintendent Hugo Hahn.[20]

Ruth von Kleist-Retzow, a matriarch of an aristocratic clan in Pomerania, where the Confessing Church was particularly strong, made her land and properties available to Pastor Dietrich Bonhoeffer, his Finkenwalde students, and their families. Finkenwalde lay within the realm of Frau von Kleist's hereditary influence, where she signed on as one of the first members of the Pomeranian Confessing Church. Because the Finkenwalde seminary began with nothing but its house on the North Sea, it was dependent on gifts from individuals and Confessing congregations for furniture, books, and food. Frau von Kleist not only saw that the seminarians were provided with groceries, but provided writing paper as well. Wives and fiancées of imprisoned seminarians found a haven of comfort and rest at von Kleist's Klein-Krössin estate. When Bonhoeffer was barred from Berlin, he found a home in von Kleist's house in Stettin. "Her hospitality," wrote Finkenwalde seminarian Eberhard Bethge, "knew no bounds."[21]

On the scene at Finkenwalde was Erna Struwe, the housemother who cooked and cleaned for the young men. Struwe bore the brunt of the news when Himmler declared all of the Confessing Church's schools illegal. She was at Finkenwalde with just a single student on 29 September 1937 when the police padlocked the doors and shut the students out, and she made the move to serve the Bonhoeffer Vikare at their new, illegal arrangement in Hinter-Pomerania.[22]

When the Nazis closed Finkenwalde, the Confessing *Superintendenten* in the area, Friedrich Onnasch in Köslin and Eduard Block in Schlawe, conspired to persist in the training of young pastors. Pretending to assign the Finkenwalde students as Vikare to surrounding parishes, the Superintendenten in fact established the young men in two "collective vicariates."[23] Superintendent Onnasch took six to eight of the young men into his own spacious parsonage in Köslin, a decision that certainly impacted the life of his wife Mia Onnasch.[24] In Schlawe the other seminarians made themselves comfortable on the Sigurdshof estate of Count Ewald and Countess Margarete von Kleist-Trychow.[25] Bonhoeffer, who was officially housed in Schlawe, motorcycled sixty kilometers from the city to the estate to teach both groups of students. The arrangement in Köslin lasted until fall 1939 when it was closed for lack of students. At Sigurdshof, Countess von Kleist-Trychow arranged to feed the men and keep them supplied with firewood during an especially bitter winter, all the while keeping the Gestapo in the dark. From April 1939 until 18 March 1940, the students met with Bonhoeffer, though the number dwindled steadily as one by one the seminarians were drafted into the army. Two days after the last young Vikar had left for the armed forces, the Gestapo arrived to search the estate.[26]

Similarly hospitable was Countess Mechthild von Behr,[27] whose Behrenhoff estate was the scene of Confessional meetings and lectures in Pomeranian Greifswald. When Pastor Albrecht Schönherr bicycled the nine kilometers from Greifswald out to the Behrenhoff estate in 1936, it was with the intent to ask the

Countess if Schönherr's illegal confessing Vikars could use her property for an occasional retreat center. With the initial conversation Schönherr realized that the countess knew almost nothing about the Confessing Church. However, out of antipathy to National Socialism, she agreed to help, and placed her castle at the disposal of the BK Student Fellowship for four summers, 1936-1939. That in itself was a courageous step, and all the more so because Countess von Behr had a Jewish grandparent.[28]

Aristocratic landholders in the eastern parts of Germany had the right, established by centuries of tradition in their churches, to appoint or disapprove the appointment of a pastor in their areas of influence. In numerous cases, the Confessing *feudiste* saw to the provision of the pastor and his family when times became difficult. When "German Christian" elements in Greifswald ousted the Confessing pastor, Carl Buth, help came from Countess Elisabeth von Thadden,[29] who, assisted by her mother-in-law, saw that groceries from her farms got to the parsonage. Countess Von Thadden made no attempt to hide her support of the Confessing cause. Indeed, she taught a Bible class and conducted children's church services as well.[30]

SPIRITUAL LEADERS

The engagement of the women of the Confessing Church was not limited to the traditional women's work of hosting meetings, teaching children and serving as secretaries. In a development that foreshadowed the eventual ordination of women to full pastoral office, several Confessing women served as elders, members of brotherhood councils, and even preachers and leaders of liturgical services.

Stephanie von Mackensen served as the only woman delegate at the synod that drafted the Barmen Confession in May 1934, and she voted as the only woman participant in the Dahlem Synod of October 1934 where the Confessing Church took form.[31] Because Frau von Mackensen initially saw in Adolf Hitler and his movement exactly what Germany needed to regain its rightful role in the world, she joined the Nazi Party in 1932; however, two events of the following year showed her the error of her ways. The infamous Berlin Sports Arena speech of 13 November convinced her that "the 'German Christians' aren't Christians any more." When DC Bishop Karl Thom demanded that all Pomeranian Protestants swear an oath of personal allegiance to him, von Mackensen strode from the hall along with members of the Pastors' Emergency League, who elected her into their brotherhood council.[32] Von Mackensen took a leading role in the administration of the Confessing Church in Pomerania, so much so that for a while, the entire income of the Confessing Church was poured into von Mackensen's personal bank account, from which she paid the pastors and vicars. At one point, when all the other members of the Brotherhood Council were imprisoned, she alone administered the Confessing Church of Pomerania.

Von Mackensen decided for tactical reasons to leave her name on the membership roles of the Nazi Party, a strategy that she worked out with several other Confessing pastors, who were also, technically, Nazis. Rather than resign, von Mackensen determined to remain in the Party until such a time as the NSDAP would insist on excluding her, thereby revealing its anti-Christian position.[33] When the day of reckoning came, Nazi Party authorities called Stephanie von Mackensen before a tribunal to determine her loyalties.

"Who is the lord [Herr] of your life, the Jew Jesus Christ, or the Führer Adolf Hitler?" demanded SA-leader Count von der Goltz.

"Jesus Christ alone is the Lord of my life," answered Stephanie von Mackensen.

"Should you encounter a conflict between the demands of this Jesus Christ and the demands of the Führer, whom would you obey?" asked von der Goltz next.

"When I experience such a conflict," she answered, "naturally I will obey the commands of my Lord Jesus."

The inquisitioners retired to another room to confer and after a lengthy delay, returned with the demand, "The *Gauleiter*[34] demands of you that you resign from the Party of your own free will!"

"Would you please tell the Gauleiter," Frau von Mackensen responded, "I have as much right to remain in the Party as he does. When I joined the Party, everyone knew that I was a Christian, and that I serve my church conscientiously. I have not changed. If my behavior is no longer regarded as correct, you will have to expel me from the Party."[35]

The NSDAP did not, in fact, dismiss von Mackensen. Instead the Party brought political pressure to bear on her husband, who had to leave Stettin, and it drafted Frau von Mackensen into Red Cross service in Paris and Brussels, where she could no longer work actively with the Church.

Charlotte von Kirschbaum exercised a profound influence on the Confessing Church through her intimate association with Professor Karl Barth. It was Barth whose writings set the course for the Pastors' Emergency League, who penned the Barmen Confession, and who agitated throughout the period 1934-1945 through his journal *Theologische Existenz heute.*[36] Generally recognized as Barth's secretary, von Kirschbaum did far more than take dictation and type. She generated and maintained Barth's citations catalogue, supplied him with documentation, and was at his side at every crucial turn in his academic life, including the decisive Bonn years, during which the Church Struggle broke out. She certainly had a hand in drafting the language of the Barmen Confession.[37] Barth made no effort to hide his debt to "Lollo" von Kirschbaum. He said she inspired him, and in fact, when she grew ill with Altzheimer's disease, Barth ceased to write.[38]

Another nontheologian who nevertheless exercised a theological influence on the Confessing Church, Marga Meusel composed the Confessing Church's earliest document calling for solidarity with the Jews—all Jews, not just the baptized. As the director of the Protestant Regional Welfare Office of the Domestic Mission in Berlin-Zehlendorf since 1932, Meusel and her colleague, Charlotte Friedenthal, saw firsthand the shocking social consequences of the law of 7 April 1933 on non-Aryan Protestants.[39] Friedenthal proposed to Berlin Superintendent Martin Albertz that the Confessing Church establish a Central Counseling Station for Non-Aryan Issues, volunteering to direct the work, but neither she, Meusel, nor Albertz could find a church leader with both the willingness and the experience to sponsor such a politically sensitive venture.[40] Meusel drafted an article entitled, "The Responsibilities of the Domestic Mission towards the Non-Aryan Christian" but in March 1935 she could find no editor brave enough to publish it.[41] In the meantime, the social conditions of the Jews continued to deteriorate rapidly, and though the Catholic St. Raphael Club had its "Aid Committee for Catholic Non-Aryans" the Confessing Church had nothing. In April 1935 Meusel turned to the Protestant convents for help, asking if they would accept Protestant non-Aryans as apprentice deaconesses, but with disappointing results.[42] In September 1935 the Confessing Church of Prussia called a synodical meeting in Steglitz, where Albertz read Meusel's redrafted document, "The Status of the German Non-Aryan," a title that reflected her growing concern for all the victims of Nazism, including non-Christians. Albertz read Marga Meusel's memorandum to the synod against two ominous background developments. Some Confessing congregations had openly refused to baptize Jewish converts, thus tacitly appropriating the "Aryan Paragraph" for their churches, and the Nuremberg Laws loomed on the horizon. Would the Confessing Church synod make a statement against both developments?

Meusel's introductory paragraphs reminded the readers of the Augsburg Confession's principle: laws which countermand God's commandments are unworthy of Christians' obedience. She then catalogued the extent of official and unofficial harassment, persecution, disenfranchisement, intimidation, brutality, libel, and social banishment that non-Aryans were experiencing. Did the Confessing Church have a responsibility to do something? She wrote:

> The Confessing Church has formally professed its role as "Watchman on the Walls" according to Ezekiel 3. Does she not want to express compassion towards her members and let the Watchman's call open eyes and shake consciences awake? The enemy—the idolatry of Blood and Race—threatens immediately outside the walls, perhaps even closer.[43]

> Out of Sweden comes a decimating charge: "The Germans have a new God, Race, and they bring him human sacrifice." Who would dare punish such as a lie?

> What should we answer to the question, "Where is your brother Abel?" We, the Confessing Church, have no better answer than Cain's.[44]

Meusel painted details of the persecution of non-Aryan children; the threat to marriages involving a non-Aryan partner; the impossibility of professional lives for non-Aryan doctors, dentists, veterinarians, teachers, bureaucrats, lawyers, druggists, and colporteurs. Then, under the heading "The Position of the Church," she wrote prophetically:

Persecution of Jews in the name of Blood and Race *must* [the emphasis is Meusel's] of necessity be followed by a persecution of Christians. The Confessing Church has experienced the beginning of that, especially the parsonages. But no one can claim to draw a comparison between the plight of Christians and the suffering of the Jews and non-Aryans. . . . [T]he Christian suffers personally, the Jew and non-Aryan suffers with his children and grandchildren. And even if a member of the Confessing Church were to come under the Aryan Laws, the rest of his family would not be punished. But the main difference is this: the Confessing Church suffers—and is aware of it—for its faith; the Non-Aryan is persecuted because God let him be born into a certain family. . . .

Shall the refugees starve? Who will recognize the obligation to help? Who will feed the hungry, clothe the naked, visit the imprisoned? Who will do good to all men, or even to those of the household of faith?

Why must we continually hear from the ranks of the non-Christians, that they feel the Church has abandoned them? That Jewish people and Jewish organizations help, but not the Church? That they needn't worry about their Catholic colleagues . . . . because the Catholic Church is taking care of them, but that one must say on behalf of the Protestants, "Lord, forgive them, they know not what they do?" Why is it that the Catholic Church can hire . . . . non-Aryan physicians and nurses, but the Protestant Church's Domestic Missions Board complies with the Aryan Paragraph?

Why doesn't the Church pray for those suffering guiltlessly, those under persecution? Why aren't there prayer meetings for the Jews, like there were prayer meetings when the pastors were arrested? The Church makes it bitterly difficult for us to defend her.

Since when was it anything other than blasphemy to contend that it is the will of God for us to promote injustice? Let us take care that we do not enthrone the evil of our sins in the Temple of the Will of God. Otherwise the fate of the temple defilers will be ours: we will hear the condemnation of Him Who made a whip of cords and drove them out.[45]

Meusel's articulate and passionate presentation of the case had the support of Albertz, Pastors Franz Hildebrandt, Niemöller, Heinrich Vogel, and Bonhoeffer with his Finkenwalde students, all of whom wanted the synod to make a statement of solidarity with the Jews; however, most of the synodalists quailed before such a radical step, which came perilously close to mixing politics with religion.[46] *Präses* Karl Koch of Westphalia threatened to resign from the Provisional Church Leadership if the synod adopted Meusel's strong language.[47] Pastor Gerhard Jacobi of Berlin opined that the time was not ripe for such a statement and pled that the issue of the Church and unbaptized Jews be taken up at a future synod, "where we can find the right word."[48]

In a firm statement, the synod branded as sin any refusal to baptize a Jew. However, in equally unmistakable language, the Steglitz churchmen allowed that citizenship in the Kingdom of God guarantees no civil protection. Niemöller described the statement as "a minimum," and Vogel called it "the minimum of a minimum."[49] "Jews will be baptized," Niemöller murmured sadly, "but we are not saying anything about what happens to them after that."[50]

Marga Meusel's concerns eventually made their way into the conscience of the Confessing Church's leadership. The 1936 secret memorandum to Hitler reflected her thought, and in 1937, the church established a ministry [*Büro*] to non-Aryan Christians under Pastor Heinrich Grüber.[51] The 1936 memorandum was too late. The Büro Grüber was too little.

The guilt of the Confessing Church in not speaking earlier and more forcefully against racism lies at the feet of its leading men. Women like Meusel and Friedenthal, by contrast, had an early and clear conception of what Christian discipleship meant in relation to racial persecution.[52]

ARRESTED, FINED, IMPRISONED

Women as well as men sat in German prisons for their faith during the Church Struggle. The Gestapo arrested apartment building superintendent Elfriede Daneit (née Schmidt), editorial assistant Melanie Steinmetz, bookkeeper Edith Wolff, secretaries Dorothea Herrmann, Hildegard Jacoby, and Helene Jacobs, widow Frieda Fischer (née Stiebler), office worker Elsbeth Vonhoff (née Bruchs) and two men—all members of the Confessing Church—between June and October 1943 for conspiring to falsify documents, deal in grocery coupons on the black market, and transfer identification papers to Jews in hiding.[53] A Jewish Christian physician, Franz Kaufmann, directed the operation, for which he died in February 1944.

Dora von Öttingen, a Rhineland nurse and parish assistant, spent six months in a Frankfurt jail in 1942.[54] Working with Pastor Georgian of the Lukas congregation of the Confessing Church of Hessia, von Öttingen worked from 1938 to 1942 in youth and women's circles, gave confirmation instruction, and even preached in Pastor Georgian's absence. She also cared for and hid Jewish families, but she spent half a year in jail for distributing a piece of contraband literature entitled "The Thirty Program Points of the National Reich Church," which outlined the government's plan for the eradication of Christianity after the war. The postwar "Reich Church" would supersede and exclude all other churches in Germany, promoting allegiance of all Germans to a gospel based on Nation and Race (*Volk und Rasse*) in complete submission to the state. Under the Reich Church, all vestiges of Christianity would disappear: Bibles, houses of worship, clergy, theologians, holy day observances, church presses, baptism, confirmation, and any dogma of forgiveness of sins. Replacing the Bible on altars in the Reich Church would be *Mein Kampf*, "in which is found embodied the greatest and purist ethic for the present and future life of our people." Swastikas would replace crosses on confiscated houses of worship.[55]

Seeing the document first in Wuppertal in 1941, where alarmed Christians were copying it by hand for clandestine distribution, von Öttingen brought the "Thirty Program Points" back to Frankfurt with her and disseminated it among her trusted acquaintances. During a Gestapo house search, agents found a copy among her books and arrested her forthwith. Von Öttingen spent the first weeks in prison in solitary confinement with brutal interrogations. The Gestapo tried to find out from whom she had got her copy of the document, where it originated, and to whom she had given further copies, but learned nothing. The balance of her prison time was spent in a crowded communal cell with several other women. Releasing her after six months, an agent accompanied von Öttingen to the Frankfurt train station and sent her home to Wuppertal with an order to desist from her chosen profession as a parish assistant.

When Leni Immer, the twenty-four year-old daughter of Pastor Karl and Tabea Immer in Wuppertal, received a summons to appear before the Gestapo to explain why she had been mailing unauthorized literature, she thought immediately of the cruel mistreatment of her friend, Dora von Öttingen. The ostensible reason for the Gestapo's interest in Immer was the church bulletins she was mailing to soldiers at the front without prior submission for government approval, but the Immers feared that the investigation into the church bulletins was a ruse to interrogate the girl and extract sensitive information about the Confessing Church.

Karl Immer, a consistently intrepid leader in the Protestant resistance, had entrusted many of the most intimate secrets of the Rhineland Confessing Church to his responsible daughter. He feared for her safety, and also feared that under Gestapo pressure she would betray too many confidences. "My child, you can't take it. Dealing with these people, you can't do it!" Leni Immer confronted his fear with two questions: "Do you think you are the only Christian in Germany? Can't you imagine that younger people can find the right words, too?" With that she prepared herself for the Gestapo inquisition.

Deep within the secret police's Wuppertal office building, with a series of locked doors behind her and the experience of Dora von Öttingen in mind, Fräulein Immer faced her interrogators with calculated charm, a disarming smile, and a stack of the offending church bulletins. Yes, she readily admitted, she had sent these church bulletins to soldiers on the front, men who were members of her father's Barmen-Gemarke Reformed Church, but this should in no way be construed as subversive. She showed the Gestapo officers the articles and news items and explained that if anything, this kind of news from home bolstered the soldiers' spirits.

At the end of her defense, the leader of the interrogation squad cleared his throat and, with some hesitation and embarrassment, extended an unusual request: since Fräulein Immer could type, and since she had studied at the better schools in Wuppertal and since she had such a good way with words, would Fräulein Immer mind formulating and typing up the minutes of this little meeting between herself and the gentlemen from the Secret Police? Leni Immer was happy to comply and came away from her questioning with more than just a moral victory![56]

The Gestapo interrogated Senta Maria Klatt scores of times. They imprisoned her once for eighteen days in Alexanderplatz, but in spite of her official designation as a *"Mischling ersten Grades"*—half-Aryan of the first degree—she was able to escape the concentration camps. On one occasion when she was arrested, she was informed that her papers for Concentration Camp Ravensbrück were ready. In a somewhat agitated state, she fainted in the ladies' room, and in falling, she hit her chin on the edge of the porcelain sink. When she revived she realized that she was wet and bleeding, but rather than improve her appearance, she stuck her finger in the wound to make it larger, smeared her face with blood "like a Sioux Indian," and let herself be discovered by the soldiers in this condition.

They dragged her, now a bleeding, weeping, piteous creature, into the Kommissar's office. He shoved the Ravensbrück papers across the desk to her and roared, "Just read through that!" However, he then pulled the papers away before she could see them, tore them in pieces, and discharged her with the order to register with a war industry firm and report to the Gestapo on a regular basis.[57]

THE MARTYRS

No description of Confessing women would be complete without mentioning those who paid for their commitment with human life. By far, most of the recorded Confessing martyrs were men, but as each man went to his death, the women in his life suffered along with him. From the standpoint of Christian faith, loss of life is not the greatest tragedy. Those who did not die themselves but were robbed of their loved ones suffered psychologically and spiritually long before and after the physical martyrdoms.

Friedrich Weissler, the Confessing Church's first martyr, unwittingly leaked the Confessing Church's 1936 secret Hitler Memorandum to the foreign press. The Gestapo arrested Weissler on 3 October 1936 and put him immediately in solitary confinement. Left behind in the apartment were his wife Johanna

Weissler (née Schäfer), and two sons. Ordinarily, the Confessing Church would have put Weissler's name on the list of those who, "persecuted for righteousness' sake," would be the object of special prayer, but Frau Weissler specifically asked the Church not to do so, as such attention to a Jewish Christian would only make the family's situation worse.[58] In February 1937 prison officials transferred Weissler to the Sachsenhausen concentration camp just outside Berlin. There, separated from the others who were arrested on the same grounds, he died under mysterious conditions. One assumes murder.[59]

The Nazi practice of *Sippenhaft*, the arrest of relatives of alleged criminals, endangered the innocent family members. For example, the police arrested Friedrich Justus Perels, an attorney in the service of the Confessing Church, on 5 October 1944 in connection with the wave of arrests that followed the attempted assassination of Hitler the previous 20 July.[60] Helga Perels, who was not at home at the time of his arrest, wandered through the streets of Berlin for days before locating her husband's cell in the Prinz Albrecht Strasse prison. Her visits were dangerous. She came perilously close to losing her own freedom when a *Kriminalkommissar* discovered a letter that F. J. Perels tried to smuggle out with her. Because the location of the prison, next to the train station, made that part of Berlin a favorite bombing target, each of Helga Perels' visits was potentially life-threatening. Furthermore, she was particularly vulnerable because of her position since 1938 as secretary of the Brotherhood Council of the Confessing Church of the Old Prussian Union in Berlin.

On one prison visit, Frau Perels asked the prison guard to deliver a basket of food and clothing to prisoner Perels. When he responded with the question, "Which prisoner Perels?" she knew immediately what that meant: her father-in-law, Professor Ernst Perels, had also been arrested under *Sippenhaft*. The older Perels died in Buchenwald on 10 May 1945.

Police arrested Anneliese Kauffmann and her brother Hans Kauffmann, cousins of F. J. Perels, in October 1944 because, through questioning Perels, the agents had determined that the Kauffmanns had three Jewish grandparents, making them full Jews (*Volljuden*). They died in February 1945. During all this time, Helga Perels, who was living without a regular income, was constrained to sublet part of her apartment.

When the infamous Nazi judge Roland Freisler condemned F. J. Perels to death on 2 February 1945, Helga Perels initiated every possible legal maneuver to appeal the decision and lengthen the time between sentencing and execution. She succeeded until 23 April 1945 when, with Russian troops entering the city, a squad of SS men directed Perels and other prisoners to walk out of the prison and cross an open field. The SS shot the prisoners in the back, subsequently administering coups de grace with bullets in the neck.

These women suffered in the martyrdoms of the men while other Confessing women paid directly with their lives for their commitment. Inge Jacobsen worked in the Büro Grüber with Pastors Heinrich Grüber and Werner Sylten, both of whom later languished in Dachau, where Sylten died. A "non-Aryan"

Christian, Jacobsen came under arrest and, facing certain deportation to a concentration camp, died while attempting to flee.[61]

Hildegard Jacoby, the daughter of a Jewish physician and an Aryan woman, worked as a church secretary for the Brotherhood Council of the Confessing Church of Berlin-Brandenburg. In spite of—or perhaps because of—her double jeopardy of being both Jewish and a Confessor, Jacoby joined the Kaufmann conspiracy with Helene Jacobs and supplied falsified identification papers and groceries to hiding Jews. After her arrest in August 1943, she began a sentence of eighteen months in prison, but then became gravely ill. When officials released her because of her frail condition on 2 June 1944, she went directly to the home of Margot Kaufmann, the widow of her already executed colleague, where she suffered a heart attack and died within the hour.[62]

The Confessing Church may look like a men's organization in some history books, but those who know them best recognize the debt to countless, and in many cases now forever nameless Confessing women. Each of the documentable cases must stand as a representative for many other stories that now, with the rapid disappearance of the eyewitnesses, are irretrievable. Little, almost insignificant acts, meant resistance: getting the children ready for church instead of encouraging them to participate with the Hitler Youth or the BDM; putting a coin in the collection plate for the Confessing Church; signing and carrying a red BK membership card; going door to door to collect contributions for the salaries of the "illegal" Vikare; taking membership in the Protestant Women's Auxiliary instead of in the Nazi Party "Frauenschaft," or attending a prayer meeting for an imprisoned pastor.

Still more intense were the flagrant violations of the law: hiding illegal seminarians, caring for Jews, and publishing forbidden journals and pamphlets. Taken together, such deeds by tens of thousands of Confessing women insured the survival of the Confessing Church and contributed to the fall of the Nazi regime. Every movement has its leaders, and it is now to the leaders among the women that we turn. We will investigate the ways in which pastors' wives inspired resistance and maintained order in a threatening, chaotic world, and at the same time prepared the way for women to be ordained to ministry in the Protestant Church in Germany.

NOTES

1. Werner Öhme, "Frauen als Märtyrer der Bekennenden Kirche," *Standpunkt* (DDR, May 1985), p. 16.

2. The women's auxiliary organization was known as the *Evangelische Frauenhilfe*. For full discussions of the women of the Evangelische Frauenhilfe see Fritz Mybes, *Geschichte der evangelischen Frauenhilfe in Quellen* and *Geschichte der evangelischen Frauenhilfe in Bildern* (both Gladbeck: Schriftenmis-

sions Verlag, 1975); and Fritz Mybes, *Agnes von Grone und das Frauenwerk der Deutschen Evangelischen Kirche* (Düsseldorf: Presseverband der Evangelischen Kirche im Rheinland, e.V. n.d.); Günther van Norden and Fritz Mybes, *Evangelische Frauen im Dritten Reich* (Düsseldorf: Verlag Presseverband der Evangelischen Kirche im Rheinland, 1979).

3. Indispensable—*"unentbehrlich."* Eberhard Klügel, *Die Lutherische Landeskirche Hannovers und ihr Bischof 1933-1945* (Berlin: Lutherisches Verlagshaus, 1964), p. 415.

4. Wolfgang See and Rudolf Weckerling, *Frauen im Kirchenkampf: Beispiele aus der Bekennenden Kirche Berlin-Brandenburg 1933 bis 1945* (Berlin" Wichern Verlag, 1986), cover of the book.

5. *"Die Frauen machten Mut zum Durchhalten."* Cited of Dr. Joachim Beckmann in an article by K. Rüdiger Durth in *Unsere Kirche* (Bielefeld). Extensive efforts to determine the date and page number of this article, a copy of which is in the author's files, have been unsuccessful.

6. From the author's interview with Senta Maria Klatt, January 1990, Berlin. See also Beate Schröder and Gerdi Nützel, eds., *Die Schwestern mit der roten Karte* (Berlin: Alektor, 1992), pp. 97-108; and Wolfgang See, "Schwestern im Bruderrat. Frauen der Bekennenden Kirche von Berlin-Brandenburg" (radio program of the RIAS Bildungsprogram, Berlin, 7 April 1984), p. 2.

7. Irene Breslauer was a secretary in the Protestant State Church of Wurttemberg. See Hans Prolingheuer, *Kleine politische Kirchengeschichte: 50 Jahre evangelischer Kirchenkampf von 1919 bis 1969* (Köln: Pahl-Rugenstein, 1984/1985), p. 182, note 104.

8. On Charlotte Friedenthal, see Hartmut Ludwig, *Die Opfer unter dem Rad Verbinden. Vor- und Entstehungsgeschichte, Arbeit und Mitarbeiter des "Büro Pfarrer Grüber"* (Dissertation, Berlin, 1988), pp. 32-39, 196-97.

9. On Hildegard Jacoby, see Bernhard Heinrich Forck, *". . . und folget ihrem Glauben nach": Gedenkbuch für die Blutzeugen der Bekennenden Kirche* (Stuttgart: Evangelisches Verlagswerk, 1949), p. 95; and Prolingheuer, *Kirchengeschichte*, p. 190.

10. Court record of the Sondergericht bei dem Landesgericht Berlin, 5 November 1943, pp. 2-6. Evangelisches Zentralarchiv in Berlin: Bestand 50/23, pp. 33-36. Herrmann and Jacobs were involved in the plot with Hildegard Jacoby.

11. Letter to the author from Leni Immer, 29 June 1990.

12. Ibid.

13. Wilhelm Niemöller, "Verkündigung und Fürbitte. Der Prozess des Hauptpastors Wilhelm Jannasch," *Zur Geschichte des Kirchenkampfes. Gesammelte Aufsätze* (Göttingen: Vandenhoeck and Ruprecht, 1971), pp. 161-62.

14. Hugo Hahn, *Kämpfer wider Willen*, (Metrzingen: Brunquell Verlag, 1969), pp. 120, 167, 286.

15. This according to Gertrud Freyss, a member of the Confessing Berlin-

Dahlem congregation, as related in Schröder, *Die Schwestern*, pp. 81-82. Hildegard Hannemann reports that the same thing happened in the Gossner-Mission in Berlin-Friedenau. See, "Schwestern im Bruderrat," p. 18.

16. Court document 3 Cs. 10/39, Neuruppin, 2 August 1939. Evangelisches Zentralarchiv in Berlin, Bestand 50/46, pp. 152-155. Judges acquitted Eckart and her colleague, Vikar Heinz Petermann, on the basis that children need physical and mental changes of pace in order to learn. The court agreed that having the children play games was sound pedagogy.

17. Frau Helmbold's title was *Studienrätin*.

18. Dagmar Maess, "'Ich tue das Meine, solange Gott mir Zeit lässt.' Erinnerungen an eine ungewöhnliche Frau." *Glaube und Heimat. Evangelisches Sonntagsblatt für Thüringen* (Jena), No. 31 (1985).

19. Marie Baum, *Anna von Gierke* (Weinheim, Berlin: Verlag Julius Beltz, 1954), pp. 102-105.

20. Hugo Hahn, *Kämpfer wider Willen*, pp. 166; 299-300, n. 19; 307, n. 15.

21. For details of Frau von Kleist's association with Bonhoeffer, see Eberhard Bethge, *Dietrich Bonhoeffer: Theologie—Christ—Zeitgenosse* (München: Christian Kaiser Verlag, 1970), pp. 613, 658, 672, 675, 792; and Jane Pejsa, *Matriarch of Conspiracy: Ruth von Kleist 1867-1945* (Minneapolis, Minn.: Kenwood Publishing, 1991).

22. Ibid., pp. 660, 668.

23. *Sammelvikariat*.

24. Mia Onnasch, née Frisius. Frau Onnasch's first name was either Mia (according to a 23 September 1994 letter to the author from Henner Grundhoff, Evangelisches Zentralarchiv in Berlin) or Maria (according to a 31 August 1994 letter to the author from Dr. Rita Scheller, Evangelische Gemeinde aus Pommern Hilfskommittee e.V., Hannover).

25. Bethge, *Bonhoeffer*, p. 667.

26. Rita Scheller, "Kreis Schlawe: Vom Strickverein zum illegalen Predigerseminar." In Rita Scheller, ed., *Unsere Pommersche Heimatkirche* (Hannover: Konvent evangelischer Gemeinden aus Pommern, e.V., 1992), pp. 22-23.

27. Bethge, *Bonhoeffer*, p. 601.

28. Countess Mechthild Behr, née von Heyden-Kartlow. See Brigitte Metz, "Frauen, die widerstanden," pp. 8-9 in Rita Scheller, ed., *Unsere Pommersche Heimatkirche*, Hannover: Konvent Evangelischer Gemeinden aus Pommern, e.V., Advent 1992.

29. Countess Elisabeth von Thadden, née Baroness von Thüngen, the wife of Count Reinhold von Thadden, an outstanding lay leader in the Confessing Church of Pomerania; not to be confused with her husband's sister of the same name. See note 63.

30. Bethge, *Bonhoeffer*, p. 490; and the author's interview with Frau Annemarie Tiedtke (daughter of Bertha and Carl Buth and the widow of one of

Bonhoeffer's seminarians), in February 1990, Minden.

31. This information on Stephanie von Mackensen is taken from the following sources: Carsten Bruns, "Fragen an Zeitzeugen: Interview mit Frau von Mackensen" in Hans-Ulrich Stephan, ed., *Das eine Wort für alle* (Neukirchen-Vluyn: Neukirchener Verlag, 1986), pp. 298-315; and the author's two interviews with Ingeborg von Mackensen in June 1987 in Iserlohn, and February 1990 in Minden.

32. Bethge, *Bonhoeffer*, p. 501.

33. Bruns, "Fragen," p. 308.

34. *Gauleiter*. A Nazi territorial political functionary.

35. Bruns, "Fragen," p. 308.

36. This sketch of Charlotte von Kirschbaum draws on material from the following sources: Charlotte von Kirschbaum, *Die wirkliche Frau* (Zollikon Zürich: Evangelischer Verlag, 1949); Renate Köbler, *Schattenarbeit: Charlotte von Kirschbaum—Die Theologin an der Seite Karl Barths* (Köln: Pahl-Rugenstein, 1987); Prolingheuer, *Kirchengeschichte*, p. 195; and the author's interview with Ruth Bockemühl, January 1990 in Wuppertal.

37. Köbler, *Schattenarbeit*, p. 48.

38. Ibid., p. 72; information replicated in the Bockemühl interview.

39. Information on Marga Meusel is from: Ludwig, *Die Opfer*; and Wilhelm Niemöller, *Die Synode zu Steglitz: Geschichte—Dokumente—Berichte* (Göttingen: Vandenhoeck and Ruprecht, 1970), p. 29.

40. Friedenthal proposed that the counseling center be called the *Zentrale Beratungsstelle für Nichtarierfragen*.

41. *"Die Aufgabe der Inneren Mission an den nichtarischen Christen,"* Ludwig, *Die Opfer*, p. 35.

42. The Protestant convents were called *Diakonissenhäuser*. Of the twenty-seven convents she wrote, four agreed to consider non-Aryan apprentices, but only under certain conditions. Ludwig, *Die Opfer*, p. 196, n. 24.

43. Niemöller, *Steglitz*, p. 36.

44. Ibid., p. 44

45. Ibid., *Steglitz*, pp. 46-48.

46. As observers of the synod, not participants, Bonhoeffer and his students could neither vote nor even be recognized to speak.

47. The information on Präses Koch was offered by Bishop Kurt Scharf in extemporary comments offered in a question-and-answer session following a debate in the Urania, Berlin, on 12 January, 1990. Notes of his comments are in the author's files.

48. Niemöller, *Steglitz*, p. 307.

49. Niemöller, *Steglitz*, pp. 286, 300.

50. See Wilhelm Niesel, *Kirche unter dem Wort: Der Kampf der bekennenden Kirche in der altpreussischen Union 1933-1945* (Göttingen, Vandenhoeck and Ruprecht, 1978), pp. 75-79.

51. *Evangelische Hilfestelle für nichtarischen Christen im Auftrag der Bekennenden Kirche.* Bethge, *Bonhoeffer*, p. 324, n. 51a.

52. Ludwig, *Die Opfer*, pp. 32-33. The only other clear voice on behalf of the Jews in the earliest days of the Confessing Church was that of Pastor Dietrich Bonhoeffer. No indication of Meusel's influencing Bonhoeffer, or vice versa, has surfaced.

53. Court records of the Sondergericht bei dem Landgericht, 1. Gew. KLs. 203/43, 5 November 1943. Evangelisches Zentralarchiv in Berlin, Bestand 50/23, pp. 32-36.

54. Information on Dora von Öttingen is from the author's interview with her in February 1990, Frankfurt am Main, and from "Dora von Oettingen" in the *"in Friedrichsdorf zu Hause"* column of the *Taunus Kurier* (Frankfurt), 25 June 1987.

55. A copy of the "Thirty Program Points" supplied by Frau von Öttingen is in the author's files.

56. The information on Leni Immer is from the author's interviews with her in Wuppertal in June 1987 and February 1990.

57. From the Klatt interview. See also See, "Schwestern im Bruderrat." p. 1.

58. Kurt Scharf, Urania comments.

59. Forck, *"und folget,"* pp. 22.

60. A complete study of F. J. Perels is Matthias Schreiber, *Friedrich Justus Perels: Ein Weg vom Rechtskampf der Bekennenden Kirche in den politischen Widerstand* (München: Chr. Kaiser Verlag, 1989).

61. Werner Öhme, *Märtyrer, der evangelischen Christenheit 1933-1945. Neunundzwanzig Lebensbilder* (Berlin: Evangelische Verlagsanstalt, 1980), pp. 247-248; and Öhme, "Frauen," p. 16; and Prolingheuer, *Kirchengeschichte*, p. 190. Jacobsen's biographers know only the barest details of her life and death, and not even her birth and death dates. "Wenn wir auch so wenig von ihr wissen, wollen wir sie doch nicht vergessen." Öhme, "Frauen," p. 16.

62. Öhme, *Märtyrer*, pp. 144-146; Öhme, "Frauen," p. 16; Prolingheuer, *Kirchengeschichte*, p. 190.

Elisabeth von Thadden lost her life to the Nazis, but she remains outside this discussion because, although her family were among the elite leaders of the Confessing Church, she evidently never officially joined. She died in the wave of executions that followed the assassination attempt on Hitler on 20 July 1944. At an afternoon coffee circle in the home of Anna von Gierke, a spy picked up on von Thadden's antipathy toward Nazism. This marked her for observation, arrest, and execution on 8 September 1944. See Öhme, *Märtyrer*, pp. 147-152; and the full biographical treatment in Irmgard von der Lühe, *Elisabeth von Thadden: Ein Schicksal unserer Zeit* (Köln: Eugen Diedrichs Verlag, 1966).

A similar case is that of Cato Bontjes van Beek, a member of the resistance group led by Schulze-Boysen and Harnack in Berlin. Van Beek came to the Christian faith as a young adult and was baptized by her own request, but no documentation links her to the Confessing Church. Upon her execution on 5 August 1943, the pastor in her hometown of Fischerhude rang the church bells in her memory, an act for which he sat for weeks in prison. See Klügel, *Die lutherische Landeskirche Hannovers* pp. 499-500.

Chapter 3

Pastors' Wives of the Confessing Church

When you've locked away all our pastors, we women will take their places, and then you can lock us up!

—Mechthild Kehr[1]

Dating from long before the outbreak of the Church Struggle, German women who married clergy assumed the distinctive burden of broad expectations for the pastor's wife (*Pfarrfrau*), not the least of which was the knowledge that she could make or break her husband's career. Church law forbade a pastors' wife to pursue a separate career, and the congregation's tacit expectations of the Pfarrfrau left neither time nor energy to pursue anything else.[2]

The common assumption in German society in 1933 was that the pastor's wife was to be a woman of faith, a model housewife and mother who was committed to home, church, school, and community. She would be a member of the Protestant Ladies' Auxiliary, if not its leader. Her house would be open to members of the church who came to see the pastor, and she was expected to be hospitable. Parishioners who did not want to bother the pastor with petty concerns felt free to unburden themselves on his wife, confident that she would convey the information to her husband. The pastor's wife typically served as keeper of her husband's calendar as church members came to the parsonage with their announcements of intentions to marry, requests for a baptismal date, or news that a family member had died and would the *Herr Pastor* please come by to make funeral arrangements? The dutiful and concerned Pfarrfrau would respond to such doorway conversations appropriately by inviting the visitor in for a cup of tea and a chat. On the day of the baptism, funeral, wedding, birthday celebration, or silver wedding anniversary, the pastor's wife accompanied her husband to the event, remaining very much at the center of the community's social whirl. If she could play the organ, lead a children's choir, teach a Bible class, and keep the financial records, so much the better. There was never a lack of things to do.

The outbreak of war exacerbated the pressure on pastors' wives. The draft took husbands away from home for extended periods of time sometime forever. The pastor who was not drafted faced multiplied responsibilities at home because he had to substitute for absent colleagues in nearby congregations. In either case, the pastor's wife saw even less of her husband during wartime.

The women whose husbands were aligned with the Confessing Church shared in all these burdens but they were even more acutely vulnerable to stress and danger than colleagues who were aligned with the "German Christians" or were attempting to remain neutral in the Church Struggle. Confessing pastors preached to congregations in which Gestapo officers took notes on the sermons, and they lived in parsonages in which the secret police had placed eavesdropping devices. The men and their wives had to deal constantly with the possibilities of house searches, fines, jail terms, and death for what they said and did.

The material in this chapter illustrates two facts of the German Church Struggle. First, the Confessing Church would not have been viable without the support of the ministers' wives, and second, the roles that these women played during the Church Struggle contributed substantially to the eventual ordination of women in the German Protestant Church.

Who were the pastors' wives of the Confessing Church? They were middle class women who occupied prominent places in the social structures of their communities, especially in rural areas, and who became even more central when their husbands were absent. They were women whose social positions made them the center of appreciative attention, but also the target of Gestapo suspicion and persecution. They were women whose loneliness in the Church Struggle bred independence. Some of them, consequently, crossed the gender line to do what their husbands could not: they demonstrated both to the laity and to colleagues in the clergy that women were capable of pastoral ministry.

THE WOMEN'S SOCIAL BACKGROUNDS

The wives of the pastors of the Confessing Church were women of social backgrounds and status similar to those of the broad membership of the Confessing Church, a fact that facilitated their ability to lead in the crisis. The women who married pastors of the Confessing Church were overwhelmingly from the middle class (as were most of the men whom they married).[3] In general, the families out of which these women emerged were neither working class people nor intellectuals. Politically, the homes in which they grew up were conservative and nationalistic. Among the men and women of the Confessing Church, only a few had been distressed about Hitler in 1933.[4] The Führer exploited the hopes and fears of this generation of post-World War I citizens, including those who would later be members of the Confessing Church.

The families who supplied the Protestant Church with pastors' brides were something of a social elite, though it was not one marked by wealth or education. The young women were the daughters of independent shopkeepers, physicians, educators, entrepreneurs, and professionals, many of whom were active lay leaders in their churches; but more than any other single profession represented among the fathers of the Pfarrfrauen was the pastorate, the significance being that many of the women brought into their marriages experiences of the parsonage and the Church.

Most of the pastors' wives were not themselves trained theologians.[5] Their education typically consisted of public school terminating with the *mittlere Reife* (after ten years) or an Abitur (usually thirteen years of school in preparation for university study). It appears that most set as personal goals marriage and motherhood.

The Confessing pastor's wife did not enjoy an easy life. Although the bride of a pastor who had been ordained before May 1934 moved, in most cases, into a sizable, furnished parsonage and could be assured of reliable, and even generous, income, circumstances changed during the Church Struggle. Young pastors ordained by the Confessing Church were considered "illegal," and they received a minimal salary of approximately 150 Reichmarks (RM), less than a quarter of what Gertrud Arndt, for example, had earned as a secretary before she married.[6] Martin Niemöller suffered a 20 percent cut in salary in 1938, and then had his entire salary stricken in June 1939. His family was forced to move out of the Dahlem parsonage.[7] At times during the Church Struggle, some pastors received their salary in groceries in lieu of cash, although until the economic debacle at the very end of the war, the pastors' families did not suffer hunger. Because the pastors on regular salary had committed themselves to contribute a tenth of their income to the support of their "illegal" colleagues who could expect nothing from the official church headquarters, the Confessing pastors survived, but this meant that the most comfortable of Confessing pastors' wives ran their households on 90 percent of a normal salary.

Confessing pastors who were ordained after May 1934 did not enjoy the perquisites that augmented the salaries of their senior colleagues. When Karl Immer, Jr., for example, announced that he was going to marry, he had to sign a statement that he understood that should he fall in the war, the Confessing Church of the Rhineland would not be responsible for the usual pension to his widow.[8]

THE SOCIAL IMPORTANCE OF THE PFARRFRAU

Because the Confessing pastor's wife was middle class and educated (but not so highly educated as to be intimidating), and typically came to her position with a young lifetime of experience within the Church, she enjoyed a certain respect that elevated her above other women in her community, especially in rural areas.

What she might have enjoyed in respect, however, she paid for with the uncomfortable scrutiny of Nazi authorities.

The parsonage was a focus of attention to which Protestants looked for role models and leadership. The presence of the pastor and his wife at a milestone birthday or a golden anniversary was the symbol of the esteem of the Church and the community. In difficult times, their presence offered at least the symbol of hope. In rural areas especially, when people lay ill or when mothers went into labor, they called on the pastor's wife for advice and help.[9]

However, the Gestapo also knew who was socially prominent and influential, and they made a custom of invading Confessing parsonages to search the cabinets, attic, drawers, and closets for contraband material. More often than not, it was not the pastor, but the Pfarrfrau, who received the unannounced callers. "The Gestapo was in our parsonage numerous times," recalled Gisela Lutschewitz. "Usually they found [only] me at home, because my husband was somewhere in the community."[10]

Irmgard Vogel dealt in her own way with such visits. When the Gestapo car pulled up in front of the parsonage in Dobbrikow, Frau Vogel retreated to the attic. While the children and the maid greeted and occupied the Gestapo downstairs, Frau Vogel grabbed the important papers the police were seeking, went to a window, and threw the contraband across a garden fence into the waiting arms of her neighbor, Elfriede Schneider. When the Gestapo left, Frau Schneider, who in this way repeatedly risked her own freedom, returned the papers.[11]

Being the wife of the Confessing pastor made the woman herself a target. In mid-1943 Thea Werthmann, wife of Pastor Wilhelm Werthmann in Wahrenholz, answered the door one day to greet a Gestapo officer who accused her of defaming the Führer. Postage stamps carried the chancellor's's portrait, and a domestic helper in the parsonage had accused Frau Werthmann of giving her a postage stamp to put on a letter with the remark, "Here you have a Hitler you can spit on." In spite of Frau Werthmann's protestations of innocence, the officer led her away, leaving her three children alone at home. (Their father was away at war.) Frau Werthmann spent a year in the concentration camp at Wolfsburg. She later discovered that her accuser, who never appeared in court to testify against her, had accepted a bribe to denounce her.[12] The incident was simple harassment of the Confessing Church. In this case, the pastor's wife, because of her social prominence, had provided a convenient target.

The importance of the social position of the pastors' wives became most acute in the turbulent, terrible days at the close of the war. Konrad Vogel remembered a harrowing event from the last weeks of the war in Brandenburg. Villagers in Dobbrikow had taken notice of a mysterious character, a man who only appeared on weekends. The whispered speculation was that he was a Gestapo officer or an SS man from Berlin who sought quiet in the countryside. In the spring of 1945, when Russian tanks surrounded Dobbrikow, the local SS officers called the populace to the village center and ordered them to resist the Russian artillery and infantry with broomsticks, rakes, and shovels. At the edge of the crowd of civilians stood the mysterious stranger. Irmgard Vogel, the pastor's wife, approached the mystery man and beseeched him to do something. Did she know who he was or was she acting on intuition? Did she have any confidence that he could tell the SS what to do? Konrad Vogel only knows that after his mother's intervention with the stranger, the man held a brief conversation with the SS officers, who then ordered their troops to leave the town. The ensuing battle took place elsewhere; Dobbrikow and its citizens were spared.[13]

In the eastern provinces, Soviet columns rolled over villages and people on their march to Berlin, and the Polish militia followed thereafter with a push to drive the Germans from the coveted Pomeranian territory. Gerda Zieger, the wife of Confessing Pastor Egbert Zieger in Arnhausen, led her villagers in the exodus from the eastern front. After several days' of forced wandering, she brought her troop of women and children back home to Arnhausen, where she found her home occupied by Soviet troops. When she protested to the soldiers that they were in her house, they brought her to the *Kommandant.*

The officer demanded to know her husband's profession and where he was to be found. Frau Zieger answered truthfully that he was the pastor of the village and was, the last she knew, serving as a first lieutenant in Greece. The Kommandant then asked Frau Zieger whether she was aware that he had orders to shoot the wives and children of German officers? Frau Zieger reported her response:

> I answered, I knew nothing of the sort, and I couldn't believe that Stalin would allow such a thing. After this bold assertion, the Kommandant pulled a photograph out of his pocket—a photograph of our family, in which my husband was clearly recognizable as a German officer. What would have happened if I had lied to that man! He counted the children in the picture (the youngest one was not in the photograph), and then said, amicably enough, we could live in the local inn until his regiment left town.[14]

Life in Arnhausen with the Soviets was difficult, especially when the vodka flowed, and the vulnerability of the women grew more acute. When the Soviets put all the women to work as forced labor tearing up one of the rail lines, Gerda Zieger went to work as well. She was always mindful to take her Bible along, from which she read to the women during their breaks. At the end of the workday, drunken soldiers would approach the women with the dreaded words, *"Frau komm!"* This was a prelude to rape. By sheer dint of personality, Zieger was able to protect the women around her.[15]

The details of Frau Zieger's experience are similar to stories told by her friend Felicitas Vedder in nearby Gross Poplow.[16] Throughout 1945, Frau Vedder, carrying a Bible and hymnal and wearing a self-made Red Cross arm band, walked from village to village, visiting and encouraging the members of her churches. One day Vedder saw a Soviet soldier marching a teenage girl whom she had taught in Confirmation classes across the village square. She asked young Hertha where she was going, to which the girl replied that the Soviets had caught her taking food out to German soldiers hiding in the forest. She had fallen ill in prison, and now the solder was taking her to the doctor for an examination. Vedder stepped in with the soldier and her young friend and accompanied them to the doctor's office. She knew the physician; she also knew about the Soviet soldiers and was determined to save Hertha from assault. When the teenager was called into the examining room, Frau Vedder went in with her and explained the situation to the doctor. She suggested to him that he "discover" that the young lady had a contagious disease that would soon infect both her fellow prisoners and the Soviet guards. The good doctor cooperated, and the soldiers immediately released Frau Vedder's young friend from jail.[17]

Mina Reger (the wife of Pastor Christian Reger of Schneidemühl, who spent 1940-1945 in Dachau), held together her little congregation in Stieglitz with similar bravery. When the Soviets burned the houses, Mina Reger gathered the women into the mill for protection. Her particular power emanated from the fact that the Soviets knew her husband to be an enemy of the fascists. She banked on his reputation to save her charges from rape.[18]

Finally, the experience of Luise Fahrenholz illustrates how socially prominent and important to the congregation the pastor's wife could be. Pastor Joachim Fahrenholz was a corporal in the German army and attached to a heavy mobile artillery unit in Russia when his superintendent wrote him a letter in the field, offering him a pastorate in Eschbruch, which included three separate congregations. Frau Fahrenholz, who was living with her year-old child in her parents' home, received a carbon copy of the letter. She read with growing alarm:

> This pastorate is yours under the following conditions: that your wife moves to Eschbruch immediately, that she reorganizes the Ladies' Aid Society, that she conducts Children's Worship Services, that she keeps the accounting books for two of the three congregations . . ., that she issues Aryan identification papers for people in all three congregations, etc.[19]

"Joachim will certainly not accept this position," Frau Fahrenholz commented to her parents. "He knows I have no training in these areas. I must write him right away."

However, her father was of another opinion. "You dare not block the road of your husband's profession. This is a decision he alone must make."

"By that evening, however," reflected Frau Fahrenholz later, "I was of the belief that I could not follow such advice, and I decided to write my husband immediately to impress on him that I could never measure up to the expectations." However, that night, at 12:45, the phone rang. It was Joachim Fahrenholz and he was bursting with good news. Before his young wife could say a word, he reported out of a heart full of joy and thanksgiving all that had happened: he was not in Russia at all, as they all had presumed, but had returned with his regiment and was in Zeitz. He had received a letter from *Superintendent* Schendel, and Schendel had offered him a pastorate in Eschbruch.

> I sent a telegram immediately saying "Yes." And I have received a telegraphed answer. The installation is day after tomorrow. You must catch a train tomorrow morning at 4:00 A.M. . . . We'll start off with the bicycles early Sunday morning. I'll meet you at the train station in Altkarbe!

"That was just too much," recalls Luise Fahrenholz. "I stuttered, 'Ja,' and stood there as speechless as a fish."

Superintendent Schendel's letter reflects the crucial role that people expected the pastor's wife to play in a rural church, and Joachim Fahrenholz's response illustrates how easily a pastor might take his wife's contributions for granted. In spite of her initial trepidation, Luise Fahrenholz took the position for her husband and served in all the capacities. She demonstrated to lay people that women could, indeed, successfully bear the physical and emotional burdens of the pastorate.

What would have happened to the fledgling Confessing congregations had these women not performed so ably? Both physical survival and theological integrity could have been lost; but through intrepid and imaginative leadership, the Confessing communities survived destruction, and the congregations maintained their faithfulness to the Reformation confessions and their opposition to the "German Christian" heresy.

ADVICE AND COLLABORATION

The battle for theological integrity did not begin in the pulpit, but in the hearts of the pastor and his wife. Stories from World War II survivors make it clear how pastor's wives advised their husbands, helping them to sort out the social, political, and theological issues.

The opening years of Hitler's rise to power were confusing for German Protestant clergymen who, with the rest of their countrymen, felt the shame of the defeat in World War I. They shared the national disdain for the inefficiency, slowness, and the awkwardness of the democratic government that had been imposed on them by the Western allies. Many longed for a return of the monarchy—and of Germany's place as a leader in the world community. Hitler promised to change all this, and most Protestant clergymen warmly greeted his accession to power on 30 January 1933.[20] However, the pastor's wife often helped her husband and his friends to see, over the course of 1933 and 1934, what Hitler and the "German Christians" would do to the Protestant Church.

Ruth Bockemühl, for example, was the teenage bride of the established, thirty-one-year old pastor of Cronenberg, Peter Bockemühl, when they married in 1929. Pastor Bockemühl later distinguished himself as a courageous fighter in the Church Struggle, publishing, editing, printing, and distributing illegal journals, but his initial leanings were toward the other side.[21]

"At first my husband was aligned with the 'German Christians,'" offered Frau Bockemühl in a 1990 interview. "I was opposed. I had gained my conviction from my father, who was opposed to the 'German Christians' from the very beginning. It was a real crisis in our marriage." After crucial discussions that threatened the stability of their home, the pastor came to see things his wife's way. Certainly, she had a profound effect on his change of heart.

Saxon Bishop Hugo Hahn reports how his wife, Erika Baggehufwudt Hahn, urged a young associate, Wolfgang Müggenburg, to align himself with the Confessors. "I was always very circumspect about exercising such influence," wrote Bishop Hahn, "but my dear wife, with her truth-loving demeanor, could not do other than speak her mind clearly and without reservation." Müggenburg became a faithful associate of the Hahns in the Church Struggle in Saxony.[22] Hahn further reports that the Confessing pastors' wives of Saxony were among "the bravest supporters of the cause of our Lord Jesus Christ."[23]

The pastors' wives served as advisers throughout the Church Struggle, at times restoring their husbands' resolve, which tended to erode under the pressure of persecution. "Don't consider what might happen to me. Do what you think is right," were Lydia Link's encouraging words to her fiancé, Bernhard Heiermann.[24] More direct was the support that one Saxon wife gave her husband as he went off to a meeting with his church officials: "I'll tell you this! If you sign anything [contrary to the Creeds], I'll never let you back in this house!"[25]

Helene Brauer-Dede and her husband, Pastor Günther Dede, were initially unequally yoked in their commitment to the Protestant opposition. The pastor was a bona fide member of the Confessing Church of Oldenburg, but he was critical of much that he saw and refused to go to the area meetings of the Confessing pastors in Rasted. Frau Dede insisted on going, at some risk, and thus represented him there and brought back news from the pastors' conferences. The contacts that she made and cultivated there stood her husband in good stead as the Church Struggle unfolded.[26]

Pastor Dede, who suffered from recurring depression, came home in a blue mood one evening to announce he was resigning from the Confessing Church.

"Where will you go, then?" Frau Dede asked.

"I'll leave the Protestant Church completely," was his answer.[27]

I then tried to make it clear to him that with such a move he would simply be stabbing Niemöller in the back, the man whose picture he displayed above his desk. Such a move would, in fact, put him in the camp of that man who was, by the grace of the Nazis, the bishop. Furthermore, such a move would be a flight from responsibility. . . . I added that he, Günther

Dede, had to carry some of the guilt if the Confessing Church did not live up to his high standards, because he refused to take on any area-wide responsibilities, wouldn't even go to the pastors' conferences in Rasted, let alone other meetings. All he did was criticize from the sidelines.[28]

The next day, after a sleepless night, Dede astonished his wife by accepting a speaking assignment for the Confessing Church in another city, and he approached the assignment with unaccustomed energy. Pastor Dede followed his wife's advice; he stayed in office and supported the Confessing Church until his death in 1942.

Another such case involved two people at the very forefront of the Confessing movement, Pastor Martin and Else Niemöller. During Pastor Niemöller's eight-year ordeal as the personal prisoner of the Führer in Dachau, he suffered understandable periods of depression. In the winter of 1939-40 his spirits dipped severely. Feeling forsaken by his Confessing Church of the Old Prussian Union, he questioned the legitimacy of the sixteenth-century Reformation and finally decided to remove himself and his entire family from the Protestant Church and convert to Catholicism. Sitting in prison, he was himself powerless to act, so he instructed his wife by letter to go to the courthouse and remove the family's names from the Protestant Church membership lists. Else Niemöller demurred, greeting his demands with a shrug of the shoulders but no action. He insisted, she stalled. She pled with him that such a move would make life difficult for her and the children. He stood resolute.

Else Niemöller eventually succeeded in persuading her husband to postpone a final decision until the end of the year. If he would not wait on behalf of her and the children, he should think about the effect his resignation from the Church would have on his Dahlem parishioners. This final argument moved him, and he agreed to wait. During the year of waiting and praying, the imprisoned pastor thought it over and decided to remain in the Church, a decision that assured his celebrity after the war. When he emerged from Dachau in 1945, he met with ecumenical acclaim for his living martyrdom, enjoyed worldwide celebrity, served as president of the Protestant Church of Hessen and Nassau, and became president of the World Council of Churches. One wonders how his career would have turned out had his wife not insisted on remaining in the Confessing Church.[29] One may also speculate how the rank and file in the Confessing Church might have felt had their celebrated leader left the fold.

From the beginning, Else Niemöller advised her husband well. On 24 September 1934 she sat in a boat on Berlin's Wannsee Lake with her husband and Pastor Fritz Müller. Together the three worked out the draft of a protest against the imposition of the "Aryan Paragraph" on the Church. The draft was refined the next day by Pastors Gerhard Jacoby and Franz Hildebrandt (both non-Aryans, according to the law), and by Dietrich Bonhoeffer.[30] Moreover, it was probably Else Niemöller who provided her husband with the "extreme unction" line that disturbed Hitler so greatly on 25 January 1935.[31]

The parsonage was not always an arena of perfect agreement. On occasion, wives questioned the cost of resistance. When, in December 1933, Reich-Bishop Müller handed over the entire Protestant Youth Organization to Nazi Party youth leader Baldur von Schirach, Pastor Karl Immer reacted strongly through his 1934 New Year's sermon in Barmen, in which he charged that the bishop's deliverance of the Protestant Youth to the Nazi Party "made the Church the State's whore." The pastor's political effrontery and bold choice of words scandalized the entire city. Not only did the Church authorities call on Immer to explain his remarks, but Tabea Immer, the pastor's wife, felt so personally wounded by the expression "whore" that for six weeks she refused to go to the church where her husband preached. Depression and paranoia plagued her for weeks until she finally demanded of her husband, "Is all of this really necessary?" Karl Immer replied: "It is absolutely necessary. The essence of our faith is being violated." Tabea Immer then agreed, "and never wavered in her agreement."[32]

In such homes there was a candid discussion of the issues. The Confessing pastor who heard his wife's emotional appeal for accommodation and moderation went through a difficult school. Such a challenge from as intimate an adviser as his wife refined the pastor's thinking. Similarly poignant is the story of Wolfgang Müggenberg's heartbreak when his fiancée broke their engagement because she was not willing to take the risk of being a Confessing vicar's wife.[33] The young man who had to choose between his beloved and his Church learned to appreciate the degree of his own commitment.

The step from adviser to collaborator was a small one. The wives of the pastors of the Confessing Church had married men whose very positions made them translate thoughts into deeds. Indeed, the sermons themselves could be interpreted as subversive. The Gestapo tapped telephones, ransacked houses in unannounced searches, and shadowed the pastors' movements. For seemingly harmless deeds, women as well as men ended up in jail.

Carrying out a relatively simple request for her husband could get a woman into trouble. Pastor Gotthold Lutschewitz of Gross-Dübsow, who would eventually declare himself with the Confessing Church, had not even been officially installed in his congregation in October 1933 when he was asked to make preparations for the church services to be held in conjunction with the harvest thanksgiving festival. Church services that Sunday morning were to be held in the open air, in Krüger's Garden, where later in the afternoon all the local Nazi organizations would convene for speeches, fanfare, and ceremony. At nine o'clock Pastor Lutschewitz asked his wife just to step out and check if everything was in readiness for the morning church service. When she got to Krüger's Garden, she saw that it was not only beflagged with swastikas, but that the speaker's stand and the table (which were to serve as pulpit and altar at 9:30) were also draped with the crooked crosses. "I said to myself," she wrote later, "for the church service that just wouldn't be right." She ran quickly to the sexton's house and asked if there were not an extra altar cloth, and if Frau Jaffke wouldn't help her make arrangements for a provisional altar. The women grabbed a cloth, a large altar Bible, a large crucifix, and some candles and flowers and went to work covering up the offending emblems, finishing just as the first worshipers appeared: a good number of SA men, Hitler Youths, and women from the Nazi Women's Organization. They all participated in what Frau Lutschewitz described as "a nice church service," but "the local teacher, who was also the Local Groups' Leader (Ortsgruppenleiter) of the Party was from that moment on never favorably disposed towards me."[34]

Lilli Muthmann provides another case of a pastor's wife coming to the unwelcome attention of Nazi authorities. Pastor Dr. Erich Muthmann moved with his wife and two sons to Helpup (Lippe) late in 1937. There, as one of his first organizational moves, Pastor Muthmann announced from the pulpit on 2 February 1938 that all the ladies who desired to "place themselves under the Word of God" were invited to a special meeting that afternoon in the parsonage. Lilli Muthmann and the congregational nurse set up chairs and greeted a large group of women who came for the meeting. "We began with song, prayer, and God's word," explained Frau Muthmann. "At the end, I asked who would like to form a chapter of the Protestant Ladies Aid (Evangelische Frauenhilfe)? A sheet of paper went through the room so that whoever wanted to could sign up. That was a step of faith and courage, because there was already a long-established Nazi Women's organization (NS Frauenschaft) in the city." Seventy women signed on as charter members.[35]

The Ladies' Aid in Helpup saw its primary responsibilities as visiting the aged and infirm, and in supporting the local deaconess house in nearby Detmold. The Nazi Party saw danger in the competition to its own women's organization. The Party forbade the Ladies' Aid to knit, sew, go on field trips, collect money, or drink coffee together, insisting that the group limit itself solely to study of the Bible. As a result, "the Nazis believed that soon the younger women would stay away from the gatherings, but more and more women came."[36] The women of the Ladies' Aid skirted the letter of the law. They undertook field trips using privately owned automobiles and drank coffee under the guise of birthday parties—not Ladies' Aid meetings—albeit confined to the parsonage.

Eventually, local Nazi authorities called Lilli Muthmann in for a public interrogation because she refused to join the NS Frauenschaft. She explained her distaste for the secularized, politicized "Christmas" songs that the Nazi women sang, in which Jesus was never mentioned. "The Nazis wondered why so many women were coming to me in my Ladies' Aid meetings when their own Frauenschaft found such weak support." Finally, the county leader demanded that Frau Muthmann be ordered to go to work in the local factory (thus eliminating her from the leadership of the Ladies' Aid). Unexpectedly, an officer from the Employment Office, a woman, intervened. "No," she insisted. "She has two small children who need their mother." The county leader flew into a rage. "Dismiss the woman," he thundered. "We have no use for her anyway! Heil Hitler!"

General harassment followed. The parsonage suffered some break-ins and the radio cable was destroyed. The Muthmann children suffered hazing at school. The police arrested Pastor Muthmann in 1940 with a charge with of violating the "Law for the Regulation of Public Collections," for which he paid a fine of 200 RM.[37] But the Ladies' Aid survived, and in the economic collapse at the end of the war the women kept busy supplying clothing and food for the stream of refugees from the east.[38]

Marianne Albertz found herself in still deeper trouble because she helped her husband. The legal brief describing her trial and conviction in Berlin in December 1941 tells the story.[39] Superintendent Martin Albertz was the head of the testing and certification committee to qualify men and women for offices in the Confessing Church of the Old Prussian Union. Heinrich Himmler had declared the Confessing Church's schools to be illegal in August 1937, but that decree did not dissuade the Confessing Church of Berlin-Brandenburg from fulfilling its perceived duty to train men and women to preach the Gospel.[40] Marianne Albertz was responsible for storing and saving all documents relating to the testing procedures. In October 1940 a Gestapo search of the Albertz apartment provided enough evidence to arraign both husband and wife, who became codefendants in a case with twenty-one others. The final verdict sent Martin Albertz to jail for eighteen months. The court found Marianne Albertz to be an accomplice and imposed a fine of RM 300.[41]

Other pastors' wives served in equally illegal and dangerous functions. Lydia Heiermann served as an unpaid secretary for the illegal Brotherhood of Vicars and Assistant Preachers of the Confessing Church in the Rhineland, of which her husband was the leader.[42] Others did the tedious research in the church records and produced the "Aryan Identification Certificates" that their parishioners needed to prove they were not Jewish. Irmgard Vogel's children remembered that when their mother discovered a Jewish grandparent in someone's family tree, she would changed the records and hand out a "clean" certificate. Her falsification of the records was a high crime, a "sin against the blood of the German race" in Nazi parlance, a felony for which she surely would have been imprisoned had she been discovered.[43]

Ruth Bockemühl was visiting in Frankfurt am Main when she learned that the printing plant where her husband's journal was produced had been raided by the Gestapo. She grabbed a telephone to alert Peter Bockemühl that the secret police had arrested his associate and had seized all the manuscripts and records. She did not know that the Gestapo was listening to every word on the other end of the tapped telephone line.

Returning home, Ruth Bockemühl found the Gestapo waiting for her. The police took her in for questioning and placed a document in front of her to sign: an affidavit attesting that she knew where and when her husband's journal was printed. Frau Bockemühl refused. Searches of the parsonage ensued, and though the police found nothing, they left a shambles behind. "They took the beds apart!" remembered the pastor's wife. "I think my husband had hidden his things under the coal pile in the cellar."[44]

When husbands were jailed, wives made arrangements to visit them, and this, too, was occasionally bound up with considerable risk. A solicitous visit at the prison was easily interpreted as a political demonstration—and perhaps it was one. Bruno Tecklenburg was among the many Brandenburg pastors imprisoned because they read a forbidden pulpit declaration. "They were in jail three days," recalled Louise Tecklenburg, "and we church members and pastors' wives brought them meals. We were still allowed to do that." When the congregation gathered before the prison to sing to the pastors in their cells, the Police Commissioner threatened to fire on them.[45]

The pastors were not the only ones to see the inside of jail cells. Mechthild Kehr in Seelow demonstrated reckless courage when she visited her imprisoned husband. While she was there to visit, Gestapo agents took her aside to press her to urge him to sign a retraction of his association with the Confessing Church. "I hope my husband signs nothing," she said, and she further declared that if the Gestapo should imprisoned all the men, "we women will be there to fill their places, and you'll have to lock *us* up!" The Nazi officer responded: "And we'll do it! Don't think we would shrink from doing that very thing!" Whereupon Frau Kehr retorted: "We never imagined anything different!"[46]

Kehr did exactly as she threatened. Her husband was arrested, and she took the pulpit the following Sunday. It happened like this. When a German invasion of Czechoslovakia seemed imminent in 1938, the brotherhood council of the Confessing Church of Berlin-Brandenburg prepared and circulated a prayer liturgy and a pulpit declaration to be read in all the Confessing congregations, a liturgy which condemned the expected war and confessed the sin of German nationalistic bellicosity. The police in Seelow forbade Pastor Rudolf Kehr to use the liturgy, and jailed him when he insisted that he would. Frau Kehr later wrote in her diary, "On that Sunday, when the church bells rang as usual, *I* read the forbidden pulpit declaration."[47]

Mechthild Kehr sat for four days in a jail in Frankfurt an der Oder, experiencing something of what Felicitas Vedder suffered when she peeled potatoes for three weeks in a Belgard jail.[48] Thea Werthmann could tell similar stories from the Wolfsburg concentration camp.[49] Was prison harder for women than men? When Mechthild Kehr was imprisoned in the fall of 1937, the authorities threatened to take her children away from her because she could not possibly be a fit mother.[50] Was such pressure ever applied to a man?

The Confessing pastor's wife had to be constantly alert to a possible visit by the local police or the Gestapo, who would search the house thoroughly for forbidden literature, lists of names and addresses, illegally collected money, mimeograph machines, and other contraband. Early in the Nazi period, reported Pastor Leni Immer, such searches were not much more than rude inconveniences, but later the inspections became more severe. She reported an occasion when the Gestapo came to search the house as she lay in bed with tonsillitis. The dangerous documents were shoved under the bed covers with her, and "my tonsillitis almost escalated into a heart attack!"[51]

INVOLVING CHILDREN IN COLLABORATION

Young Leni Immer's fright points out that Confessing parsonages in which there were children had problems of their own. The care and coaching of the children was the particular responsibility of the pastor's wife during the Church Struggle, a burden that the pastor, because of his absence and his involvement in the issues beyond the walls of the parsonage, did not share equally. If the parents decided to let their children participate in the Church Struggle, the mother had to be concerned with schooling them in confidentiality.

The Immers decided to involve their seven children (the oldest was eighteen years old in 1933) in the Church Struggle. "They should know as much as possible," said Karl Immer. "Only in this way can they develop an allegiance with us."[52] One can imagine the danger of confiding life-and-death secrets to a house full of children. The family knew, for example, that because the house had been bugged, even casual conversation was dangerous. Suspecting a Gestapo microphone in the telephone, it was muffled with a coffee cozy at all times.[53]

Tabea Immer and the children were enthusiastic co-conspirators in the general illegal activities of the Confessing Church. The children of Heinrich and Margarete Grüber were similarly involved in Berlin, working with their father's Jewish-Christian secretary, Inge Jacobsen.[54]

Heinrich and Irmgard Vogel at first kept information about the Church Struggle from their seven children because they deemed them far too young to understand or be responsible with the secrets. However, the grown children remembered knowing that something was amiss, something both secret and important. When the news broke about the assassination attempt on Hitler on 20 July 1944, Konrad Vogel, who had just turned thirteen, remembered being called in to his parents' presence. They explained to him and his sister Ilse (fourteen) that what they had heard about the attempt on the Führer's life was true, and that furthermore, they, the Vogels, had been in moral support of it: "We support the attempt. Disobeying God's commandments is terrible, but it is sometimes necessary in order to prevent something even worse. Now we must learn to live on the basis of His forgiveness." Konrad Vogel remembered a feeling of relief that swept over him as a result of this conversation: "Finally! Finally you are talking about it!"[55]

Lilli Muthmann's experience with the way in which Nazis put pressure on school-aged children of Christian parents is typical of the experiences of hundreds of others. Pastor Dr. Erich Muthmann's parishioners complained about daily hateful, anti-Semitic, and anti-Christian harassment in the school in Helpup. "Whoever still goes to church is himself a Jew," declaimed an elementary school teacher in Helpup, disturbing children and parents alike, as did the teachers' "unbelievable fanaticism against anything that had to do with

Jews, Christianity, the Bible, Church, and the priests."[56] In a history lesson about Charlemagne, who was vilified as Karl the Saxon Slaughterer in Nazi parlance, after vividly describing how Karl decapitated Saxons who refused to be baptized, the Helpup teacher concluded with the prediction, "Some day it will be the other way around." When alarmed parents protested, the teacher took his wrath out on the terrified schoolchildren with a desk-pounding tirade and threats about reprisals against "the gentlemen" (their fathers) who had raised objections. One of the Muthmanns' sons came home from school that day, pale and quaking, with the plea, "Mommy, I would rather die. Just don't make me go into that school again." After a move from Helpup to Detmold, the boy was amazed that he experienced no hazing from his class mates. "What Christian mothers in Helpup suffered for their children through all those years," wrote Pastor Muthmann later, "is indescribable."[57]

Conditions for children were better in Detmold than in Helpup, and so not every Confessing family's experiences were the same, nor did every family feel compelled to involve the children in the Church Struggle. The Niemöllers did as much as they could do—notwithstanding the fact that the father was in prison for eight years—to protect the children from the details of the Church Struggle. The children were unaware of the financial worries their mother bore, as Else Niemöller successfully kept her concerns from them.[58]

THE EXPERIENCE OF LONELINESS

With a husband away from home and with a head full of secrets she could not share with her children, many a Confessing pastor's wife found herself steeled in loneliness. Alone in the home, the wife had to decide by herself whether to harbor non-Aryan refugees, how parish affairs should be handled, and whether to remain in the parsonage or to flee to her family. The loneliness enforced a discipline that often bred independence in thought and action.

Separation was a common lot of clergy wives in the Third Reich. Military inductions of the clergy numbered over 10,000, and hundreds of Confessing clergy wives had to live through fearful days when their men were imprisoned.[59] By December 1937 over 800 Confessing pastors had seen the inside of jails and interrogation cells.[60] Wives of the leaders of the Confessing Church functioned alone at home while their husbands went on weeks-long speaking tours or participated in synodical meetings. When men went into temporary hiding, it was expedient that their wives not know where they were. For example, Pastor Hans Asmussen intentionally did not tell his wife of his hiding places in case the Gestapo questioned her.[61] In the absence of the men, women often demonstrated to the congregations their ability to take up the slack in church leadership in addition to the arduous challenges of day to day survival.

Especially in rural areas, life could be hard. Typically, a rural clergy couple's family consisted of several children living in a large manse. It was not unusual for the pastor's wife in the hinterlands to manage a large vegetable garden, a field of potatoes, and barnyard animals, including a dog, cats, goats, pigs, a donkey, a cow or two, and poultry. In extreme situations, water for drinking and bathing might be drawn from a well in the front courtyard while a pond in the back provided a place to do the laundry. Where the homes were not electrified, light glowed from petroleum lamps whose glass cylinders had to be cleaned daily. There was no guarantee of indoor plumbing, or if so, then perhaps only in the kitchen.[62] Even in prosperous areas where electricity and indoor plumbing were the rule, war-time economy led many clergy families to cultivate small livestock and large gardens.

Taking care of the manse and children would appear to have been more than enough to fill each day, but the rural Pfarrfrau had to do even more as she assumed the major burden of administering the parish in her husband's absence. The normal parade of parishioners graced the parsonage door throughout the week, but as Sunday approached the pastor's wife had to find someone from a nearby congregation to take the vacant pulpit.[63] This entailed correspondence, planning, and perhaps providing food and lodging in the parsonage for the visiting preacher. When there was no pastor to be found, the woman resorted to other measures, namely, preaching herself or training laymen in the congregation to do the work. Irmgard Vogel begged the men of Dobbrikow to read the liturgical services on Sundays: "Can't you help just once? I can't do it every Sunday!"[64] The idea was so radical to these peasant farmers that most simply refused. However, one valiant man, Herr Nöthe of the hamlet Nettgendorf, was brave enough to try, though he approached the new duty with awe: "But *I?*, Frau Pastor, *I* should proclaim the Word of God?" He agreed to do it, but only if he could come to the parsonage on Saturday evenings and practice in front of Frau Pastor Vogel.[65]

Irmgard von Derschau found herself in a similar position.

In the early Fall of 1943 Herr Dr. August Knorr and my brother Fritz Onnasch called for a meeting of laymen in Zezenow. These men were to be responsible for preaching services, because more and more pastors were being drafted. The elders of our three village congregations then chose twenty men who, on the basis of their gifts, their faith and their conduct were suitable people to lead a Sunday service. I had sermons sent to me on a regular basis from Stettin and Breslau, and I picked out the best ones. Then I invited these men into our parsonage to demonstrate to them, on the basis of the scriptures, that they were called to this service. Initially they tried to talk me out of it, maintaining that I myself was better suited for this work than they. "But if you think so, little lady, we'll give 'er a try."[66] . . . We met every month, and those who were to conduct the services met with me early in the week.[67]

Such conditions prevailed in the countryside, but in urban areas as well women felt compelled to carry on the work of the Church in the absence of their husbands. Margarete Grüber in Berlin remembered one of the first things that crossed her mind when her husband was arrested on 19 December 1940: "If my husband doesn't return home," she said to herself, "you must maintain the congregation in such a manner that you can give it back to him later, just as it was when he left it." She labored to get men to take the pulpit or to lead Bible studies, but only men of the Confessing Church.[68]

Louise Tecklenburg faced a tremendous challenge when, while her husband was away with the army, the church administration transferred him in absentia from rural Brandenburg to Berlin's fashionable Lichterfelde suburb. Frau Tecklenburg made the move in 1942 with her children, including a set of newborn twin girls, but without her husband. Taking on the responsibility of administering the church and gaining the church's confidence for her husband, she made arrangements for a series of monthly "Open Houses" in her home, to which parishioners could come for religious discussions. In this way she got to know the congregation and the people got to know her and the children. The congregation offered her a place on the church's board of elders, where she represented her absent husband until he returned in 1945.[69]

WIVES CROSSING THE GENDER LINE

Alone in the parsonage, wives sometimes found themselves having to do substantially more than make provisions for other men to fill their husband's pulpits. Many a pastor's wife stepped across an invisible but imposing gender line and did what German Protestant women had not done since the Reformation: because of the shortage of men, Confessing pastors' wives found themselves baptizing babies, burying the dead, preaching in church services, and distributing Holy Communion.[70] In short, they themselves often did the work that their husbands were not there to do, and in so doing, they reshaped the image of the pastorate in the minds of the lay people whom they served: the pastor could be a woman. German Protestants learned that fulfilling clergy responsibilities was no longer exclusively "men's work."

Emmi Hof Groh Blöcher offered an illuminating example.[71] Having grown up in a pious home where her storekeeper father read with dismay and alarm passages out of *Mein Kampf* to his children, young Emmi Hof had no illusions about the Nazis and their plans to control the Protestant Church. Even as a youngster, she resisted.

When her young husband, Pastor Theo Groh, died in France in 1940, young Frau Groh saw her way clearly: "My future was clearly laid out for me. . . . For one thing, I had learned to love this kind of work, and furthermore, I thought I could continue my husband's work."[72] After she finished additional study in Berlin, the Protestant Church of Nassau assigned Emmi Groh to work with scattered groups of women, girls, and children. During the war years she traveled through the territory, visiting congregations, and putting on programs for women, girls and children, but always operating only on the distaff side of church life. However, changes in rural life brought about changes in Emmi Groh's work. At the late stage of World War II, as the draft was growing to its maximum involvement of all men between the ages of sixteen and sixty, a local church elder asked Groh to conduct a church service, though she had neither the official commission nor permission to do so. Other local elders also asked her to preach, and she agreed to help as she could. Sometimes, the sermons were liturgical in nature, prepared by headquarters to be read when, in an emergency, there was no pastor to preach. At other times, Emmi Groh brought her own message. For a woman to preach was highly unusual, but so were the circumstances: there were not enough pastors, as so many were serving in the army, and Emmi Groh could preach because no one consulted the higher church authorities for permission.

Why did the men in the congregations not take this responsibility upon themselves? Frau Blöcher reflected that because of the war, the healthy, younger, better educated men were mostly absent from the Nassau countryside, and the older congregational elders from the peasantry, with their rough village dialects, did not trust themselves to preach. That a woman should preach, especially in the northern reaches of the Nassau Church, was a rare thing, as in pietistic circles the phrase "The woman should keep silent in the churches" was well known.[73] "But no one said anything to me about it," recalled Emmi Hof Groh Blöcher.

For Herta Gadow-Meyer, the invitation to preach came from more official quarters.[74] Pastor Hartmut Gadow in Zühlsdorf (Pomerania) grew sick with a lung disease in October 1944, and could no longer carry out his pastoral duties. The neighboring pastor offered to help, but Superintendent George Gramlow of Arnswalde convinced the Protestant Consistory of Pomerania to offer the pastoral position to the pastor's wife, Herta Gadow-Meyer, who was a trained *Theologin*. On 30 November 1944 Generalsuperintedent Dr. Paul Gerhard Wahn of the official consistory of the German Protestant Church of Pomerania signed the empowering certificate, which read:

> In re: Care of the Zühlsdorf congregation. In the place of your invalid husband we impart to you herewith permission to hold worship services in the Zühlsdorf congregation, to offer religious instruction, and otherwise to practice aspects of pastoral care.[75]

Although Herta Gadow-Meyer was "illegal"—she had taken her examinations before Confessing Church commissions, not organs of the German Protestant Church—the certificate protected her from Gestapo harassment. Hartmut Gadow reported that in nearby Sellnow, the Arnswalde Consistory similarly commissioned Frau Christine vom Stein to lead her husband's congregation while he was away at war, and she continued to do so after he was killed.[76]

Figure 3.1
Sketch for a Preaching Robe for Theologinnen

What should a woman wear while preaching? Herta Gadow-Meyer initially resisted the ostentation of a preaching robe until low temperatures in the churches and the encouragement of her Pomeranian parishioners persuaded her of the practicalities of the vestments. Theologinnen in Baden suggested this sketch for a preaching robe which would keep them warm on cold, winter Sundays, and would obviate the need of carrying a change of clothing while bicycling through inclement weather to their preaching appointments. Source: Landeskirchliches Archiv Stuttgart, Bestand 356 a II.

Even with official papers, Gadow-Meyer was exceedingly circumspect in the way she approached her office, in which she ministered to three separate congregations within her pastorate. "In all three churches I avoided stepping into the pulpit until some of the farmers insisted that I do so," she later wrote. "Furthermore, they insisted that as it got colder in the unheated chapels I should wear clerical robes over a fur coat which they leant me." Practicality motivated the peasants of Zühlsdorf to persuade Gadow-Meyer to wear a heavy preaching robe. The alternatives were to wear a simple dress (and run the risk of catching a cold), to risk soiling her dress while travelling to her preaching appointments by foot or bicycle, or to carry a change of clothing which was difficult on a bicycle. Thus, in Gadow-Meyer's case, practicality won out. However, more than practicality was involved. In Germany, where every profession was marked by its prescribed uniform, a woman preaching in clerical vestments made a strong symbolic statement. Standing before her parishioners in her preaching robe, Herta Gadow-Meyer modeled a new role for women in Germany (see Figure 3.1).[77]

Certainly not all the women who stepped in for their husbands were university educated. Felicitas Vedder in Gross Poplow had been a nanny before marrying Pastor Martin Vedder, and Gerda Zieger in nearby Arnhausen had little formal education beyond high school, but both women were resourceful, quick-witted, and faithful to the causes they had joined. At the end of the war, Frau Vedder was a war widow with two children, while Frau Zieger and her five children did not know the whereabouts of Pastor Egbert Zieger. As the social order in rural Pomerania began to collapse in 1945, both women took over the leadership of their communities and their churches.

A distant relative of Frau Vedder's husband, Superintendent Johannes Zitzke of Belgard, gave special papers to both women which eased their way as they ministered from village to village to protect them from the potentially abusive Soviet soldiers or Polish police.

On a simple piece of paper, dated 7 July 1945, adorned with his official seal and written in German, Polish and Russian, Superintendent Zitzke commissioned Gerda Zieger and Felicitas Vedder to conduct church services, burials, weddings, and children's Bible classes, and to do spiritual counseling (see Figure 3.2). The document was far from an official ordination, but the Soviet and Polish soldiers who saw it were sufficiently impressed. Illiterate soldiers were even more impressed by Frau Zieger's white arm band with a violet cross, and with Frau Vedder's homemade Red Cross arm band.[78]

Still another example of a woman stepping into traditionally male roles comes out of the East Prussian Church. Felix and Gertrud Arndt arrived in Gross Tromnau, East Prussia, in 1938 to the typical huge parsonage, garden and potato field, animals, and congregation. When, in September 1939, war with Poland broke out and Felix Arndt was drafted, it fell to Gertrud Arndt to find someone to conduct the church services. She was delighted when an emeritus pastor moved to nearby Garnsee to escape the bombing attacks on Berlin. Willing to

Figure 3.2
Felicitas Vedder's Commission

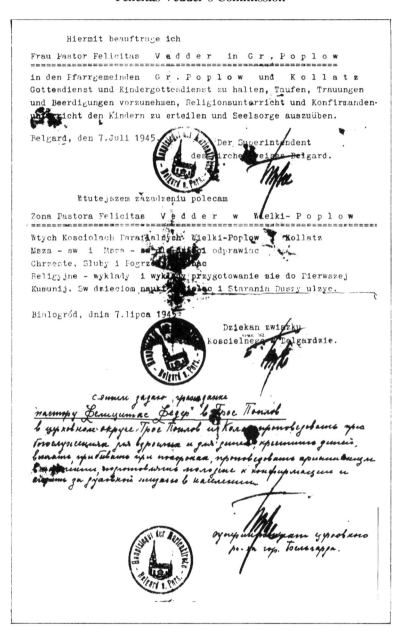

Hiermit beauftrage ich

Frau Pastor Felicitas V e d d e r in G r . P o p l o w

in den Pfarrgemeinden G r . P o p l o w und K o l l a t z
Gottesdienst und Kindergottesdienst zu halten, Taufen, Trauungen
und Beerdigungen vorzunehmen, Religionsunterricht und Konfirmanden-
unterricht den Kindern zu erteilen und Seelsorge auszuüben.

Belgard, den 7.Juli 1945.   Der Superintendent
                                             des Kirchenkreises Belgard.

            W.tutejszem zazadzeniu polecam

Zona Pastora Felicitas V e d d e r w W.ielki- P o p l o w

W tych Kosciolach Parafialnych Wielki-Poplow i Kollatz
Msza - sw i Msza - sw. dla dzieci odprawiac
Chrzeste, Sluby i Pogrzeby naac
Religijne - wyklady i wyklady przygotowanie sie do Pierwszej
Kumunij. Sw dzieciom naukit wiele i Starania Duszy ulzyc.

Bialogród, dnia 7.lipca 1945.

                                Dziekan zwiazku
                                koscielnego w Belgardzie.

Translation: "I hereby commission Frau Pastor Felicitas Vedder, in the congregations Gr. Poplow
and Kollatz, to conduct worship services, Sunday school, baptisms, weddings and funerals, and to
carry out religious instruction, confirmation classes and spiritual counseling." Signed:
Superintendent Johannes Zitzke. Source: Frau Felicitas Vedder.

take over the church services for her absent husband, the elderly gentleman came by train every Saturday and spent the night in the parsonage. All went well for awhile, but one morning the elderly pastor failed to appear for breakfast, and Frau Arndt discovered he had fallen victim to a stroke. "Precisely on this same Sunday," wrote Frau Arndt:

> there were three baptisms to perform, and I was determined to find a neighboring pastor to come over and do them. But the distances were too great, and one of the pastors advised me, in light of the emergency situation, to baptize the babies myself. I asked the families if they wanted to wait until next Sunday, or whether they would allow me to do the baptisms. One couple wanted to wait, but the other two thought that since they had made all the preparations and the relatives were already there, I should go ahead. I quickly grabbed the liturgical manual, got dressed a bit more formally, and with a fervent supplication for God's help, I managed the baptisms.[79]

Frau Arndt described a similar occasion later on when she could not find a pastor to offer Holy Communion to a dying woman. Again on the advice of a pastor, and with the permission of the dying woman's family, the pastor's wife administered the sacrament.

The wives took on their absent husbands' work in much less pleasant ways as well. "The most difficult," remembered Gertud Seyler of Zorndorf, "was to have to call on the families whose fathers or sons had fallen in the war."[80] There were also the funerals. On 7 May 1945 Irmgard von Derschau returned to her village of Zezenow, from which she and others had earlier fled from the Soviet advance. Church members from three villages, who had been orphaned of their pastor, asked Frau von Derschau to bury the dead and hold the appropriate funeral services for them. "I didn't feel equal to the ministry, but I saw under the circumstances it was my duty." She gathered a choir of girls, arranged for an adult soloist, and carried out the services.[81]

Funerals were hard. Mechthild Kehr reported thirty burials in one month:

> Devastating cases. Young women, little girls, children. Most died because of starvation with typhoid or dysentery. . . . There were emergency baptisms of little children who had the faces of old people, marked by death. In the church services I tried to pull the people out of their desperation, to let them know about a gracious, merciful Lord, in spite of the destitution and death surrounding us. *"Nevertheless, I am with you always . . . "* That was my first sermon text.[82]

Frau Kehr had dreamed as a twelve-year-old girl of someday being a pastor, and exulted later in her diary, "And for a few weeks I really was one!"[83] She might have continued to serve in this way for years had she not become severely ill with typhus.

Most cases of women stepping into roles that only men had previously exercised occurred in rural areas. In the cities, circumstances were different. The concentration of population in the urban areas meant that neighboring parishes were just a few minutes away from each other, whereas in the country, miles of poor roads separated the congregations. Thus, a pastor in a city parish could serve several neighboring congregations. He would preach on Sunday morning at one, officiate at a second in the afternoon, and conduct services in still a third on Sunday evening.

Nevertheless, urban women, too, stepped across the gender line. Lydia Heiermann in Elberfeld admitted to preaching and conducting one church service in 1943.[84] Pastor Leni Immer reports that Marianne Albertz and Frau Peccina in Berlin preached.[85]

The Protestant-Lutheran Provincial Church of Hanover has collected quantifiable data of the activities of urban pastors' wives from 1933 to the end of World War II. Shortly after the war, in order to determine the recent history and status of the Lutheran Church of Hanover, the church consistory sent out a questionnaire to each of its 1,022 congregations. The questionnaire asked about the size of the congregation in 1939, the names of the pastor(s), and to which of three ecclesiastical and political parties the pastors belonged: NSDAP, "German Christian," or the "Confessional Fellowship," meaning moral alliance with the Confessing Church.[86] Question 27 asked, "To what degree did the pastor's wife take on congregational responsibilities during the war?"[87]

Of 1,022 churches, twenty-eight (2.52%) reported that the pastor's wife had conducted liturgical services at least once between 1933 and 1945. Apparently, for ten of these twenty-eight women, this was not a regular practice but rather something they did once or twice during those years, when there was no other alternative. One woman's husband reported, "She served for a while as organist, and sometimes offered liturgical services, but always with a racing heart."[88] Nine of the respondents indicated, however, that the women read liturgical services on a frequent, or even regular basis. In five cases, the women performed burials, and one woman of the Protestant-Lutheran Provincial Church of Hanover baptized a child. The women of Hanover, which was more heavily populated than Pomerania or East Prussia, did not have as frequent a need to do "men's work," but when the needs arose, the problems and solutions were the same: unavailable men, capable women, willing parishioners.

Hilde Enterlein Schönherr, the pastor's wife in Brüssow, took on her husband's church work in a most unusual way.[89] One day in 1945, while Pastor Albrecht Schönherr was in a prisoner of war (POW) camp in Italy, and Frau Schönherr and her two small children, Oswald and Barbara, were taking refuge in the local drug store after the destruction of their house and possessions in a bombing raid, the Russian officer overseeing the local Soviet occupying force in Brüssow called Hilde Schönherr to his headquarters. The officer received her warmly, graciously offered her a glass of vodka, and then, in broken German,

asked her, "Why here no church services?" Frau Schönherr explained that her
husband the pastor was a POW in Italy and that until he returned, there was no
one ordained to carry out the services. The Russian officer then insisted,
pointing at her and saying, "*You* church services!" Frau Schönherr, who
possibly knew what other women were doing and who herself had six semesters
of a theological education, still demurred. She protested that the church had
suffered war damage and was neither a clean nor a safe place to assemble.
Undeterred, the Soviet officer called in the mayor of Brüssow and gave orders
that of all the public buildings that were to be repaired, the church was to be
placed first on the list. Consequently, on Pentecost Sunday 1945, Hilde
Schönherr, wearing a white apron and sturdy wooden shoes as her only clerical
vestments and acting at the behest of the Red Army, conducted her first church
service in Brüssow. Shortly thereafter, the re-emerging Protestant Church
administration in Berlin, under the guidance of Kurt Scharf, issued a formal
assignment for her to act in Brüssow in her husband's absence until his return.[90]
For over a year she served in this way, administering the parish, counseling the
parishioners, preaching, leading the prayers, and distributing the elements of the
Lord's Supper. Primarily, however, she conducted funeral services, which were
required on almost a daily basis, sometimes up to seven times a day. When her
husband returned from the camps in May 1947, she gladly relinquished her
office to him.[91]

SUMMARY

The wives of pastors in the Confessing Church were as involved in the
Church Struggle as their husbands. In fact, in many cases they remained in the
battle while the men languished in prisons or died in the war. In this regard,
they resembled their secular sisters who stepped in to fill the places vacated by
men. As in World War I, in this new national crisis, German women of all
descriptions took unaccustomed places in shops, factories, bus and train depots,
the mines, and the barns and fields.[92] In most cases women crossed traditional
gender lines and did "men's work" for the first time because of economic
necessity: the family's major breadwinner was at war—or dead. Of course, the
national economy also forced the Nazi government, in contradiction to its earlier
espoused ideals, to recruit women for factory work. Financial desperation,
patriotism, and government recruitment all motivated German women to work in
positions they had not previously filled.

However, the engagement of the pastors' wives differed from the involvement
of German women in industry and commerce, as the Pfarrfrauen were not driven
by economic necessity to do their husbands' work. Wives of legally ordained
pastors continued to receive salary checks, even if their husbands were far from
the parish; moreover, the pastors' wives certainly got no encouragement from
the government to step in for their husbands. Ideology, theology, loyalty—these

factors motivated the Confessing women of the parsonages.

Another point distinguishes the pastors' wives from other German women who went to work in their husbands' places. After the war, the pastors' wives apparently gave up their positions gladly, returning the responsibilities of the parish to their husbands or to the ordained pastors who replaced them. These women never expected to move into full-time positions as pastors. Feminist ideology was not a motivator.

A particular legacy of the pastors' wives remains visible in the structure of German society today, where women now serve as pastors. Wilhelm Niesel testified to the influence of the pastors' wives on this development while debating the issue of the ordination of women at the Twelfth Confessing Synod of the Protestant Church of the Old Prussian Union in Hamburg in October 1942. Niesel, who opposed the ordination of Theologinnen, expressed his regret that

> under emergency situations, in not a few congregations, women, mostly pastors' wives, have preached in the churches in the absence of the pastors who were either at war or in prison. They carried out the functions of the office. In this round-about way, Vikarinnen, too, have been allowed to preach in church services, but they have not been ordained to that service![93]

Niesel's testimony is especially important in two regards. He asserted, first, that the phenomenon of pastors' wives preaching was observable in "not a few congregations." The phrase compensates for the lack of quantifiable data and the dwindling number of sources that could corroborate the contention that women filling their husbands' pulpits was a widespread phenomenon. However, Niesel's contention that pastors' wives set a precedent that the Theologinnen followed is less defensible. Well before the war, Theologinnen were engaged in full pastoral service—without ordination yet—in Brandenburg. Pastors' wives stepped in to fill the vacancies in their communities primarily after the outbreak of war, when so many of their husbands were drafted. One trend did not necessarily spring from the other. Pfarrfrauen and Theologinnen were doing similar work simultaneously.

Niesel's testimony and the foregoing pages of documentation, anecdotes, and memoirs confirm the two theses of the chapter. Without the leadership and support of the pastors' wives, the Confessing Church could not have survived the Nazi dictatorship. The women could have kept their husbands from serving in the Confessing cause, or at least have severely limited their effectiveness, and in fact, some women did.[94] However, there were others, as in cases cited here, who encouraged their husbands, occasionally showing even more determination to resist the Nazification of the Church than their men would have otherwise exercised. Bishop Hahn remarked that an "anxious, sniffling pastor's wife can be a tremendous stumbling block to her husband, as opposed to a brave wife—like mine—who can be a tremendous support to his steadfastness in the Creeds."[95]

Secondly, pastors' wives modeled behavior that prepared German Protestant lay people to accept women in public leadership roles in the church. These women did not aspire to a career in the ministry, and yet they helped prepare the way for the women who did want to become pastors. When Emmi Groh preached, Felicitas Vedder officiated at a grave site, Mechthild Kehr read a pulpit declaration, Hilde Schönherr led a worship service, Gertrud Arndt baptized a baby and carried bread and wine to a Communion-hungry parishioner, Irmgard Vogel listened to a farmer practice his sermon on Saturday night, and Herta Gadow-Meyer pulled on a preaching robe, they all demonstrated something that German Protestants had not seen since the days of the Reformation: women in public roles of spiritual leadership.

Another set of women, who had worked side by side with some of these pastors' wives, would carry the developments a step further. The Vikarinnen, the female theologians of the Confessing Church, would seek not just informal leadership roles, but official recognition in the form of ordination. When ordination for women finally came, it came about partly as a result of the precedent-setting work that the pastors' wives did under the observant eyes of their grateful flocks.

NOTES

1. Mechthild Kehr's diary entry of 1937, in the author's files. The diary does not give the month, but the incident took place in late August or September.

2. Only in 1960 did the Church laws permit a pastor's wife to be professionally engaged outside the parsonage. *Kirchenrätin* Gesa Conring discussed the pros and cons of pastors' wives having independent careers in a report to the Church Conference of the Protestant Church in Germany on 28 November 1962. Landeskirchliches Archiv Stuttgart, Bestand 315e, no. 4366.

3. Wolfgang Scherffig, *Junge Theologen im "Dritten Reich"* (Neukirchen-Vluyn: Neukirchener Verlag, 1989) 1:1, describes pastors' wives in the Rhineland as all originating from the bourgeoisie. However, as more aristocracy lived in the eastern regions of Germany than in the west, one discovers in Pomerania a few aristocratic names among pastors' wives. For example, Pastor Hans Dietrich Pompe married Spes von Bismarck, and Dietrich Bonhoeffer's fiancée was Maria von Wedemeyer. Irmgard von Derschau was a member of the Onnasch family, who provided several Confessing Pastors to the Church Struggle.

4. These characterizations offered by Scherffig have been corroborated in letters to the author from Pastorin Leni Immer, Pastorin Sieghild Jungklaus and Martha Link and in these books: Helene Brauer-Dede, *Frau Pastor* (Oldenburg: Verlag Klaus Dede, 1986) p. 109; Anneliese Hübner, *Wenn Stürme toben*

(Neuhausen-Stuttgart: Hänsler Verlag, 1984) p. 21; and Hans Prolingheuer, *Kleine politische Kirchengeschichte* (Köln: Pahl-Rugenstein, 1984-1985). Those who were worried about Hitler before 1933 were the exceptions, as related to the author in letters from Emmi Blöcher. Pastorin Marlies Fleisch-Thebesius, whose father was Jewish, reports that even members of her family were of divided opinions on Hitler in 1933. See her *Hauptsache Schweigen: Ein Leben unterm Hakenkreuz* (Frankfurt: Radius Verlag, 1988), pp. 27-29.

5. Among the exceptions the author has discovered: Emmi Mühlen-Bach, Maria Vetter Berendts, Herta Gadow-Meyer, Annemarie Götz-Schilling, and Hilde Enterlein Schönherr.

6. Gertrud Arndt, *Als Pfarrfrau zur Zeit des Nationalsozialismus* (Oldenburg: privately published, undated), p. 1.

7. James Bentley, *Martin Niemöller, 1892-1984* (New York: Free Press, 1984), pp. 144, 146.

8. Related by Leni Immer during an interview with Lydia Heiermann and Ruth Eissen in Wuppertal in February, 1990.

9. Attested by Arndt, *Als Pfarrfrau*, the Kehr interview, and a letter to the author from Gisela Lutschewitz of 28 March 1991.

10. Lutschewitz letter.

11. Interview with Dr. Christa Vogel, Pastor Konrad Vogel, and Maria Vogel in Berlin 14 January 1990.

12. Anita Schileker, "Wahrenholzer Pastorenfrau saß 1943 in Wolfsburg in KZ. "... und dat hett se nich secht!" in *Evangelische Zeitung* (Wolfsburg), no. 37 (13 March 1987): 6. The story is confirmed in a letter from Frau Werthmann to the author of 8 September 1991.

13. Vogel interview.

14. Gerda Zieger, "Von der Kriegswalze überrollt in Arnhausen Kr. Belgard/Pommern. Nach Kalendernotizen von Januar bis Ende September 1945," (privately published, n.d.), p. 3.

15. From the interview with Pastor Egbert Zieger and Frau Gerda Zieger in Winsen/Aller 30-31 January 1990.

16. From the interview with Frau Felicitas Vedder in Oldenburg in 27-28 January 1990; and from Frau Felcitas Vedder's memoirs which are contained in several scattered articles listed in the bibliography.

17. Vedder interview.

18. Robert Wise. *The Pastors' Barracks* (Wheaton, Il.: Victor Books, 1986), pp. 171-176.

19. This citation and the following material is from Luise Fahrenholz, "Bericht der Pfarrfrau Luise Fahrenholz (Eschbruch)" in Wilhelm Brix, ed., *Erinnerungen an Stadt + Land Friedberg Nm [sic, for "Neumark"]* (Berlin: Selbstverlag des kirchlichen Betreuungsdienstes für Friedberg in Berlin, 1974), p. 312.

20. For detailed accounts of the early enthusiasm of the German Protestant leaders, including some who would later be at the helm of the Confessing

Church, see Friedrich Baumgärtel, *Wider die Kirchenkampf-Legenden*
(Freimund: Verlag Neuendettelsau Mfr., 1958); and Prolingheuer, *Kirchenges-chichte.*

21. Bockemühl coedited *Unter dem Wort* with Pastors Karl Immer and
Hermann Klugkist-Hesse, all three men of the Wuppertal region; the other
journal's title was *Wo stehen wir heute?*

22. Hugo Hahn, *Kämpfer wider Willen* (Metzingen: Brunquell Verlag,
1969), p. 164.

23. Ibid., p. 66.

24. Heiermann interview.

25. Hahn, *Kämpfer wider Willen*, p. 66.

26. See Brauer-Dede, *Frau Pastor*, p. 140.

27. In German, that entire sentence was said with one word: *"Austreten."*
Ibid., p. 156.

28. Ibid.

29. Martin Niemöller's letters of 7 January 1940, 1 April 1940, 6 September 1940, and 6 October 1940. In Edita Sterik, ed., *Else Niemöller: Die Frau
eines bedeutenden Mannes* (Darmstadt: Zentralarchiv der Evangelischen Kirche
in Hessen und Nassau, July 1990), pp. 126-127.

30. Bentley, *Martin Niemöller*, p. 71.

31. "Extreme unction" or *"letzte Ölung."* See Chapter 1, p. 14. Hahn,
Kämpfer wider Willen, p. 50, attributes the phrase to Else Niemöller. Bentley
holds open the possibility that the words were supplied by Martin Niemöller's
secretary, who was also in the room at the time. Bentley, *Martin Niemöller*, p.
84.

32. Immer, *"Pfarrhaus;"* interviews with Frau Pastor Leni Immer in July
1987 and 12-13 February 1990; Hartmut Weber, ed., *"Und Sara zog mit:"
Frauen in der Bekennenden Kirche* (Bayrischer Rundfunk-Kirchenfunk, 6 April
1986).

33. Hahn, *Kämpfer wider Willen*, p. 165. Müggenberg was in Saxony; the
Heierman interview related similar cases in the Rhineland.

34. Lutschewitz letter.

35. Lilli Muthmann, "Mein Grusswort in der Kirche zu Helpup am
11.9.90 [sic] zum 50. Geburtstag der Frauenhilfe," p. ii. The handwritten document in the author's files has the erroneous 1990 date in the title. In fact, the
speech was given in 1988, as Frau Muthmann clarified in a letter to the author
of 18 November 1993, and as is evident from contemporary newspaper articles.

36. Ibid., p. iii.

37. Karl Schreck, *Aus dem Kampf der Bekennenden Kirche in Lippe 1933-
1945* (Varenholz: privately published mimeograph, 1969), p. 2.

38. Two published reports on the Muthmann cases: "Wort und Tat: Von
der Gruppe geht viel spontane Hilfe aus. Helpuper Frauenhilfe vor einem halben
Jahrhundert gegründet," *Neue Westfällische* (Oerlingahusen), no. 213 (13 September 1988); and "50 Jahre Frauenhilfe: Nicht immer nur "ja" gesagt. NW

sprach mit der Gründerin," *Neue Westfällische* (Oerlinghausen), (September [1988?]).

39. A copy of the official trial record of Marianne Albertz is available in the Evangelisches Zentralarchiv in Berlin, Bestand 50/8, pp. 1-115. In the same collection (unnumbered page) is a letter signed by "Rott" and addressed to "Dear Brethren." Dated "Berlin, Ende Dezember 1941," it is a Confessor's description of the trial.

40. Himmler's declaration was described in legal parlance as "(Sond. 1) P.K.K.Ms.5.41 (362.41)," Albertz trial record, p. 42.

41. The list of codefendents reads like a "Who's Who" of the Confessing Church. In the order in which they appear in the record they were: Martin Albertz, Hans Asmussen, Hans Böhm, Günther Dehn, Elisabeth Grauer, Günther Harder, Hellmut Hitzigrath, Hans Lokies, Wilhelm Niesel, Willy Prätorius, Barbara Thiele, Heinrich Vogel, Gerhard Jacoby, Ferdinand Vogel, Bruno Violet, Theodor Moldänke, Marianne Albertz, Frieda Arnheim, Margarete Michels, August and Anna Schröder, Ottonie Blanck, and Hermann Lossau. Rott letter, and Albertz trial record, p. 1.

42. The activities of this group are described in great detail in Scherffig, *Junge Theologen.*

43. Vogel interview.

44. From the author's interview with Ruth Bockemühl, Wuppertal, 13 February 1990.

45. See, "Schwestern," p. 17.

46. From the author's interview of Mechthild Kehr, 16 January 1990 in Berlin; corroborated with transcripts from her diary and in letters from her to the author of 5 May 1990 and 25 May 1990.

47. Kehr interview; Kehr diary.

48. Re Felicitas Veddder, see Vedder interview.

49. Concerning Thea Werthmann, see Schileker, "Wahrenholzer Pastorenfrau."

50. Kehr diary, 1937, cited in a letter of 10 May 1990 from Mechthild Kehr to the author. The diary entry does not give the month, but the event took place shortly after "the end of August [1937]."

51. Immer, *Pfarrhaus.*

52. Ibid. One might also wish to read Karl Immer's letter from jail, addressed to his children, in Bertold Klappert and Günther van Norden, *Tut um Gottes willen etwas Tapferes!* (Neukirchen-Vluyn: Neukirchener Verlag, 1989) pp. 100-107.

53. Bockemühl interview; the author's interview with Emmi Blöcher in her home in Sinn-Dill, 19 February 1990; the Immer interviews.

54. Heinrich Grüber, *An der Stechbahn* (Berlin: Evangelische Verlagsanstalt, [1953]), p. 5. Like the Immers, the Grübers harbored non-Aryans in their home.

55. Vogel interview.

56. From Pastor Erich Muthmann's letter of 15 June 1945 to Herrn Oberschulrat Dr. Kühn, Landesregierung Lippe, Abt. III, Detmold; copy supplied by Lilli Muthmann in the author's files.

57. Ibid., p. 2.

58. The testimony of Hertha von Klewitz, neé Niemöller, in W. See, "Schwestern," p. 5.

59. The induction figure is from Richard Solberg, *God and Caesar in East Germany: The Conflicts of Church and State in East Germany since 1945* (New York: Macmillan Co., 1961), p. 18. Solberg's statement is that "more than 60% of all German clergymen had been inducted into regular military service during the war." Literature on the Church Struggle frequently estimates the size of the German clergy before the war at about 18,000.

60. Hubert G. Locke, ed., *Exile in the Fatherland: Martin Niemöller's Letters from Moabit Prison* (Grand Rapids, Mich.: William B. Eerdmans Publishing Company, 1986), p. 78.

61. Bentley, *Martin Niemöller*, p. 128.

62. This composite picture is drawn from Arndt, *Als Pfarrfrau;* Brauer-Dede, *Frau Pastor*, pp. 41-43; Gertrud Seyler, *Aus meinem Leben* (Minden: privately published, n.d.); the Vogel interview; and Cläre Wetzel, "Bericht von Frau Cläre Wetzel (ehemals Büssow)" in Schendel and Schauer, eds., *Erinnerungen*, pp. 314-18; and letter to the author from Ilse Härter, 29 December 1992.

63. Bockemühl interview; Brauer-Dede, *Frau Pastor*, pp. 17, 43, 91; from the author's interview with Lydia Heiermann, Wuppertal, 13 February 1990; Seyler, *Aus meinem Leben*, pp. 3, 8; and Vogel interview.

64. Quoted by her daughter Maria during the Vogel interview.

65. Vogel interview.

66. "Aber wenn Sie meinen, Frau Pasterchen, denn wollen wir's mal versuchen."

67. Irmgard von Derschau, "Die Arbeit in Kirchengemeinden der Synode Stolp-Land 1945-1946," (Hannover: Konvent Evangelischer Gemeinden aus Pommern Hilfskommittee e.V., n.d.).

68. See, "Schwestern," p. 5.

69. From the author's interview with Louise Tecklenburg, Berlin, 16 January 1990. Women serving as elders was rare, but not unprecedented. The examples of Stephanie von Mackensen and Louise Helmbold have already been cited.

70. Research has failed to discover a single case of a pastor's wife's confirming children, unless she was also a trained theologian. Pastor Otto Berendts wrote in a letter to the author of 29 October 1991, that his wife, Maria Berendts (née Vetter), who substituted for him in every pastoral function in Schermeisel, Neumark, did not confirm children simply because she had to travel frequently to her sick mother in Berlin and could not keep the regular confirmation instruction schedule. He then added, "But as far as the congregation and the *Bruderrat*

were concerned, they would have had no objection to her doing it." Contributing to their willingness may have been the fact that Maria Berendts was a trained *Theologin*.

71. The following information on Emmi Hof Groh Blöcher is from the Blöcher interview.

72. Blöcher interview.

73. 1 Corinthians 14:35.

74. The data on Herta Gadow-Meyer are from Hartmut Gadow and Herta Gadow-Meyer, *"Geflüchtet—Gejagt—Bewahrt. Brandenburg-Pommersche Erinnerungen 1944-1945"* (Hannover: Konvent evangelischer Gemeinden aus Pommern e.V., 1991) pp. 10, 28-30.

75. Ibid., p. 27.

76. Ibid., p. 28.

77. The symbolic importance of the vestments was not lost on church authorities in Baden and Wurttemberg who, in 1942, overruled the arguments of *Theologinnen* who petitioned for the privilege to wear clerical robes for the practical reasons that concerned Frau Gadow-Meyer's farmers. Landeskirchliches Archiv Stuttgart, Bestand 356 a II, nos. 245, 246, 258.

78. From the author's interviews with Pastor Egbert Zieger and Frau Gerda Zieger, Winsen-Aller, 30-31 January 1990; and with Frau Felicitas Vedder.

79. Arndt, *Als Pfarrfrau*. The initial report from Frau Arndt is augmented with a letter to the author from 20 March 1990.

80. Seyler, *Aus meinem Leben*.

81. Von Derschau, *Die Artbeit*. Frau von Derschau was not the only woman doing similar service in her area of Pomerania. Her memoir mentions "Frau Pastor Kaun, who faithfully carried out the ministry of the late Pastor Kibelkas, as well as the wife of Pastor Fürstenburg . . . and the pastor's wife in Schurow."

82. Kehr diary, dated simply "1945."

83. Kehr diary, 1945.

84. Heiermann interview. It was in a convalescent home, but men were present, and she preached her own sermon, not a prewritten one provided by headquarters in Düsseldorf or Koblenz.

85. Immer interview.

86. The term *"Bekenntnisgemeinschaft"* referred to the fellowship of pastors who supported the aims of the Confessing Church as it existed in other Landeskirchen.

In fact, there was not a "Confessing Church" in Hanover, because the Protestant-Lutheran Provincial Church of Hanover was a so-called "intact" church, one that (along with the Protestant-Lutheran churches of Bavaria and Wurttemberg) had not been taken over by "German Christians." Confessors had not found it necessary to establish a rival ecclesiastical government because the Hanoverian Church was not in heretical hands. Nevertheless, as the questionnaire makes clear, there were allegiances to the Confessional Movement among the pastors.

87. *Fragebogen zur Geschichte der Landeskirche von 1933 bis Kriegsende*, issued by the Protestant-Lutheran Church of Hannover. The results of the questionnaire are filed with the Landeskirchliche Archiv, Ev.-luth. Landeskirche Hannovers, Collection SI H iii.

88. Frau Pastor Otto Fischer of Hillerse and Höckelheim, a double congregation of 1664 souls. Landeskirchliche Archiv, Ev.-luth. Landeskirche Hannovers, Collection SI H iii, 417 Hillerse und Höckelheim.

89. Information about Hilde Schönherr is from interviews with her husband, Bishop Emeritus Albrecht Schönherr, conducted in July 1987 in East Berlin, and in March 1992 in Seattle, Washington.

90. The assignment was termed an *Auftrag*, but it was nothing approaching ordination.

91. Schönherr interview. Details of the story were confirmed by the Tecklenburg interview in which Superintendent (retired) Joachim Stein reported that the Soviets ordered regularly scheduled church services to resume in their zone on Pentecost Sunday, 1945. In the Soviet zone, in which people worked Monday through Saturday and were expected to turn out for city renovation work on Sundays, Soviet officials exempted from the "volunteer" work those who desired to go to church. Solberg, *God and Caesar*, p. 31, reported that German church leaders in the Soviet zone held Colonel Tulpanov, chief cultural officer, and his Captain Yermolajev, a religious affairs officer, in high regard for their cooperative attitude toward the churches.

92. Katherine Thomas, *Women in Nazi Germany* (London: Victor Gollancz, 1943), p. 15, quoting from Marie Elisabeth Lüders, *Das Unbekannte Heer* (1936).

93. Wilhelm Niesel, *Kirche unter dem Wort: der Kampf der Bekennenden Kirche* (Bielefeld: Ludwig Bechauf Verlag, 1948) p. 241.

94. Frau Lydia Heiermann (Heiermann interview); and Bishop Emeritus Albrecht Schönherr (oral testimony in Seattle, Washington, at the 22nd Annual Scholars' Conference on The Holocaust and the German Church Struggle: Religion, Power and the Politics of Resistance; Scholars Colloquium IV: "Women, Gender and the Church Struggle," Tuesday, 3 March, 1992). Both eyewitnesses attested to numbers of women who discouraged their husbands from aligning with the Confessing Church.

95. Hahn, *Kämpfer wider Willen*, p. 66.

Initially Pastor Peter Bockemühl was drawn to cast his lot with the "German Christians." His teenage bride, Ruth Bockemühl, persuaded him to go the way of Karl Barth and the Confessing Church. Barth performed the couple's wedding ceremony. Source: Frau Ruth Bockemühl.

"Threatening measures of the Nazi State naturally had an impact on the family, too," recalled Dr. Petrus Bockenmühl, here pictured as a boy (left) with his brother Justus and his parents, Pastor Peter Bockenmühl and Ruth Bockenmühl. Simply naming their son "Petrus"—not an Aryan name—was an act of resistance on the part of the Bockenmühls. Source: Frau Ruth Bockenmühl.

The family of Superintendent Carl and Bertha Buth, Greifenberg, Pomerania. The children are, from left to right, Günther, Annemarie, Renate, and Christel. When DC church officials cut off Pastor Buth's salary, the family nevertheless ate well due to provisions from the estate of Countess Elisabeth von Thadden. Source: Frau Christel Aden.

Superintendent Karl and Bertha Buth (née Steffler), Greifenberg, Pomerania, ca. 1942. Source: Frau Christel Aden.

Wilhelm and Nina Hof of Weidelbach were among the first Confessors in the Nassau churches. Wilhelm Hof, one of the relatively few who actually read Mein Kampf, shared his growing alarm with the entire family, equipping Emmi Hof, the older girl in the middle, to counter the influence of the "German Christians" and the Hitler Youth on the young people of Weidelbach. Left to right: Gertrud, Wilhelm Hof, Emmi, Heidi, Nina Hof, Alfred. Source: Frau Emmi Blöcher.

The army drafted "illegal" Confessing Vikar Theo Groh in 1939, shortly after he received a call to serve a church in Biedenkopf. He and Emmi Hof married just four days before he had to report for duty. He fell in France in June 1940. Emmi Hof Groh then prepared herself for church service in Berlin, and later preached among Confessing churches in Nassau. Source: Frau Emmi Blöcher.

Pastor Karl Immer, seated right, called Confessors to his Barmen-Gemarke church in Wuppertal in May 1934, where the Barmen Confession was drafted by Professor Karl Barth and signed by Confessing delegates from throughout Germany: 137 men and one women.

Seated with him in this 1936 photograph is his wife Tabea Immer (née Smidt) surrounded by the couple's children, clockwise from the left: Friederike (15), Waltraut (17), Karl, Jr. (20) in uniform, Alida (16), Leni (21), Adalbert (13) and Udo (10), all of whom were intimately involved in the illegalities associated with the Church Struggle. Source: Pastorin Leni Immer.

The last photograph of Tabea and Pastor Karl Immer, of Wuppertal, 1944. Source: Pastorin Leni Immer.

Mechthild Kehr, who took the place of her husband in his parish in Seelow, Brandenburg, led the "Collection Struggle" there. She suffered imprisonment in Frankfurt an der Oder, hid Jewish refugees, fled before the Soviet army in February 1945, and returned in June to pastor the parish. Frau Kehr now lives in Berlin. Source: Frau Mechthild Kehr

Lilli Muthmann defied local Nazi Party officials in Helpup, Lippe, by offering Christian women an alternative to the Nazi Frauenschaft. She founded the Protestant Ladies' Aid in Helpup on 2 February 1938. She sat for this oil portrait by Maria Wisselhorn, "The Young Pastor's Wife. Source: Frau Lilli Muthmann.

Post-war photograph of Pastor Bruno Tecklenburg of the Johannes congregation of Berlin-Lichterfelde, with his wife and seven children. Source: Frau Louise Tecklenburg.

The 1928 wedding procession of Pastor Martin Vedder and his bride, Felicitas Adami. Source: Frau Lieselotte Fendler.

Pastor Martin Vedder with his wife Felicitas Vedder and their nine-year-old daughter Lieselotte, 1942. The pastor died in military service in Crimea, leaving his wife to minister to the churches in Gross Poplow, Pomerania. Source: Frau Lieselotte Fendler.

This 1942 photograph of Felicitas Vedder and her children Hellmut and Lieselotte was taken three years before Vedder was arrested and her children shunted to an orphanage on the Baltic Sea island Rügen. Source: Lois Vedder.

Hilde Schönherr (née Enterlein) and her two children, Oswald and Barbara, at the train station in Brüssow 1942, the year Pastor Albrecht Schönherr went to war. In 1945 a soviet military officer insisted that Frau Schönherr conduct worship services in Brüssow. Source: Bishop emeritus Albrecht Schönherr.

Hilde Enterlein Schönherr in 1947, after two years of pastoring the church in Brüssow during her husband's absence. Pastor Albrecht Schönherr, who entered military service 1942, returned from an Italian POW camp in May 1947. Source: Bishop emeritus Albrecht Schönherr.

The family of Pastor Heinrich and Irmgard Vogel, of Dobbrikow, Brandenburg, in August 1942. Left to right: Pastor Heinrich Vogel (in uniform), Maria, Irmgard Vogel, Martin, Brigitta (on her mother's lap), Ilse, and Konrad. Source: Dr. Christa Vogel.

Pastorin Ilse Härter refused "ordination" when the Confessing Church of the Rhineland offered to consecrate her in 1939. She was one of the first two women whom the Confessing Church of Berlin-Brandenburg fully ordained, without gender-based restrictions, on 12 January, 1943. Source: Pastorin Ilse Härter.

Vikarin Sieghild Jungklaus, the first woman in Berlin-Brandenburg to wear a preaching robe, leads her confirmation class out of the side portal of the Hoffnung Church of Berlin-Pankow. This photograph from 1944 illustrates a gender-based limitation placed on Jungklaus even after her ordination. She was allowed to confirm young women, but not young men. Source: Pastorin Sieghild Jungklaus.

Sieghild Jungklaus and her fiancé Siegfried Anz, at a 1937 or 1938 Ascension Day gathering of BK students in the garden of a non-Aryan Christian, a member of the Confessing Church. This annual outing was a gesture of solidarity with the non-Aryan Christian sculptor. Source: Pastorin Sieghild Jungklaus.

Pastorin Aenne Kaufmann settled the question of appropriate clothing for a preaching woman by commissioning a tailor to make a traditional Talar—a preaching robe—for her. This was the only one she ever owned. Source: Pastor Uwe Kleinhückelkoten.

Pastorin Elisabeth Charlotte "Lieselotte" Lawerenz rode a circuit through Brandenburg as an "illegal" Vikarin, preaching from town to town, an activity which eventually landed her in prison. She was the first woman to serve as an assistant at an ordination ceremony—the service in which Ilse Härter and Hannelotte Reiffen were ordained to full pastoral ministry on 12 January 1943. Source: Pastorin Elisabeth Charlotte Lawerenz.

The girls in Vikarin Herta Meyer's class did not want to disband after their confirmations, so they continued to meet with the "illegal" Vikarin in the Berlin-Pankow Confessing Church. Source: Pastorin Herta Gadow-Meyer.

Theologinnen had no traditions to guide them in the question of appropriate dress. Vikarin Maria Vetter wore a simple black dress, adorned albeit with a silver cross that bore the date of her "ordination," (2 July 1936) and the inscription "Acts 20:17-36." Source: Oberkirchenrat Otto Berendts.

Chapter 4

Theologinnen in the Confessing Church

[Pastor Schlingensiepen] pointed out that I was a woman. To that I could only truthfully affirm, I had never had any doubt about it.

—Pastorin Ilse Härter[1]

The pastors' wives were not alone in modeling a new professional role for women in Germany. Another group of women shared the theological commitment and the years of practical experience of the wives, but they differed from them in significant ways. Unlike the *Pfarrfrauen*, they were single and academically trained in theology, and they vigorously aspired to remain in positions of professional church leadership after the war. Having passed the same theological examinations required of the pastors, these women were the *Theologinnen*—the female theologians—of the Confessing Church.

Like so many pastors' wives during the Church Struggle, Theologinnen began to do what only men had previously been permitted to do. They preached, baptized, buried, married, gave Holy Communion, published, and administered parishes. Although they initially worked in all these areas with the understanding and at the request of their male supervisors, peers, and parishioners, they served without the recognition and comfort that full ordination would have afforded. That situation was to change. By 1945 Theologinnen of the Confessing Church had overthrown eighteen centuries of Christian tradition and opened doors to a new professional opportunity for women: German Protestant women could aspire to become ordained pastors.

This chapter identifies seven factors that contributed to this remarkable social and theological change: one hundred years of German feminism, a demographic crisis after World War I, Nazi persecution, modeling of the capabilities of women by pastors' wives and *Vikarinnen*, a new approach to Scripture, one man's dissatisfaction with and unilateral rebellion against a synodical decision, and the willingness of the people in the pews to accept women in new roles.

ONE CASE HISTORY AND ITS BACKGROUND

Late on the afternoon of 6 December 1935, Vikarin Aenne Kaufmann of the Market Church in Essen, having just finished teaching her regular Friday afternoon Ladies' Bible Class, made her way to keep an appointment with Johannes Böttcher, her pastor and a leader of the Confessing Church of the Rhineland.[2] As a Vikarin, Kaufmann's work was pleasantly challenging, though limited to ministry with women, girls, and children. She taught, counseled, and developed and carried out church programs, but because she was a woman the Church did not allow her to perform sacerdotal functions. Even among groups of women, she had no authority to offer Holy Communion, preach from the pulpit, confirm catechumens or baptize infants and converts. Like almost every other Theologin in Germany she had cast her lot with the Confessing Church in the emerging Church Struggle, which put her in a precarious political and professional position.[3]

Arriving in Böttcher's office, Kaufmann was asked, "Are you prepared to be ordained?" Böttcher explained that several brothers of the Confessing Church wanted to be present to assist in the ordination service, but that otherwise no one, not even her parents, was to know about this ahead of time. Secrecy was important lest the Gestapo get involved. On the following Sunday, 8 December 1935, at the early service of the Market Church in Essen, Pastor Johannes Böttcher, assisted by four other pastors, "ordained" Aenne Kaufmann to Christian ministry in the Confessing Church of the Rhineland.[4]

In spite of what appears to have been a precedent-setting event of theological and social importance, Aenne Kaufmann's "ordination" brought about no apparent changes. Afterwards, no one addressed her as *"Frau Pastorin"*; she remained "Fräulein Kaufmann." She did not wear clerical garb, her salary did not increase, and she was not included in the preaching cycle in the Market Church.[5]

The evidence indicates that the men who agreed to "ordain" Aenne Kaufmann on Sunday, 8 December 1935, did not *intend* for anything to change. Their intent was not to elevate a woman to the rank of colleague, but rather to make a defiant gesture to Nazi Minister of Ecclesiastical Affairs Hans Kerrl who, on the previous Monday, had decreed that no church could ordain candidates without his approval. When word of Kerrl's ruling reached the Brotherhood Council of the Confessing Church of the Rhineland, they decided summarily to defy it, resolving to ordain someone—anyone!—at the earliest possible opportunity.[6] When, after examining the field of candidates, they found they had ordained all the usual candidates just the previous September, they agreed to make their statement by "ordaining" three Vikarinnen.[7] Böttcher "ordained" Kaufmann in Essen while Pastor Heinrich Ibeling of the Matthai Church in Düsseldorf "ordained" Hannah Klein and Emilie Bach at later services the same day.[8] Was the move theological, or political, or both? What did the "ordination" of Aenne Kaufmann achieve? If for the men involved the ceremony was a symbolically defiant gesture against the ambitions of Hans Kerrl, from Aenne Kaufmann's perspective it was something much more: the act was an ecclesiastical recognition of her God-given spiritual gifts and her professional training. Having studied the issue of ordination of women, Kaufmann had long since concluded that it was theologically defensible, although she would never have initiated it. Once the ceremony was over, she quietly assumed all the responsibilities of full ordination. For example, when, shortly after the ordination service, the parents of a newborn baby asked her to baptize their infant, she agreed to do so. Without fanfare (and hence, without resistance), she preached and presided over Holy Communion on the hospital wards. When she was asked whether men were present on these occasions, she replied, "I never looked."[9]

"Ordination" evidently meant different things to different people. For Kaufmann, it represented a change. For the men, their defiance was intended to preserve the status quo: the Church must operate independently of the state. That the men had no intention of making changes is further illustrated in the language of the certificate that they issued attesting to Kaufmann's "ordination" (see Figure 4.1). Boldly inscribed with the title *Ordinationsurkunde* ("Ordination Certificate") the subsequent text stated that the ordainers, "exercising *emergency rights . . . consecrate . . .* the candidate Aenne Kaufmann [emphasis added]."[10] The men saw their action as an emergency, temporary measure; they did not issue to Kaufmann a document identical to what they were giving to men. The use of the word "consecrated" (*eingesegnet*) instead of "ordained" (*ordiniert*) is crucial in ecclesiastical law.[11]

The ceremony of 8 December 1935 cannot, then, be regarded as a bona fide ordination because it laid restrictions on women that were not applied to men. Nevertheless, the event was part of a growing trend within the provincial Confessing churches as they "ordained" dozens of Vikarinnen, taking tentative steps toward culmination in full ordination for women. Although the full ordinations would not take place until 12 January 1943, in the intervening six years Confessing women with limited "ordinations" performed every sacerdotal and sacramental function of the Church.

Of course, the very idea of ordaining a woman would never have occurred to the men of Essen without the women's social and intellectual preparation. The women's movement in Germany in the nineteenth and early twentieth centuries had set the stage for the idea that women, too, could do what men did in the pastorate.

GERMAN FEMINISM AND ORDINATION OF WOMEN

Women whose interests were not primarily Christian—and were, in some cases, anti-Christian—prepared the way for the eventual ordination of German Protestant women. Initially, most Christian women opposed liberating measures

Figure 4.1
Aenne Kaufmann's Ordination Certificate

Ordinations - Urkunde

In Ausübung des von der Bekenntnissynode der Deutschen Evangelischen Kirche am 20. Oktober 1934 verkündeten Notrechtes haben wir gemäss dem Beschluss des Rates der Evang. Bekenntnissynode im Rheinland die zur Vikarin in *die Gemeinde...Essen -Altstadt......* berufene Kandidatin

A e n n e   K a u f m a n n
....

geb. am *4. Septemb.03* in *Bremen.........*
am heutigen Tage
im Gottesdienst der *evangelischen.* Kirchengemeinde

Essen-Altstadt

eingesegnet. Gegenüber den Irrlehren der Gegenwart hat die Vikarin die theologische Erklärung der ersten Bekenntnissynode der D.E.K. zu W.-Barmen vom 29. bis 31.Mai 1934 als für ihre Amtsführung massgebend anerkannt. Wir bezeugen solches glaubhaft und ordnungsgemäss. Die Vikarin aber befehlen wir dem alleinigen Herrn der Kirche Jesus Christus, dem alle Gewalt im Himmel und auf Erden gegeben ist. Er erfülle an ihr die Verheissung: Siehe, ich bin bei euch alle Tage bis an der Welt Ende!

...Essen...... den *8. Dezemb.35.*

Der Präses
der Evang.Bekenntnis-
Synode im Rheinland

i.A.

Die assistierenden
Pfarrer:

The certificate is not identical to what the Confessing Church of the Rhineland issued to men who were ordained in 1935. Line 11 reads "consecrated" (eingesegnet) instead of "ordained" (ordiniert). Source: Archiv der Evangelischen Kirche des Rheinlands, Düsseldorf, Nachlass Aenne Kaufmanns, Akte 17.

on their behalf because they feared that the women's emancipation movement was "of the world."[12] They associated it with communism or Social Democracy, with political liberals and radicals. Cooperation with the leftists demanded more toleration than most Protestant women of the nineteenth century could muster, although later Christian women would readily admit their debt to the secular movement.[13]

The establishment of the General German Women's Association (Allgemeiner Deutscher Frauenverein, or ADFV) in 1865 was the beginning of a successfully organized effort to secure equal rights for women in Germany. By 1870 the ADFV's cofounders, Luise Otto and Auguste Schmidt, boasted ten thousand members. That same year, Jenny Hirsch began publication of the *Women's Advocate* (*Der Frauen-Anwalt*) which gave German women a mouthpiece as well as an ear through which they could learn of the progress of women in other countries. Hirsch reported on women serving as librarians, druggists, teachers, and physicians in France, Great Britain, Russia, Switzerland, and the United States of America.[14] The feminist agenda of the 1870s, as outlined in articles in the *Advocate*, demanded equal standing with men before the law, basic educational opportunities for girls, and the right to vote.[15] In 1885 the Socialist August Bebel published *Women and Socialism*, which called for similar reforms: freedom for women to marry for love and not out of mere economic necessity; general employment and education for women; economic independence for women from their families, even from their own husbands; and the right of women to play a role in civic affairs.[16] Bebel's ideas generated a political bloc. By 1919, women comprised one third of the membership of the Social Democratic Party (SPD).[17]

Most Christian women, however, were suspicious of anything that the SPD promoted. From their perspective, socialism was tainted with Marxist atheism and with cultural and religious iconoclasm. If religiously conservative women were to become feminists, a more moderate spokesperson had to emerge, and she arose indeed in the person of Helene Lange. A self-described Christian and an indefatigable reformer intent on integrating women into every aspect of German society, Lange held chief among her goals the reform of education so that women could enter the professions.[18]

In 1893, after establishing the General German Female Teachers Association (Allgemeiner Deutscher Lehrerinnenverein or ADLV), Lange founded a high school in Berlin where young women could study the same subjects as their male counterparts: mathematics, the natural sciences, economics, Latin, and history. Because no German university admitted women, Lange prepared her students for Swiss institutions while simultaneously lobbying for coeducation at home. In 1894 she called numerous women's organizations together to establish the Federation of German Women's Associations (Bund Deutscher Frauenvereine or BDFV), which in 1896 called for women's suffrage, using Lange's tract, "Women's Right to Vote" to articulate the position.[19] In 1901 the 40,000 members of the ADLV began agitating for better professional training, higher

pay, and recognition as professionals. Since such training could only take place
on the university level, Lange lobbied the universities to open their lecture halls
to women. The state of Baden was first to comply in 1902. Bavaria and
Wurttemberg followed in 1903-1904, Saxony in 1906-1907, and then Prussia,
Hessia, the Rhineland, and Mecklenburg in 1908-1910.[20]

By the time of Helene Lange's death in 1930, German society had changed
fundamentally. In 1908 only 3,436 women were studying in German
universities, but by 1930, nearly 20,000 women were preparing themselves for
professional careers in nearly every academic field.[21] Already by 1925, the
professions census of Germany counted 97,675 women teaching; 2,720 serving
as druggists; 2,572 practicing medicine; 921 working as chemists; 835
practicing dentistry; 160 in positions as religious clerics; and 54 practicing
law.[22] After the Weimar Constitution opened suffrage to women, at any one
time between 1919 and 1930 between four and five hundred women were
serving in elective offices at the city, state, and federal levels.[23] Helene Lange's
self-identification as a Christian made feminism palatable for other Christian
women. An emerging Christian women's movement opened up new professional
fields for Protestant women, but at the time of Lange's death in 1930, there was
still no terminal position open for women in theology.

THE CHRISTIAN WOMEN'S MOVEMENT

In 1899 Elisabeth Gnaucke-Kuehne, Lic. Weber and Paula Müller-Ottfried
cofounded the German Protestant Women's Association (Deutsch-Evangelischer
Frauenbund or DEFB), a clear expression that feminism was alive within limited
circles of Christian women, although the Christian movement distinguished
itself subtly from its secular counterpart.[24] Weber, in a June 1899 speech,
recognized that the "radical [i.e., secular] women's movement" had helped
Christian women, admitting that although Christian women had been late in
asserting themselves on behalf of their sex, they were "now ready to help—but
in their own way." He cautioned that because "Protestant women recognize the
limitations within which a Christian German woman can operate. . . no woman
from this group would attempt to influence legislation at the parliamentary
level."[25] In this way, the women heard a man remind them of their limitations.

Helping "in their own way" meant that these women would work within their
churches to effect change. Adelheid von Bennigsen wrote to the editor of *The
Women's Movement* that Christian women had their own unique agenda.
Moreover, she wrote, she was thankful that advances were being made across
the entire spectrum and were "happy to represent the right wing of the women's
movement."[26]

Step by step, a Christian feminist agenda unfolded. In 1903 the DEFB
demanded that women be permitted to vote in church elections and be given the
right to be elected to chair benevolence committees.[27] In April 1903 a certain

Fräulein Pappertz issued a call for women's suffrage, which was a step toward "parliamentary" involvement.[28] In September, in a significant step toward solidarity with the secularists, the DEFB invited representatives from all the other major women's groups in the country to participate in their convention as observers.[29]

From the ranks of Protestantism came a new generation of educated women, heir to the reforms of the secular movement, and eager to study at the German universities. Because of educational preparation and religious conviction, some of these women inevitably chose to study theology—but what would they do with a degree in a field that was exclusively male?

For years theology professors forestalled their decision on whether to admit women on the basis that there was no career open to a Theologin. The leaders of the feminist movement themselves advised their sisters against theology on the same basis.[30] However, in 1914 Lydia Schmid enrolled to study theology under the Protestant theological faculty of Tübingen. She won a degree in 1921 with which she taught religion in a girls' high school in Stuttgart until 1928.[31]

The idea spread to other universities. By 1925 nearly fifty women were studying theology in Germany, as evidenced by the forty-eight who met in Marburg to form the Union of Protestant Theological Women of Germany (Verband evangelischer Theologinnen Deutschlands or VETD). The membership expanded to seventy within a year: by 1926 there were about a hundred women in theological study in Germany.[32] The VETD's announced goals included the establishment of new positions for women that would lighten the loads of the pastors, specifically, in chaplaincies on women's wards of hospitals and prisons, counseling in homes for girls, teaching, youth work (with girls), and administrative positions within para-church organizations.[33] No official statement emerged that women might someday seek ordination, but the new organization provided a forum where women shared ideas and dreams, raised the level of consciousness of the whole group, and garnered courage from their growing numbers.

The move to employ theologically trained women began with Lydia Schmid in Wurttemberg in 1921. In 1926 the Protestant Church of Thuringia provided the first guidelines for the employment of women as pastors' helpers (*Pfarrgehilfinnen*). In 1927 the Protestant Church of Mecklenburg-Schwerin followed suit, and in November 1928 the Protestant Church of the Old Prussian Union (APU) created the office of curate (Vikarin), a position that was open to single women.[34] All the APU member churches had adopted the law by the end of 1928.[35] Hamburg went one step further when it allowed women with "proper theological accreditation" to conduct services "in institutions for women and in women's wards of general institutions."[36] Mecklenburg-Schwerin joined Hamburg in allowing women, in special individual cases, to administer Holy Communion, but not until 1930 did a woman take her theological examination before a church board.[37]

THE DEMOGRAPHIC CRISIS

The late 1920s saw a great deal of activity among women in the Protestant Churches of Germany because of a demographic crisis brought about by casualties in World War I (and also, perhaps, because of growing feelings of secularism). There were no longer enough men in Christian ministry. In 1928, of 112 pastorates in and around Stuttgart, for example, 41 were empty, and 24 were filled with pastors who had been called out of retirement.[38] In 1935 the Protestant Church of Pomerania reported that of 801 pastorates, 229 were empty.[39] By the end of the war, 325 Thuringian pastors were responsible for 1500 congregations.[40] Because the situation prevailed all over Germany, the churches looked to women to fill the vacant posts.[41]

As a result, the theological faculties of the universities found themselves training women for a growing number of careers. Not only would women teach religion in public schools, they could look forward to being administrative assistants, counselors, teachers of adult women, and leaders of youth ministries. The Church leaders insisted that the women have university training in the same skills and disciplines as the men, a traditional curriculum that required two major examinations. The First Theological Examination covered theoretical material: Scripture, theology, apologetics, hermeneutics, ethics, church history, and ancient languages (Greek, Hebrew, Latin). The Second Theological Examination, usually taken two years later, was generally written after a period in pastoral apprenticeship and covered the practical material of day-to-day ministry.

This curriculum presented problems in one area in particular: homiletics, the preparation and delivery of sermons. The question was, Should the women be required, indeed, should they be allowed, to preach? The High Church Council of the Protestant Church of Wurttemberg decreed that the women could take the First Theological Examination but that they might not preach. "In place of the sermon, the female students of Protestant theology will give a 'talk.'"[42] A talk was later defined as a presentation to be delivered from a position before the altar in the church, but not from the pulpit; furthermore, the talk would be given to an audience consisting solely of women, with the exception of course of the male faculty member who of necessity would be present.[43] The Tübingen theological faculty never accepted this ruling of the High Church Council. Professor Faber in Tübingen told his women students that because the winter was so harsh, and because on the day of the examination he feared he might suffer from a head cold, their examination would, indeed, be held in the heated sacristy of the church, and not at the cold, drafty position before the altar in the nave. This difference between the academics and the clerics manifested a crack in the wall that centuries of Church tradition had built up to keep women and men separated in their ministries.

With increasing exposure to a wider variety of ministry experiences and opportunities, Theologinnen revised their professional goals. Just three years after the Union of Protestant Theological Women (VETD) called for professional positions that would ease the loads of the pastors, some of the women expressed discontent with the prospects of playing only auxiliary roles in the church.[44] In a 1928 speech to the VETD in Marburg, Annemarie Rübens delivered the credo, "The Theologin has not only the possibility, but the duty to proclaim [the Gospel] with whatever means possible, and that includes striving for full pastoral recognition."[45]

Two years later Rübens joined Ina Gschlössl in writing an open letter to church leaders on the pages of the *Christian World*. They decried the pastoral monstrosity that so often occurred in hospital and prison work: when Theologinnen worked long and lovingly to bring a penitent prisoner to the point of faith, spiritual progress often suffered a setback after the new believer learned that a stranger, a man, would come in to administer the baptism or extend the elements of Holy Communion. "Working under such conditions provides daily inward pain," they wrote, "and in the long run destroys the joy and initiative of serving." Rübens and Gschlössl further maintained in their letter that lay people despised the Church's stance. "What makes the Church behave as if women are less gifted than men for ecclesiastical functions" when in so many other professions women were stepping in beside men and working competently? Rübens and Gschlössl pulled no punches, concluding their letter with a rebuke:

> The motive behind such a law is neither practical nor theological. . . . There is only one other explanation, namely this: Behind this ruling is—let us say it clearly—a certain attitude about the inferiority, that is, the ineptness of women to hold their own office within the Church.[46]

THE THEOLOGINNEN IN THE CONGREGATIONS

The Rübens-Gschlössl letter laid the axe to one root of patriarchy in the Church: churchmen viewed women as inept, inferior, emotionally unstable, and constitutionally unsuited for the rigors of the pastorate. How could women possibly have the time to be wives and mothers, and pastors, too? During the Church Struggle, Theologinnen not only proved themselves physically and emotionally capable of carrying a pastor's load, they also disproved the contention that the congregations would not accept women in the pulpits.

Indisputably, Theologinnen shared fully in carrying the Confessing Church through the Church Struggle and the war. *Präses* Kurt Scharf "ordained" Vikarin Liselotte Berli in 1937 in Berlin with the official understanding that her ministry would be limited to work with women, girls, and children, but he nevertheless placed her in a position where she worked in full pastoral capacities from 1937 on, well before the heightened crises associated with the war.[47] When Hannelotte Reiffen entered the service of the Confessing Church of Brandenburg in 1937, Scharf set her into service as a circuit rider among villages in the southeastern section of Brandenburg. In Worbis she established a regular preaching service. Later Reiffen substituted full-time for Pastor Jochen Kanitz in Ilmersdorf.[48] There she persuaded the pastor's wife, Ilse Kanitz, an erstwhile parish assistant, to hide a Jewish woman for several weeks.[49]

The war exacerbated the need for women to step in to pastoral work. Emilie Bach, "ordained" along with Aenne Kaufmann in 1935, married Pastor Karl Mühlen in 1940, a step that would ordinarily have obligated her to lay down her office as Vikarin, as there was no provision for married women in the office. In fact, however, she continued to work:

> I did not stop my activity as a Vikarin even though at the time married Theologinnen were not allowed to serve in the Church. This is the way it happened: When my fiancé [Pastor Karl Mühlen] received his draft notice on the Saturday before Pentecost, 1940, which ordered him to appear for induction on the Tuesday after Pentecost, we were able, with the help of a colleague, to be married in a [civil] "war wedding" (for engaged couples in which the man was to be drafted within a few days). On the same day we had a church wedding in Duisburg-Bissingheim, where my husband was serving with the Confessing Church. The next day my husband went off to war, that is, to basic training. I worked, in addition to my position with the Protestant Ladies' Auxiliary of the City League of Duisburg . . . in my husband's congregation, giving, for example, catechism and confirmation instruction, because my husband was gone.[50]

In 1943 Emmie Mühlen-Bach answered the call of the Confessing Church of the Rhineland to go into the Oberbergisches Land to take over administration of another parish whose pastor had been drafted. She remained in that office until the birth of her first child.[51]

Theologin Gustel Steil substituted for her husband, Pastor Ludwig Steil, in Wernereiche after he was drafted.[52] Scharf assigned Ilse Fredrichsdorff to Lietzen immediately after her Second Theological Examination—but well before her full ordination on 14 September 1943. There she pastored two congregations, which suffered agonizingly at the end of the war. Her villages fled the approaching Soviet Army. Fredrichsdorff led the people over the countryside, where she found them food and water and shelter, and tried to reach and cross the Elbe River before the Soviet advance. However, the villagers were overrun by the Red Army and had to return to their devastated villages, where a typhus epidemic broke out. Fredrichsdorff buried ninety-nine of her typhus-ridden parishioners before one of her own flock buried the one hundredth victim: Vikarin Ilse Fredrichsdorff herself finally succumbed.[53]

Gertrud Grimme, who was "ordained" on 25 September 1938 with the usual limitations for women, went to Dahl where she would have continued within those limitations throughout the war except for the fact that one day the Brotherhood Council of Dahl asked, "Why don't you hold a Communion service for us?" They argued that she knew them, was already leading liturgical services, was teaching their children, and was visiting their sick. "Why should a stranger come to hold a Communion service?" Although Grimme explained the legal situation, after discussions with the provincial brotherhood council, she took over all pastoral responsibilities, not only in Dahl, but in Zurstrasse as well. "How I would love to have remained as the regular pastor in Dahl. But after the war I had to turn it over to a man."[54]

Ilse Härter worked as a Vikarin with the Confessing Church of the Rhineland, where in 1939 she refused "consecration" because it was inferior to ordination.[55] When she transferred to the Confessing Church of Berlin-Brandenburg in 1941, one of the first questions Pastor Martin Albertz asked her was, "Are you ordained?" He promised to "ordain" her forthwith, but church-political considerations required that it be postponed. On 1 March 1941 Martin Albertz gave still "un-ordained" Vikarin Ilse Härter the assignment of gathering and organizing a Confessing congregation in Berlin-Wannsee, where the existing church was under a "German Christian" pastor. From February through July, Härter pursued the task successfully, but then, because she refused to take an oath of loyalty to Adolf Hitler, or to bring to DC Church officials proof of her pure Aryan heritage, the "German Christian" presbytery dismissed her.[56] Consequently, in August 1941 Scharf directed her to step in for Pastor Günther Harder, the imprisoned pastor of Berlin-Fehrbellin.[57] In April 1942 the Confessing Church of Brandenburg loaned Vikarin Ilse Härter to the Protestant Church of Wurttemberg so that she could step in for Pastor Hermann Diem, who had been drafted.[58] There she worked in full pastoral capacities until 1944 when she returned to southern Brandenburg to pastor seven villages in and around Meinsdorf.

In Berlin, Sieghild Jungklaus, took over responsibilities for part of the large Pankow parish after its Pastor Erhardt was drafted. Well before her full ordination on 16 October 1943 she was preaching for the church.[59] Lieselotte Lawerenz, although legally not permitted to do so, nevertheless traveled from congregation to congregation in Brandenburg, where she preached, held worship services, baptized, and distributed Holy Communion, even in the presence of men. She spent time in a Gestapo jail for her efforts.[60] In Westphalia, Ruth Mielke held Sunday services in Häverstädt and Buchholz, presided over Holy Communion, and baptized infants.[61] Theologin Charlotte Rose was serving in the east when Russian troops broke into her town. She blocked the door of the church wearing her black preaching gown and white clerical collar, and so protected the girls whom she had gathered together.[62] In Silesia, Vikarin Katharine Staritz publicly appealed to all pastors of Breslau to take an open stand in defense of Christian Jews. For this she spent a year in Ravensbrück Concentration Camp.[63]

It is impractical here to name all the Theologinnen who served their Church bravely and well as secretaries, teachers, hospital chaplains, counselors, smugglers, and administrators. They sheltered Jews, spoke out against injustice, stood up against Nazi chicanery, inspired the young, consoled the bereaved, and sat with the dying. Not all the Vikarinnen necessarily stepped into what had previously been men's territory, but some were undeniably functioning as pastors before the Church made legal provision for them to do so.

There was no guarantee, however, that women would have these same liberties of ministry after the emergency of the Church Struggle and the war had ended. Pastors Martin Albertz and Kurt Scharf would certainly be supportive, but there were other men (as well as women) who demanded theological justification before what might be allowed in an emergency could become the norm for quieter times. Theological justification for ordaining women to the pastorate could only come if theologians could honestly adopt a new way of looking at Scripture. Contributing to the theological debate were two indisputable facts: women were daily proving themselves capable of leading local parishes; and the laity accepted the women.

THE DEVELOPMENT OF A NEW THEOLOGY

The literature on the roles of women in the Church had been growing since the beginning of the century. The progressive side of the discussion emphasized the New Testament passages that describe the considerable engagement and positions of leadership of women in the primitive Church. Traditionalists spoke up on the other side of the debate with the words of St. Paul in which the apostle apparently enjoined women to silence and subservience. The two most outstanding passages were 1 Corinthians 14:33b-35 and 1 Timothy 2:12.

As in all the churches of the saints the women should keep silence in the churches. For they are not permitted to speak, but should be subordinate, as even the law says. If there is anything they desire to know, let them ask their husbands at home. For it is shameful for a woman to speak in church.

1 Corinthians 14:33b-35

I permit no woman to teach or to have authority over men; she is to keep silent. For Adam was formed first, then Eve; and Adam was not deceived, but the woman was deceived and became a transgressor. Yet a woman will be saved through bearing children, if she continues in faith and love and holiness, with modesty.

1 Timothy 2:12

The debaters consulted the published works of the church historians and theologians Adolf von Harnack and Leopold Zscharnack, who maintained that women, although suppressed in recent centuries, had played significant roles in the primitive Church. Priscilla, they suggested, was the anonymous author of the New Testament's Epistle to the Hebrews. Women in whose houses the churches met were described as the leaders of those churches: Mary of Jerusalem, Priscilla of Ephesus, Nympha of Rome, and Lydia of Philippi and Thyatira. They maintained that Euodia and Syntyche were leaders of two rival (and bickering) house churches in Philippi, and that Phoebe was a *prostasis* —patroness, or *Vorsteherin*—of the Christian community in Cenchraea. They reminded their readers that the Bible reports on prophetesses in Caesarea, Corinth, Jerusalem, and the hill country of Judaea, and that when Revelation 2 condemns the false prophetess Jezebel, it indicates that there were prophetic women throughout the early Turkish churches. Jezebel was not reproved because she, a woman, was prophesying, but because she was a heretic. Harnack and Zscharnack pointed out that Acts 2 and 1 Corinthians 12 promised manifestations of the Holy Spirit to every believer—male or female.[64]

Bonsett, Harnack, Schmiedel, Stoecker, and Weiss, among other leading German theologians, had suggested that neither the Corinthian nor the Timothy passage was really from the hand of Paul, and Harnack and Zscharnack both concluded that Paul had a limited view. He was a product of his own age, and he would have written differently had he lived in twentieth-century Germany.[65]

Such arguments came from theological liberals, but Protestant Germany, since the 1920s, was experiencing a shift back towards the theological center because of the influence of Karl Barth. Barth, professor of systematic theology at Marburg, and later Bonn, and author of the epoch *Romans* (*Römerbrief*), was calling pastors back to the Bible as the Word of God: inspired, binding, and authoritative. Barth became a father of the Confessing Church and drew many of his disciples, male and female, into the Confessing Church along with him. They could not, like the liberals, just dismiss Paul as a pre-Enlightenment misogynist. Instead, they saw him as inspired by the Holy Spirit to write the Word of God. For Barthians the whole New Testament had to be understood without the liberal tactic of simply discarding uncomfortable passages. This meant that despite whatever one read about prophetesses, deaconesses and spirit-filled maidservants, one still had to deal with the statement, "It is a shame for a woman to speak in the assembly."

The theological debate about the roles of women in the Confessing Church began with books, speeches, articles, judgments (*Gutachten*), essays, and papers.[66] One of the earliest of the Confessing women to publish on the issue was Lic. Anna Paulsen who, with an academic degree equivalent to a doctorate, taught in the Burckhardthaus in Berlin, training women for service as parish assistants. In 1935 Paulsen published *Mother and Maid: God's Word on Women*, in which she presents much of the material describing women's active, public roles in the earliest Christian churches. In dealing with the Corinthians and Timothy texts, she danced a clever sidestep. Recognizing that "some exegetes consider [1 Corinthians 14:34-35 and portions of 1 and 2 Timothy] . . . to be additions to the text [or] regulations and directions from another [non-Pauline] hand and from a later time," she concluded that, "one should not build a case for or against women's preaching on these two questionable passages. Instead, one should pull in observations from the broader circle of evidence."[67] Paulsen applied a traditionally valid hermeneutical principle to the "women's question:" when the preponderance of evidence supports one conclusion, one should not ignore the preponderance in favor of a peculiar, apparent exception.

In fact, however, theologians of the Confessing Church could not ignore these two passages, which are both of significant length. Hans Asmussen spoke for all the Confessing exegetes when he said that the suggestion that 1 Corinthians 11 (in which there is, indeed, mention of women praying and prophesying) and 1 Corinthians 14 were written by two different people is too superficial a solution. "We will have to have enough courage to listen to both passages, even if we cannot bring both passages into complete harmony with each other."[68] Even Confessors who disagreed with Asmussen's conclusions supported the hermeneutic principle he espoused: one must use all the material in the New Testament to develop a sound theology.

Ultimately, the Vikarinnen and the men who supported the ordination of women developed the following apologia for their point of view. They established the right of women to serve as pastors on the basis that 1 Corinthians 14 and 1 Timothy 2 were not the normative passages to apply to the question of women's position in the Church. Instead, they asserted, two other New Testament citations demonstrate what the teaching of the Lord and the apostles had been.

There is neither Jew nor Greek, slave nor free, male nor female, for you are all one in Christ Jesus.

Galatians 3:28

To each is given a manifestation of the Spirit for the common good.

1 Corinthians 12:7

On the basis of these two statements the Theologinnen argued that women had both the right and the responsibility to publicly proclaim the Gospel. On the basis of a charismatic call, women in the apostolic churches prophesied, participating in the ministry of the Word.

The proponents of ordination for women then dealt with the offending passages. They pointed out that Paul, who raised no objections to women's speaking in 1 Corinthians 11, was clearly concerned about abuses in 1 Corinthians 14, where he commanded not all women, but rather, specifically, married women to be silent because some of them had been disturbing the assembly with rude questions. He told them to save their questions for their husbands when they got home. In 1 Timothy 2:12, Paul forbade women to teach because, said the Vikarinnen, their public teaching was tied to a dangerous desire for false emancipation and, in being teachers of men, the women might forget to be submissive to their husbands. In both cases Paul was dealing only with married women who should have recognized that their primary God-given role was to be wives and mothers, for which they needed to cultivate submission and quietness. Stemming from concern to establish orderliness in the primitive Church, Paul's admonition to silence was directed exclusively to married women.[69]

In a further step toward developing a theology that would allow the ordination of women, the Vikarinnen asked the important hermeneutical question, "Is a custom, in all of its details, binding for all time?" This they answered with another question:

Doesn't the conservative attitude toward slavery in the primitive church show dependence on the social structure of the time? One should recognize that in the letters of the New Testament we do not find binding rules for order, but instead individualized instructions for specific cases.[70]

Another writer contended that in the 1 Corinthians and 1 Timothy passages, the apostle was dealing with the growing gnostic heresy. Christian women in Ephesus (the city in which young Timothy was laboring) were swayed by gnostic teachers to berate matter, the human body, and, therefore, marriage, and when such women rose to teach men, they despised their positions as wives and mothers.[71] For that reason—in light of the awakening gnostic heresy—Paul did not allow married women to have authority over men.

With such considerations, the Vikarinnen articulated still another important hermeneutical principle: The New Testament letters must be understood as specific pastoral instructions for mission churches, and not as blueprints for time and eternity.

All the arguments of the Vikarinnen and the men who supported them can be reduced to a handful of hermeneutic guidelines: one must use all the New Testament evidence; the preponderance of evidence is not to be outweighed by a rogue passage or two; and the epistles were written to address immediate issues and were not intended to bind details on all people for all time.

The arguments were formidable and swayed some opinion, but they did not convince everyone. Lic. Ernst Käsemann, Pastor Hans Asmussen, and *Präses* Heinrich Held of the Rhineland were adamant in their opposition; and Superintendent Otto Dibelius was not excited about the prospect of women preaching.[72] Barth, who had been teaching in Basel since 1935 when he was banished from Germany, did not enter the discussion, but one can assume that the arguments later collected and published by his secretary and intimate confidante Charlotte von Kirschbaum certainly represent the professor's leanings.[73] Von Kirschbaum was no friend of ordination for women.

THE APU HAMBURG SYNOD OF OCTOBER 1942

Theology is but one of the elements that contribute to ecclesiastical law. Somewhere, there must be an actual enactment of church legislation, and that is one of the functions of a synodical meeting. The full legal debate on whether the Confessing Church of the Old Prussian Union would elevate women to the pastorate came to a head at the Eleventh Synodical Meeting of the Confessing Church of the Old Prussian Union in Hamburg in October 1942.[74] The representatives from Berlin and Brandenburg leaned toward ordaining women, but men from the more conservative Rhineland resisted; thus, when a Rhinelander emerged as the chair for the meeting, the Synod passed Resolution 4 of the so-called Hamburg Resolutions, which legislated restrictions on the emerging status quo: Vikarinnen were to exercise a ministry that included the proclamation of the Word and distribution of the Sacraments primarily to circles of women, young people, and children. Should there be a man present during such a service, however, the Vikarin was not bound to be silent. Baptisms in a church service were to be performed by a pastor, but outside formal services, a Vikarin could be called on to baptize. She was not to serve during the church services, nor was she to perform weddings, confirmations, or burials. Vikarinnen might participate in presbytery meetings, but only as advisers.[75]

These were to be the rules for normal times, but 1942 was not a normal time for Christians in Germany. War raged, the government was persecuting Christianity, and pastors were few in number. Moreover, among those few, hundreds were jailed or in military service, and among those hundreds, men were dying daily. In light of such conditions, Resolution 5 of the Eleventh Synod followed Resolution 4. It was entitled, "For the Proclamation of the Gospel by Women," and in it the synod recognized:

> In times of emergency, in which the orderly preaching of the Gospel out of the mouths of men is silenced, the church administration can allow a qualified woman to preach even in church services.
> The Holy Scriptures testify that the gift of prophecy has also been given to women. . . . In the church of Jesus Christ all believers are called to a royal priesthood. . . . On the other hand 1 Corinthians 14 and 1 Timothy 2 forbid women to preach. Accordingly, we concur with Martin Luther that "for the sake of order, discipline and honor, women should be silent when the men speak. If there is no man to preach, then it would be necessary for women to do so."[76]

The synod continued with ten points:

1. It is of utmost importance that the Word be preached on Sundays.
2. If the pastor is away, a neighboring pastor should be called in.
3. If no neighboring pastor, nor any pastor at all, can be found, then the

sermon can be held by an elder.

4. If there are several elders who have been trained for this service, one should preach and the other should lead the liturgy.

5. If there are no lay preachers available, then the church administration (and only the church administration) can declare an "emergency situation."

6. Even so, in an emergency situation, it is the duty of the church administration to see that liturgical services are read.

7. Reading, however, is no substitute for a living sermon in a Protestant Church, so if there is a Vikarin available who is qualified and ready to preach her own sermon, the church administration is to direct her to do so. This assignment is to be regarded as exceptional, and the arrangement is limited to the duration of the officially recognized emergency situation.

8. If there are neither pastors, elders, nor Vikarinnen available, other women may be commissioned to read liturgical sermons or even offer their own messages.

9. In all cases in which a woman—even a theologically trained woman—is leading the services, every effort is to be made to see that a man comes in occasionally to direct. If there is a Vikarin available, she can even substitute for a pastor who might come in to preach for her congregation and may substitute for him in his own pulpit even if there is no emergency situation in his own congregation.

10. If possible, when a woman preaches, a man should conduct the liturgy.[77]

Not surprisingly, such a compromise did not please everyone. The conservatives remained adamant, as represented by Pastor Wilhelm Niesel who insisted, "Women don't preach. Elders preach!" Niesel bemoaned that, because pastors' wives had preached and carried out pastoral functions in numerous congregations, the Theologinnen now thought they could do the same thing.[78]

More progressive synodalists were equally unhappy because the compromise did not reflect the reality of the situation in Germany. In several cases Vikarinnen were already functioning as pastors. Vikarinnen were not following the lead of the pastors' wives, as Niesel contended, but instead, acting simultaneously with the Pfarrfrauen and independent of their influence, they had been leading churches since 1937—before the emergency situations caused by the war![79]

Second, the Vikarinnen and some of their male colleagues were unsatisfied with the exegesis that lay behind the Hamburg Resolutions, and they were insulted that the service of women could only be recognized in an emergency situation. Ilse Härter and Hannelotte Reiffen articulated the position of the Brandenburg Vikarinnen, rejecting the notion that only an emergency situation could be used to justify a woman's public preaching and administration of Sacraments. "If the scriptures condemn such as sin, it remains sin, even in an emergency situation."[80]

Kurt Scharf, Confessing Church Präses in Berlin-Sachsenhausen and one of the leading figures in the Confessing Church, was so distressed over the irregular parliamentary proceedings at the Hamburg synod that he resolved to act alone.[81] In protest against to what he called the "Robber Synod" of Hamburg, in which Rhinelanders had dominated the discussions and decisions, Scharf ordained two women, Ilse Härter and Hannelotte Reiffen, on 12 January 1943. He did so "without any limitations," fully intending for them to pastor churches in every sense, with no gender-based restrictions (see Figure 4.2).[82] Scharf's act was not entirely unilateral and rebellious, as it was done with the consent and support of the Brotherhood Council of the Confessing Church of Brandenburg (as the document attests) but Brandenburg acted unilaterally, without consultation with or consent of other brotherhood councils.

Naturally, there were protests, but more significantly, other pastors followed Scharf's lead. Dibelius tried to enforce the Hamburg resolutions in Berlin, but the work of the Brandenburg Vikarinnen continued unabated and unaltered.[83] Because the emergency persisted, the work remained to be done. "We had more important things to do," remembered Ilse Härter, "than to ask ourselves nervously, 'What may I do? What may I not do?' The congregations would have had no understanding for this discussion."[84] Additional full ordinations of women followed, more and more in the name of the Brotherhood Councils of Berlin-Brandenburg, and, eventually, of the Rhineland and other areas as well. Scharf ordained Ilse Fredrichsdorff on 14 September 1943. Pastor Eitel-Friedrich von Rabenau ordained the Vikarinnen Annemarie Grosch, Sieghild Jungklaus, Margarete Saar, Ruth Wendtland, and Gisela von Witzleben on 16 October 1943; and Martin Albertz ordained Lore Schlunk the same day. Günther Harder even ordained a married woman, Ilse Boelte-Thon, on 11 January 1945 in Neuruppin.[85]

Ultimately, it was the people in the pew who agitated for and accepted this change in the social structure of German Protestantism. Sieghild Jungklaus recalled that it was the congregation that came to her defense when, after the war, male elements within the church suggested that it was time for the women to lay down their ordinations and vacate the pastoral offices. In several cases it was the lower ecclesiastical officials—congregational elders—not the bishop or superintendent, who invited the women to preach and distribute Holy Communion. This was the case with Gertrud Grimme and Ruth Mielke in Westphalia, with Lieselotte Lawerenz in Brandenburg, and with Emmi Blöcher in Nassau.[86]

In the end, parity for German Protestant women carried the day. The Confessing Church moved from consecrating women with gender-specific limitations in 1935 to their full ordination to all pastoral responsibilities in 1943. After the close of the war and the subsequent dissolution of the Confessing

Figure 4.2
Ordination Certificate of Pastorin Ilse Härter

Nachdem die Vikarin

Ilse H ä r t e r

vor Gott gelobt hat, daß sie ihr Amt führen will in
Bindung an das Wort Gottes, wie es verfaßt ist in der
Heiligen Schrift Alten und Neuen Testamentes als der
alleinigen und vollkommenen Richtschnur für die Lehre,
wie es bezeugt ist in den altkirchlichen Glaubensbe-
kenntnissen, dem Apostolikum, dem Nicaenum und dem
Athanasianum sowie im Heidelberger Katechismus und wie
es gegenüber den Irrlehren unserer Zeit aufs Neue als
bindend bekannt ist in der Theologischen Erklärung der
ersten Bekenntnissynode der Deutschen Evangelischen
Kirche in Barmen, haben wir sie gemäß dem Beschlusse
des
Bruderrates der Kirchenprovinz Mark Brandenburg
vom 9. Dezember 1942   am heutigen Tage im Gottesdienst
der Kirchengemeinde Sachsenhausen-Nordbahn zur Vikarin
        in Ebersbach - Fils   ordiniert.

Wir befehlen die Ordinierte dem alleinigen Herrn der Kirche JesusChristus, dem alle Gewalt gegeben ist im Himmel
und auf Erden. Er sendet auch sie. Er erfülle an ihr
die Verheißung: Siehe, ich bin bei euch alle Tage bis an
der Welt Ende!

                Sachsenhausen-Nordbahn, den 12. Januar 1943

DER ORDINATOR: DIE ASSISTIERENDEN PFARRER:

The ordination certificate, which contains no gender-specific restictions, was signed by the
ordaining pastor, Präses Kurt Scharf, and by two assistants: Pastor Hermann Diem, for whom
Pastorin Härter substituted in Ebersbach-Fils (Wurttemberg); and Vikarin Lieselotte Lawerenz, who
was thereby the first woman to assist at an ordination. Source: Pastorin Ilse Härter.

Church, women retained their ordinations, and more of their sisters joined them. In 1945 the newly reestablished Protestant Church in Germany (Evangelische Kirche in Deutschland or EKD) recognized all earlier consecrations as ordinations, immediately raising the number of fully ordained Vikarinnen to nearly fifty.[87]

This noteworthy social and theological change came about because of a combination of social, demographic, political, and theological phenomena. German feminism and a demographic crisis after World War I opened up positions for nonordained women. Further manpower losses as a result of Nazi persecution compelled the Confessing Church to use women in more expanded ministries. While women demonstrated their capabilities in the pastorate, theologians developed a hermeneutical approach to scripture that would justify their ordination. In spite of restrictive synodical rulings, pastors in Brandenburg began to ordain women, and the laity secured the new arrangement by voicing its satisfaction with women in the pulpit.

NOTES

1. Ilse Härter and Günther van Norden, "Persönliche Erfahrungen mit der Ordination von Theologinnen in der Bekennenden Kirche des Rheinlands und in Berlin/ Brandenburg," in Günther van Norden, ed., *Zwischen Bekenntnis und Anpassung* (Köln: Rheinlandverlag, 1985), p. 196.

2. This account is taken from an interview with Frau Pastorin Aenne Kaufmann, Essen, 4 February 1990; and from Gudrun Orlt, "Das Verbot eines bösen Menschen brachte erste Frau in die Gemeinde. Vor 50 Jahren wurde Aenne Kaufmann ordiniert," *Der Weg* (Düsseldorf), 50, no. 85 (9 December 1985).

3. On the near unanimous support of Theologinnen for the Confessing Church, see Ilse Bertinetti, *Frauen im geistlichen Amt: Die theologische Problematik in evangelisch-lutherischer Sicht* (Berlin: Evangelische Verlagsanstalt, 1965), p. 71, citing Anna Paulsen, "Die Vikarin," *Evangelische Welt* 2 (1957), p. 540.

4. The following discussion will show that although this ceremony was called an "ordination," it differed from the ordination of male candidates and was not equivalent to the ordination that women would receive after 1943. When the word is enclosed in quotation marks ("ordination") it signifies something less than full ordination.

According to Lutheran tradition and Church law before 2 December 1935, any pastor could rightfully ordain a qualified person to Christian ministry. Customarily, the ceremony involved the area superintendent or the bishop, but such was not a legal requirement. Böttcher, as trustee *(Vertrauensmann)* of the Confessing Church in Essen, was fully authorized to ordain within the Confessing Church, though not within the German Protestant Church under Hans Kerrl.

5. This was also the experience of Emmie Mühlen-Bach: "At first nothing

changed in our official rights. We were still called '*Vikarin,*' and were not allowed to preach or perform other pastoral functions in worship services." Letter to the author, 26 August 1991.

6. "In an act of resistance, they wanted to assert their right to perform the functions of ecclesiastical leadership (ordination!)." Härter and van Norden, "Persönliche," p. 207.

7. Ibid., pp. 207-208. See also Orlt, "Das Verbot." The published reports are further corroborated by a letter to the author from Emmi Mühlen-Bach, 26 August 1991; by the author's interview with Pastor Hans-Gerhard Böttcher in Neukirchen-Vluyn on 5 February 1990; and the Kaufmann interview.

Mühlen-Bach, who married in 1940, nevertheless pastored a congregation during the Church Struggle, as described later in the chapter.

8. Both reports were corroborated by the Böttcher and Kaufmann interviews. Emilie Bach and Hanna Klein both married at later dates. Letter to the author from Emmi Mühlen-Bach, 26 August 1991.

9. Kaufmann interview. The remark was certainly ironic.

10. The original ordination certificate is in the Archiv des Förderkreises für das Eben-Ezer Heim in Haifa e.V. in Waldsaum 49, 45133 Essen. The copy of the document that is in the archive of the Evangelische Kirche des Rheinlands, Düsseldorf, Nachlaß Aenne Kaufmanns, Akte 17, has a hand-drawn line through the word "*Ordination,*" which was replaced with "*Einsegnung,*" (consecration). This redaction was evidently the work of *Oberkirchenrat* Johannes Schlingensiepen who, after the end of the war, opposed the move to recognize earlier "consecrations" as ordinations. "Later the Provincial Church Offices assured Frau Kaufmann of all her rights and privileges, and the ordination was no longer questioned." A letter from Pastor Uwe Kleinhückelkoten to the author, 19 November 1993.

11. Ordination was the recognition of higher office. In the words of Johannes Schlingensiepen, who spoke for the Confessing Church of the Rhineland in refusing to ordain Ilse Härter: "Pastors are ordained. *Vikarinnen* get consecrated." Härter and van Norden, "Persönliche," p. 196.

12. Helga Zimmermann Weckerling's words in Wolfgang See and Rudolf Weckerling, *Frauen im Kirchenkampf* (Berlin: Wichern Verlag, 1986), p. 57.

13. "The female theologian in Germany is in every respect the result of the emancipation movement of the last 150 years." Erika Reichle, *Die Theologin in Württemberg—Geschichte, Bild, und Wirklichkeit eines neuen Frauenberufes* (Bern: Herbert Lang, 1975), pp. 16-19.

14. See *Der Frauen-Anwalt*, Jenny Hirsch, editor (Berlin: Wedekind und Schwieger). Volume 3 (1872-1873), for example, contains such articles as "Female Physicians in America," (p. 204); "Female Druggist-Assistant" (p. 297); "The Study and Practice of Medicine by Women" (p. 277); and "Female German Teachers in England" (p. 68).

15. Count Agenor von Casparin, in an article, "Was die Frauen wollen" in *Der Frauen-Anwalt*, 4 (1873-74), 149-153, was not enthusiastic about the pros-

pects of enfranchisement: "You want universal suffrage. You won't get it." He
suggested that German women wait and see what might happen in America.

16. August Bebel, *Women in the Past, Present, and Future*, trans. by H.
B. Adam of *Die Frau und der Sozialismus* (London: Modern Press, 1885).

17. Claudia Koonz, *Mothers in the Fatherland* (New York: St. Martin's
Press, 1987), p. 34.

18. Helene Lange (1848-1930). Helpful biographical treatments of Lange
are included in two books by Gertrud Bäumer, *Gestalt und Wandel: Frauenbildnisse* (Berlin: F. A. Herbig, [ca. 1939]); and *Studien über Frauen* (Berlin: F. A.
Herbig, 1921).

19. Bäumer, *Studien*, pp. 162-165. The original title of the suffrage tract
was *Frauenwahlrecht*.

20. Gertrud Bäumer, *Die Frau in Volkswirtschaft und Staatsleben der
Gegenwart* (Stuttgart: Deutsche Verlags-Anstalt, 1914), p. 147; and Reichle,
Die Theologin, p. 42. Though women had not been admitted as bona fide students, Göttingen had admitted them as auditors since 1896-97. See Minna Sauer,
ed. *Die Frauenbewegung* Volume 2 (Berlin: Ferdinand Dümmlers Verlagsbuchhandlung, 1896), p. 204. Bäumer reported that she was permitted to audit
courses at Berlin as early as 1903. "Up until that time, the decision whether we
could audit a lecture lay in the hands of the lecturer." Gertrud Bäumer, *Im
Lichte der Erinnerung* (Tübingen: R. Wunderlich, 1953), p. 145.

21. Bertinetti, *Frauen*, p. 71; Bäumer, *Die Frau*, p. 147.

22. Reichle, *Die Theologin*, p. 58.

23. Koonz, *Mothers*, p. 30.

24. Reichle, *Die Theologin*, p. 21. Lic. Weber, whose first name
unfortunately has not surfaced in my research, was a man.

25. "Der Deutsch-evangelischer Frauentag in Cassel am 5. und 6. Juni."
Die Frauenbewegung, 5 (1899), 115.

26. Adelheid von Bennigsen, "Noch ein Wort zur christlichen Frauenbewegung," *Die Frauenbewegung*, 6 (1901), 116.

27. Reichle, *Die Theologin*, p. 23.

28. "Die Frauenfrage auf der Hauptversammlung der freien kirchlich-
sozialen Konferenz vom 14.-16. April zu Berlin," *Die Frauenbewegung*, 9
(1903), p. 75. Unfortuntaely the article does not mention a first name for
Fräulein Pappertz.

29. "Die 4. Generalversammlung des Deutsch-Evangelischen Frauenbundes in Bonn. (24.-25. September)," *Die Frauenbewegung*, 9 (1903), p. 157.

30. On the professors, see Reichle, *Die Theologin*, p. 43. In 1906
Josephine Levy-Rathenau and Lisbeth Willbrandt warned young women against
pursuing a degree in theology, as there was "not yet" any opportunity to use it in
a practical way. See Reichle, *Die Theologin*, p. 44, where she cites Levy-
Rathenau and Willbrandt, "Die deutsche Frau im Beruf—Praktische Ratschläge
zur Berufwahl," *Handbuch der Frauenbewegung* (Berlin) 5, (1906), 252.

31. Reichle, *Die Theologin*, p. 47.

32. Ibid., p. 35.

33. Ibid., p. 36.

34. Härter and van Norden, "Persönliche," p. 193.

35. The member provincial churches of the APU were the Protestant Churches of Berlin/ Brandenburg, Danzig, East Prussia, Pomerania, the Rhineland, Saxony, Silesia, and Westphalia.

36. Fritz Zerbst, *The Office of the Woman in the Church—A Study in Practical Theology* (St. Louis: Concordia Publishing House, 1955), p. 8.

37. On the administration of Holy Communion, see ibid., p. 8.

Gerda Keller made the claim to being the first women to be examined by the Westphalian Church in 1930. Gerda Keller, "Inmitten einer Kirche von Männern—Eine Frau entscheidet sich für die Theologie" in Hans Martin Linnemann, ed., *Theologinnen in der Evangelischen Kirche von Westfalen. Drei Erfahrungsberichte* (Bielefeld: Lutherverlag, 1990), p. 52. Ilse Härter recorded that Waltraud Eymal was the first, in 1931, to take the First Theological Examination from the Protestant Church of the Rhineland. Annemarie Rübens and Elisabeth von Aschoff, in the fall of 1931, took the Second Theological Examination there. Ilse Härter, "Einführung bei der Eröffnung der Ausstellung 'Das Weib schweigt nicht mehr' in der Kirchlichen Hochschule in Wuppertal am 17.1.1991," pp. 3-4. The manuscript of the speech (in the author's collection) has since been published in *Reformierte Kirchenzeitung* (Neukirchen-Vluyn: Neukirchener Verlag) 132 (1991), No. 4, 128-131.

38. Reichle, *Die Theologin*, pp. 90-94.

39. Hellmuth Heyden, *Kirchengeschichte Pommerns*, Band 2 (1957), p. 241, citing "Akten des Konsistoriums Stettin und Berichte über Provinzialsynoden."

40. Herbert von Hintzenstern, "'Für Euch bin ich Bischof, mit Euch bin ich Christ': Berichte—Dokumente—Zeugnisse," *Glaube und Heimat: Evangelisches Sonntagsblatt für Thüringen* (Jena), No. 33 (18 August 1991): pp. 4-6.

41. Reichle, *Die Theologin*, pp. 90-94.

42. Ibid., pp. 104-105. By "talk" was meant, not a *Predigt*, but an *Ansprache*.

43. Ibid., p. 107.

44. A minority within the VETD had from the beginning campaigned for full pastoral offices for women, among them Carola Barth, Elisabeth Bizer-von Aschoff, Ina Gschlössl, Annemarie Rübens, and Aenne Traube-Schuemer. Härter, "*Einführung.*"

45. Reichle, *Die Theologin*, pp. 37-38.

46. Ina Gschlössl and Annemarie Rübens, "Ein notwendiges Wort in Sachen der Theologinnen an Herrn Generalsuperintendenten D. Schian," *Die Christliche Welt*, 44 (March 1, 1930): cols. 216-220.

47. Härter and van Norden, *Persönliche*, p. 195.

48. Ilse Härter, "Theologinnen in der Bekennenden Kirche," p. 5, text of a speech delivered at the meeting "Illegals in the Confessing Church," 28 August-

1 September 1989 in Rengsdorf on the Occasion of the Eightieth Birthday of Eberhard Bethge. The manuscript in the author's collection was subsequently published as *"Zuerst kamen die Brüder"* in K. A. Bauer, ed., *Predigtamt ohne Pfarramt?* (Neukirchen-Vluyn: Neukirchener Verlag, 1993).

49. This was related by Ilse Härter to Victoria Barnett in a note further relayed to the author on 15 May 1991; and detailed further in a letter from Ilse Härter to the author, 18 November 1993. Härter cites G. Szepanski, *Frauen im Widerstand.*

50. A letter to the author from Emmie Mühlen-Bach, dated 21 November 1993.

51. From a letter to the author from Emilie Bach, 9 July 1991.

52. From the author's interview with Pastor Elisabeth Charlotte Lawerenz, Detmold, 8 February 1990.

53. Information on Ilse Fredrichsdorff is from letters to the author from Ilse Härter of 26 June 1991, 3 November 1991, and 18 November 1993; and from the author's interview with Pastor Ilse Härter, Goch, 20-21 January 1990.

54. Gertrud Grimme, "Von der Vikarin zur Oberkirchenrätin—Der Weg einer engagierten Theologin," in Linnemann, *Theologinnen*, pp. 17-18.

55. Pastor Hermann Hesse announced in March 1939 that he would ordain Vikar Harry Weisberg on one Sunday and would consecrate Härter on the next. Upon her refusal, Härter met with her male colleagues in the church to discuss the issues. According to her own account, she convinced them all that there was nothing left to do but ordain her; however, when Hesse called Johannes Schlingensiepen in Barmen, the pastor declared simply, *"Vikare* are ordained, *Vikarinnen* get consecrated." In a discussion with Schlingensiepen the next day he asked Härter if she were willing to take an oath of chastity (*Ehelosigkeit*). She asked him if the male theologians in the Confessing Church were now being asked to remain single, something she considered a real possibility in light of the Church's desperate financial condition. He said "No," but reminded Härter that she was a woman. "To that I could only truthfully affirm, I had never had any doubt about it." Schlingensiepen denied ordination, and did not encourage Härter to accept consecration. Härter and van Norden, *"Persönliche,"* pp. 196-197.

56. "It was a foolish expectation of mine that I would be given full pastoral oversight of the new congregation." Härter's friend Willi Rott told her that Superintendent Otto Dibelius intended to assume charge of the Wannsee Confessing Church himself after she had established the congregation. Härter interview.

57. On her position in Berlin-Fehrbellin, see Härter and van Norden, *"Persönliche,"* p. 200.

58. The Protestant Church of Wurttemberg was never dominated by the "German Christians" to the same extent as, for example, the United Church of the APU, so a "Confessing Church" in Wurttemberg was not a necessity. The Protestant Churches of Wurttemberg, Bavaria, and Hanover were considered

"intact" churches, not institutionally fractured by the "German Christian" heresy. Wurttemburg's Bishop Theophil Wurm nevertheless considered himself part of the Confessing Fellowship (Bekenntnisgemeinschaft), though for him, the statement issued from Barmen in 1934 was a "declaration," not a "confession." Hermann Diem, a member of the Wurttemberg "Church-Theological Society" (Kirchlich-theologische Sozietät) identified with the "Dahlemites," who regarded the Barmen statement as a confession of faith, and the edicts of the Dahlem synod of October 1934 as binding.

59. From the author's interview with Pastor Sieghild Jungklaus in Berlin, 15 January 1990.

60. Lawerenz Interview.

61. Mielke explained, "They had to give me special permission, because it was not allowed, according to the church law." From the author's interview with Pastor Ruth Mielke, Minden, 16 February 1990. See also Ruth Mielke, *Lebensbild einer westfälischen Pfarrerin: Erfahrungen mit Theologinnengesetzen 1927 bis 1974* (Minden: privately printed, 1991), p. 54.

62. *Vikarin* Klara Hunsche assumed that it was this figure standing in front of the church door that kept the rapacious soldiers from breaking in. Ilse Härter in a letter to Victoria Barnett, n.d.; relayed to the author in a letter from Barnett, 13 May 1991.

63. Letter, Härter to Victoria Barnett; see also Katharine Staritz, *Des grossen Lichtes Widerschein* (Muenster: Westfalen, 1953); Peter Hauptmann, *Kirche im Osten*, p. 193.

64. Adolf von Harnack, *Die Mission und Ausbreitung des Christentums in den ersten drei Jahrhunderten* (Leipzig: J. C. Henrich'sche Buchhandlung, 1902), pp. 395-407, 277 n. 2; H. Zscharnack, *Der Dienst der Frau in den ersten Jahrhunderten der christlichen Kirche* (1902).

65. See "The Theological Debate" in the Bibliography for bibliographical data on the books that informed an article by Ernst Käsemann who cites these authors.

66. See "The Theological Debate" in the Bibliography for a listing and discussion of the documents that contributed to the debate over the ordination of women.

67. Anna Paulsen, *Mutter und Magd: Das Biblische Wort über die Frau* (Berlin: Furche Verlag, 1935), p. 116.

68. Hans Asmussen, untitled essay beginning with the words, *"In jeder Weise tritt die Frau im N.T. zurück"*, p. 7. See "The Theological Debate" in the Bibliography for full citation and discussion.

69. This position, that the command to silence was directed to married women and that, therefore, single women could speak in a Christian assembly, is now disavowed by most women in the German Protestant Church. It was the working argument of the 1940s. Härter interview.

70. *"Äusserung der Vikarinnen auf die Gutachten,"* p. 2. See the full citation and discussion in "The Theological Debate" in the Bibliography.

71. *"Zur theologischen Besinnung über die Frage des Vikarinnenamtes."* See the full citation and discussion in "The Theological Debate" in the Bibliography.

72. On Heinrich Held, see Härter, *"Einführung,"* p. 6. Ilse Härter, in a letter of 3 November 1991 to the author, noted that Held was the *Präses* in Essen during the time of Aenne Kaufmann's "ordination." He would never have approved of any ordination for her that would have elevated her to a rank equal to that of the men.

The information on Dibelius is from the author's interview with his secretary, Senta Maria Klatt, Berlin, 12-13 January 1990.

73. Charlotte von Kirschbaum, *Die wirkliche Frau* (Zürich: Evangelischer Verlag Zollikon, 1949).

74. Prussian church leaders were meeting in Hamburg because it was safer to do so than in Berlin and environs.

75. *Ausführungsbestimmungen zu Beschluß IV*, Nos. 1-4. Zentralarchiv der Evangelischen Kirche in Hessen und Nassau, Darmstadt, Bestand 35/432.

76. *Beschluß V.* Zentralarchiv der Evangelischen Kirche in Hessen und Nassau, Darmstadt, Bestand 35/432.

77. *"Ausführungsbestimmungen zu Beschluß V: Der Dienst der Frau in Zeiten der Not."* Zentralarchiv der Evangelischen Kirche in Hessen und Nassau, Darmstadt, Bestand 35/432.

78. Wilhelm Niesel, *Kirche unter dem Wort* (Göttingen: Vandenhoeck and Ruprecht, 1978), pp. 278-279.

79. The earliest documented cases are those of Lieselotte Berli and Hannelotte Reiffen. Härter Interview.

80. Brandenburger Vikarinnen, *"Stellungnahme zu den Ausführungsbestimmungen zu Beschluss IV: Der Dienst der Vikarin,"* p. 3. See the full citation and discussion in "The Theological Debate" in the Bibliography.

81. Scharf had been *Präses* since 1935. Kurt Scharf, *Widerstehen und Versöhnen* (Stuttgart: Radius Verlag, 1987), p. 232.

82. Scharf reported the Synod's position to Ilse Härter at a retreat for pastors' wives in December 1942. He was so incensed, said Härter, that he told her he would on his own initiative ordain the two un-ordained Brandenburg *Vikarinnen* "ohne jeden Abstrich." Härter and van Norden, *"Persönliche,"* p. 204.

83. Ibid., p. 206.

84. Härter, *"Theologinnen,"* p. 7.

85. Names and dates supplied by Ilse Härter, letter to the author of 30 January 1990; and the Jungklaus interview.

86. From the author's interview with Emmi Blöcher, Sinn-Dill, 19 February 1990.

87. Ilse Härter, "Der Weg der Frauen zur Ordination und Pfarramt," *Schlangenbrut*, no. 22 (August 1988): 6.

The author's data include the names of twenty-five *Theologinnen* for whom he has evidence that they were "ordained" before 1943, and of whom he has no evidence that they married and thus had to relinquish their positions. The following consecrated *Vikarinnen* joined the ranks of the fully ordained in 1945: Elfriede Amme-Fischer, Ingeborg Becker, Lieselotte Berli, Erika Dalichow, Hilde Ermert, Gertrud Frischmuth, Elisabeth Grauer, Gertrud Grimme, Dorothea-Sophie Hamann, Helene Heidepriem, Klara Hunsche, Aenne Kaufmann, Gerda Keller, Ilse Kersten, Elisabeth Klein, Hannah Klein, Lieselotte Lawerenz, Renate Ludwig, Lic. Christa Müller, Charlotte Rose, Maria Vetter Berendts, Marta Voigt, Marta Zaum, Helga Zimmermann, and Lic. Elisabeth Zinn.

Chapter 5

Conclusions: Developments After 1945

How I would love to have remained as the regular pastor in Dahl. But after the war I had to turn it over to a man.

—Gertrud Grimme[1]

The decision to recognize earlier consecrations as full ordinations, and thus to ordain upwards of twenty-five *Vikarinnen* retroactively,[2] did not guarantee uniform parity for *Theologinnen* in the re-emerging Protestant Church in Germany after 1945. Fully ordained women still faced discrimination in the postwar readjustment period. In most cases, ordained Theologinnen working in full pastoral capacities in their congregations found themselves shoved to the side and relegated to less than full congregational responsibility when their male colleagues returned home from the prisoner of war camps.[3]

This did not nullify the ordinations. Fully ordained women continued to serve their churches as teachers, trainers, educational directors, and administrators. They preached frequently, distributed Communion, baptized infants, and served in all capacities as needed—but not as the senior pastor in the congregation. According to Ilse Härter's research, it was sometime in 1948 that the last pastorate held by a woman disappeared. A man took the position.[4] As (male) church authorities assigned pastors to parishes, they used a familiar formula which had consistently guided them in the past, when they posted Vikare and Vikarinnen: "First we place the brothers," presumably because the men were married or would soon marry and would need a professional position with a salary to support their families.[5] The women, of course, still had to remain single if they wanted to serve their churches as pastors.

The temporary disappearance of women as senior pastors in 1948 in no way rendered irrelevant the accomplishments of Confessing women of the preceding fifteen years. The theological and social developments of those years called women into the life of the church in unprecedented and irrevocable ways. First and foremost, women preached. That was perhaps the most demonstrative and impressive single act of the period, a deed witnessed by thousands of parishioners. Preaching was an act of substance as well as symbol.

The substance was that in preaching, women demonstrated to the laity and clergy that they were capable of serious, practical, theological discourse. Especially important was the positive response of the laity. Skepticism that women could not pastor and fear that congregants would storm out of the sanctuary if a woman rose to speak proved unfounded.

The symbol was equally important. The women preached, and the act itself made people sit up and take notice, talk about it, and broadcast it. The women's sermons were blows to tradition that reverberated across the land. When a particular woman preached she awakened dreams of previously inaccessible career goals in younger women in the churches. After 1945 younger Theologinnen extended the campaign to move beyond ordination and to gain the full, practical implications of ordination for women.

The record of successive ecclesiastical legislation in the Protestant Church in Germany reveals the process of a slow but certain awakening of sensitivity to the needs and desires of theological women. In 1957 the Church awarded to ordained Vikarinnen the same salary as to pastors, granted women seats in presbyteries and synodical meetings, and finally, in 1963, replaced the title *Vikarin* with *Pastorin* and *Pfarrerin*, thus eliminating confusion and discrimination. Even so, women still suffered under limitations that did not affect men. For example, a woman could only seek a pastoral position in a congregation large enough to have a three-pastor staff, and then, a woman could occupy only one of the three positions.[6] Furthermore, the laws allowed parishioners to choose whether, in planning an event such as a baptism, burial, or wedding, they would prefer to bring in a male pastor from another parish rather than have a woman preside. The law made no provision for parishioners who might want to bring in a neighboring female pastor.[7]

Not until 1970 did the Protestant Reformed Church in Northwest Germany pass legislation that awarded Pfarrerinnen completely equal legal and financial standing with their male colleagues. The Protestant Churches of Hessen-Nassau and Baden followed suit in 1971; Kurhessen-Waldeck followed in 1973; and in 1974, the Protestant Church of the Union conformed, as did Bavaria and the Rhineland (1975), Wurttemberg (1977), Brunswick and Hanover (1978), and Oldenburg (1981). The tiny Protestant Church of Schaumburg-Lippe remained the last holdout of male hegemony in the Protestant Church in Germany.[8]

In the new German Democratic Republic (DDR), the Church Struggle continued unabated against the Communists. There, in East Germany, women continued to play a stronger role within the pastoral ranks than in the West. By 1987, Bishop Emeritus Albrecht Schönherr of the "Protestant Church in the German Democratic Republic"[9] could report that approximately half of all theology students and ten percent of the pastors were women.[10] By 1986 in the

Federal Republic of Germany (BRD), 10.5 percent of the 17,102 pastors were women.[11] Women are well established within the pastorates of the Protestant Church in Germany, and although the debate about the propriety of this is still an issue in a few congregations, women have risen above the pastorate to hold leading positions in the church administrations.[12] The number of women in the pastorate does not nearly approach the number of men, but church councils hear continual calls for even further inclusion of women.[13] Especially noteworthy was the decision of the Lutheran Church in Hamburg (Nordelbische-Lutherische Kirche) on 4 April 1992 to name Maria Jepsen as bishop, nearly fifty years after the colorful synodical debate in Hamburg in 1942. The laws of the member churches of the Protestant Church in Germany today are not identical, nor have they developed uniformly, but on the whole, women are on a parity with men in the pastorate.

RESTRUCTURING THE PROTESTANT CHURCH

With the fall of Nazism, so too fell the German Protestant Church, which had, for all intents and purposes, become simply an arm of the government. In the final days of the war, with Berlin surrounded by Allied forces, Otto Dibelius called his valued secretary and said, "Fräulein Klatt, shall we re-open the Consistory?"[14] The Protestant Church started rebuilding.

Among the earliest debates was that on the nature of the relationship of the new Church to the new state. Protestants chose a name for their new church that made clear the legal separation between the two institutions: it was to be *"Die Evangelische Kirche in Deutschland"* (EKD), the Protestant Church in Germany—not "of" Germany.[15]

A second major matter dealt with the issue of guilt over the war and the Holocaust. Confessing Church leaders, now in leading positions within the EKD, did not duck their own complicity in the horrors of Nazi Germany. Pastors Martin Niemöller and Otto Dibelius drafted and read a confession of guilt at an international ecumenical meeting in Stuttgart on 19 October 1945:

> We accuse ourselves of not having confessed more courageously, prayed more faithfully, believed more joyfully and loved more ardently. Now a new beginning must be made in our churches.[16]

That confession of guilt, repeatedly offered and championed especially by Niemöller in his worldwide travels, facilitated the EKD's entry into the international ecumenical fellowship of churches. Traveling with Niemöller, and presenting a picture of the "good German" to a skeptical world, was his wife, Else Niemöller.[17] American newspaper articles introduced her as the less well-known wife of the celebrity martyr who, during the Church Struggle, "encouraged and advised" her husband, and visited him monthly in prison. The

St. Petersburg Times announced her speaking engagements in Florida with reports of how she had "carried on the work of [Pastor Niemöller's] Berlin parish and trained their seven children to give Christian witness whenever the church was attacked, at school or at public meetings."[18]

The new beginning for German Protestantism also involved dealing with the erstwhile "German Christian" pastors. Though the Though the Nazi Government had begun gradually to disassociate itself from the radical wing of the "German Christian" party shortly after the Sports Arena speech of 13 November 1933, the "German Christians" remained in pulpits across the land, and were especially strongly represented in Thuringia.[19] The Protestant Church of the Rhineland issued a statement on 13 July 1945 that because the "German Christians" had abandoned orthodoxy, "no one who takes this point of view may administer an office in the Christian Church."[20] The Westphalian Church similarly demanded, in August 1946, that all "church officials who, in the considered judgment of the church, had departed from the true basis" be stricken from the church rolls, removed from office, or transferred. Seven and a half percent of Westphalia's 730 Protestant ministers came under scrutiny.[21] Saxony similarly examined its pastors' histories as did other provincial churches.[22] However, such house cleaning was not uniform throughout the country. A transfer from one city to another allowed unrepentant "German Christian" pastors to take up their work elsewhere without any confession of remorse or wrongdoing.[23] Although the EKD emerged from the war institutionally victorious over the "German Christian" heresy, the germs of the contamination were not completely eradicated.

Practical secularization remained a problem for the new Protestant Church as well. On the one hand, in spite of everything Hitler, Rosenberg, Müller, Jäger and Nazi propagandist Joseph Goebbels had done, after the war, ninety-five percent of all Germans—well more than half of them women—retained their church affiliations.[24] On the other side, except for the hungry years immediately after 1945, Protestant as well as Catholic churches remained largely underutilized on Sunday mornings. The Nazis had not been able to destroy the cultural attachment to Christianity, nor had the experience of the Third Reich changed the church attendance habits of the pre-Nazi years. Those who were regular in church attendance and active within their parishes experienced a profound change in the church's life: women had joined men in leading positions in parishes in both East and West Germany.

THE FEMINIST MOVEMENT AFTER 1945

Feminism did not survive National Socialism as well as the institutional Church. Nazism temporarily destroyed the campaign among women for civil equality in West Germany. The flowering movement that had placed women in almost every area of public life (except in the pastorate) before 1933 lay wilted and, apparently, dead after just a few months of the Nazi takeover. In the social devastation following the war women as well as men had much more immediate and pressing problems than the campaign for equality. Hunger stalked the cities and provinces.[25] The winter following the armistice was especially cold. Refugees streamed from the east to the west, and the displaced people brought their own crises of poverty and resettlement with them. Rubble in ruined cities covered decomposing bodies, which contaminated air and water. Families remained divided for years. For more than two decades the needs to survive and reestablish their families' economic foundations occupied the time and energy of women who had survived twelve years of Nazi misogyny. Consequently, as Renate Wiggershaus has noted of West German women, it was only at the end of the 1960s or the beginning of the 1970s that they discovered that for the previous century there had been an active women's movement. Twenty-five years after the end of the war, most young adult West German women knew nothing of their feminist heritage.[26] In the German Democratic Republic, on the other hand, what would have passed as feminism in the West was absorbed into gender-equal socialism.

The continual and increasing emergence of women in the Protestant pastorates of both Germanies during the postwar years offered women a new picture of themselves, and may have contributed to the awakening feminist movement of the succeeding decades.

SUMMARY

We have entertained four theses. The first is that though the women of the Confessing Church shared experiences with their predecessors in the Protestant Reformation, the Confessing women succeeded in establishing the social and theological gains they won during the Church Struggle, while the Reformation women did not.

The question arises, why were the women of the Confessing Church able to leave a more lasting legacy? Not until the twentieth century did a crucial number of factors convene to bring about permanent change for church women. The ordination of women in twentieth century Germany was the result of a combination of seven conditions: (1) a preexisting secular feminist agenda that Christian women slowly but surely adopted; (2) a rising level of academic training among Protestant women; (3) a demographic crisis, following World War I and exacerbated by World War II, that prompted the Church to introduce unordained women into ministerial work; (4) persecution at the hands of the Nazis, which both sharply defined the theological and political issues, and crucially reduced the number of available men to fill church offices; (5) modeling of new behavior by women in the churches; (6) a corps of academically trained women who articulated in sophisticated, theological terms the arguments in favor of their ordination; and, finally, (7) male colleagues who took up the banner for and with the women.

The women of the sixteenth-century Reformation shared the factors of demographic crisis, persecution, articulate spokeswomen, and a handful of male colleagues who supported their public roles, but these alone could not bring about a permanent change. Crucial to the success of churchwomen in the twentieth century were some additional conditions: a broad social climate that was ready for women in the pulpit and access for women to university educations. When the Christian women's movement capitalized on what secularists had won, it catapulted numbers of young Christian women into university study that prepared them for careers in the churches just at a time when the churches desperately needed the infusion of talent, conviction, and training.

The second thesis is that in spite of superficial similarities, different and conflicting motives energized the two groups of women under consideration. Both Theologinnen and Pfarrfrauen broke through gender barriers to do what only men had previously been allowed to do. The primary difference was that the Theologinnen consciously sought to make gender-role changes in the midst of the chaos of the Third Reich, while the pastors' wives struggled to maintain the status quo. Ironically, to maintain normalcy, the wives stepped into abnormal roles.

The Theologinnen were consciously influenced by the general women's movement in Germany, even if some of them denied it.[27] The theologically trained women desired empowerment, and they defended their claim on ordination with intellectual arguments. They promulgated a new understanding of Scripture. The Theologinnen were committed to changing the Church to create a new profession for women. On the other hand, the pastors' wives did not hesitate to lay down their pastoral responsibilities when their husbands returned, or when another man arrived to take over the parish.

An important economic element separated the pastors' wives from the theologians and contributed to the difference in their attitudes. The wives of "legal" pastors could live on their husbands' salaries or, in tragic cases, widows' pensions. The Theologinnen were generally both "illegal" and unmarried: they needed salaries. This by itself was a motivation to carve out a permanent, professional niche.

The data support, thirdly, that the overt misogyny of the Nazi Party had relatively little effect on the Theologinnen of the Confessing Church. Ironically, during the era of the most overtly misogynist regime of Europe, women made a profound incursion into a previously exclusive, professional male domain, which is, however, not to be compared with the experience of their proletarian sisters who found work in steel mills, factories, and mines; nor with women entering the Nazi Party. The Theologinnen stepped into a professional, elite club of men, made all the more exclusive because of an 1,800-year-old tradition of scriptural interpretation.

Comparisons with laboring women are untenable. The Theologinnen did not undertake to do "men's work" in order to survive economically, nor to support government programs, nor because state propaganda urged them to. They moved into pastoral work at financial cost and at great risk of life and liberty precisely because they opposed the government's policy toward the churches. Their work was in distinct dissent and resistance to the government propaganda.

Furthermore, if the Nazi Party finally opened its membership to increasing numbers of women for purely pragmatic reasons, this did not correspond to the Church's reasons for admitting women to the pastorate. The Hamburg synodalists of 1942 were content to exploit women's energies as temporary, emergency preachers, agreeing that full ordination was not necessary for allowing the women to preach. Albertz, Diem, Harder, von Rabenau, Scharf, and others ignored the synod's consensus and ordained women in spite of the synodical ruling because they had come under conviction of a new theological insight. There was no parallel shift in Nazi ideology regarding women.

Fourth, the study demonstrates yet another case in which theology is informed by its secular circumstances. Both men and women in the Confessing Church opened their eyes to the world around them and discovered that the secularists had articulated a biblical position better than had the Church. Secular feminists had long maintained that fairness demanded equal rights and opportunities for women in every professional field. When the Christian women's movement adopted the same ideal, it was important to them to be able to defend it by citing Galatians 3:28 and 1 Corinthians 12:7. Those passages had been in the Bible for 1,800 years, yet it was the secularists' pressure that made the Christians read their Bibles more carefully. The same phenomenon runs through church history as illustrated in the attitude of the papacy to democracy, in the American clergy's attitude toward slavery, and in the hesitancy with which conservative American churches supported the civil rights movement.

To be sure, the Confessing Church did not adapt to everything in National Socialist culture. This is how it differed with the "German Christian" regime. Where the Confessing Church realized that society had outstripped it in articulating what was already in the Bible, the Confessors changed; and that change was on the basis of what the Bible taught, now that it was read with new eyes. The Confessing Church upheld the authority of the Bible while allowing for the necessity to revise interpretive approaches.

The pastors' wives and Theologinnen of the Confessing Church were responsible in large measure for the very survival of the Confessing Church. In that respect they were like the largely anonymous thousands of Confessing secretaries, teachers, nurses, clerks, housewives, organists, pastoral assistants, businesswomen, and teenagers who collected funds, hid Jews, printed contraband documents, typed pulpit declarations, wrote letters, mailed illegal materials, hid radios, and otherwise participated in dissent and resistance. Women made up the majority of the membership of the Confessing Church. See and Weckerling were right to aver, "without the women, there would have been nothing."[28]

118 WOMEN AGAINST HITLER

Pastors' wives and Theologinnen, working through a political, social, economic, demographic, and theological catastrophe, established a new profession for women within the German Protestant Church. Building on the gains of secularists, an emerging Christian women's movement supplied young women to study theology under Protestant faculties. With the demographic crises of the World Wars, the Church found increasingly more work for the newly trained women to do. Women entered pulpits and pastorates. Some sought ordination and argued successfully enough to convince power-holding men in the churches to ordain women and thus affirm and recognize their God-given spiritual gifts. The ordinations of women were precedent setting. The ministry of women in the crisis years was in some cases literally legendary, so that both in substance and symbol, pastors' wives and Theologinnen of the Confessing Church established a new set of expectations for those who should serve as pastors.

In the years following World War II, in spite of temporary setbacks in the distribution of positions, Protestant women moved increasingly and ineluctably into the structure of the Protestant Churches in East and West Germany. Their commitment and talent proved that women *can* be pastors; their scholarship sought to demonstrate that women *may* and *should* be pastors. Protestant women, who had always heard that they were to be silent in church, broke their silence and, together with men, protested Hitler's attempt to take over Protestantism. That resistance led to persecution, a persecution in which the women shared, and through which, ironically, they emerged as overt, recognized leaders, and so changed the pitch of the Church's voice.

NOTES

1. Gertrud Grimme, "Von der Vikarin zur Oberkirchenrätin—Der Weg einer engagierten Theologin" in Hans-Martin Linnemann, *Theologinnen in der Evangelischen Kirche von Westfalen* (Bielefeld: Luther-Verlag, 1990) pp. 17-18.

2. See p. 109 n.89 for the names of Vikarinnen whose consecrations were retroactively recognized as full ordinations.

3. Dagmar Henze, "Die Geschichte der Evangelischen Theologin—Ein Überblick," *Reformierte Kirchenzeitung* (Neukirchen-Vluyn), March 1991:98.

4. Ilse Härter, "Einführung bei der Eröffnung der Ausstellung, 'Das Weib schweigt nicht mehr' in der kirchlichen Hochschule in Wuppertal am 17.1.1991," *Reformierte Kirchenzeitung* (Neukirchen-Vluyn), 132, no. 4 (1991):6.

5. Ilse Härter, "Theologinnen in der Bekennenden Kirche," published as "Zuerst kamen die Brüder" in K. A. Bauer, ed., *Predigtamt oder Pfarramt?* (Neukirchen-Vluyn: Neukirchener Verlag, 1991), p. 3.

6. Härter, *"Einführung,"* p. 7.

7. Ibid.

8. Henze, "Geschichte," p. 98. Information on the Rhineland is from Härter, *"Einführung,"* p. 7. The names of the churches reflect changes that were made after the reorganizations following World War II.

9. Church leaders had chosen the name carefully: not *"of* the DDR," but *"in* the DDR."

10. From the author's interview with Bishop Emeritus Albrecht Schönherr, East Berlin, July 1987; and Schönherr's letter to the author of 26 November 1993.

11. "Immer mehr Frauen im evangelischen Pfarramt," *idea-spektrum.* [*sic*] *Nachrichten und Meinungen aus der evangelischen Welt* (Wetzlar: Informationsdienst der Evangelischen Allianz e.V.) 38 (1986): 3. The article notes the continual rise of women in the pastorate of the Protestant Church in Germany (EKD). In 1964, by comparison, 1.9% of the 13,452 EKD pastors were women.

Another *idea-spektrum* article (25, 1985, p. 8), *"Hört Vormarsch der Pfarrerinnen auf?"* noted that in 1984 34 percent of the 995 theology students who took the EKD's First Theological Examination were women. Among the 752 participants in the Second Theological Examination, 30 percent were women as well.

12. Random issues of *idea-spektrum* reveal the ongoing debate among fundamentalists. See, for example, articles regarding the ordination of women in Bavaria, "Junger Pfarrer legt Amt nieder. Viele Amtsbrüder haben resigniert" (9, 1986, p. 11); "Nein zur Frauenordination" (7, 1986, p. 8); and in Lower Saxony and Braunschweig, "Bekenntnisbewegung in Niedersachsen: Kritik an Frauenordination; Gegen eine falsche Religions-toleranz" (25, 1987, p. 10).

13. "Mehr Frauen in Kirchengremien! Frauen als 'sehr geehrte Herren'" in *idea-spectrum* 46 (1984), 5.

14. From the author's interview with Senta Maria Klatt, Berlin, 12-13 January 1990.

15. The EKD is still an umbrella organization including all the re-organized provincial churches—the *Landeskirchen*—Lutheran, Calvinist, and United. The political structure of the EKD remains essentially what it was before 1933, a situtation that deeply disturbed Karl Barth but greatly pleased Otto Dibelius. See James Bentley, *Martin Niemöller, 1892-1984* (New York: Free Press, 1984), pp. 168-170.

16. The complete text of the Stuttgart Confession of Guilt can be found in English in Otto Dibelius, *In the Service of the Lord* (New York: Holt, Rinehart and Winston, 1964), p. 259; and in Bentley, *Martin Niemöller,* p. 176.

17. Bentley, *Martin Niemöller,* pp. 179-198.

18. "Niemoellers Here. German Pastor Will Address Church Assembly." *St. Petersburg* [Florida] *Times,* 8 February 1951. Martin Niemöller noted in his diary of 11 February 1951, "Sunday. St. Petersburg . . . Else preaches twice. I give a short greeting." Edita Sterik, ed., *Else Niemöller* (Darmstadt: Zentralar-chiv der Evangelischen Kirche in Hessen und Nassau, July 1990), p. 139.

19. Erich Stegmann, *Der Kirchenkampf der Thüringer Evangelischen Kirche 1933-1945* (Berlin: Evangelische Verlagsanstalt, 1984).

20. Stewart W. Herman, *The Rebirth of the German Church* (New York: Harper and Brothers, 1946), p. 13.

21. Ibid., pp. 13-14.

22. Regarding the Saxon church's actions see ibid., p. 4.

23. Susannah Heschel has reported on the case of Thuringia's unrepentant "German Christian" Professor Walter Grundmann of Jena whose postwar career in Leipzig and Eisenach flourished. Susannah Heschel, "Jesus Was an Aryan: Walter Grundmann and the Nazification of Germany," a paper read at the 22nd Annual Scholar's Conference, "The Holocaust and the German Church Struggle: Religion, Power and the Politics of Resistance," University of Washington, Seattle, 2 March 1992.

24. Herman, *Rebirth*, p. 18.

25. Much of Else Niemöller's work after the war was involved with raising funds and food for hunger relief from benefactors in the United States and the United Kingdom. Bentley, *Martin Niemöller*, pp. 189-192.

26. Renate Wiggershaus, *Frauen unterm Nationalsozialismus* (Wuppertal: Peter Hammer Verlag, 1984), p. 5.

27. Erika Reichle, *Die Theologin in Württemberg* (Bern: Herbert Lang, 1975), pp. 18-19: "The female theologian in Germany is in every respect the result of the emancipation movement of the last 150 years." Nonetheless, every Confessing *Theologin* interviewed for this book denied being a "*Feministin*," at least in the radical ways in which the word was being used in the 1980s and 1990s.

28. Wolfgang See and Rudolf Wecklering, *Frauen im Kirchenkampf* (Berlin: Wichern Verlag, 1986), cover of the book.

Sources and Bibliography

EYEWITNESS INTERVIEWS

The following eyewitnesses and participants in the Church Struggle agreed to be interviewed for this book.

Pastor Otto Berendts, Pastorin Elma Berendts
Pastor Berendts, a Vikar working in Berlin during the Kirchenkampf, met and in 1938 married Vikarin Hanna Elisabeth Charlotte Maria Vetter, a Theologin who had been consecrated 2 July 1936 by *Präses* Gerhard Jacobi of the Confessing Church of Berlin. After his wife's death in 1971, Pastor Berendts married Pastorin Elma Waubke, herself a younger eyewitness of the events of the Church Struggle, and an acquaintance and friend of some of the principle players.
The Berendts granted interviews, reviewed files, and offered personal glimpses into the personalities and events of the Church Struggle during a visit in the author's home in October 1993.

Emmi Blöcher
The widow of Confessing Vikar Theo Groh, Frau Emmi Hof Groh Blöcher trained at the Burckhardthaus in Berlin, following which she preached and taught in the Protestant Church of Hessen and Nassau.
Frau Blöcher granted an interview in her home in Sinn-Dill on 19 February 1990. Also present for the audio-recorded interview was Käthe Haag.

Ruth Bockemühl
Frau Bockemühl, the widow of Confessing Pastor Peter Bockemühl of Wuppertal, supported, influenced, and protected her husband and raised two

sons during the years of the Church Struggle. The family was closely acquainted with Professor Karl Barth, who performed the Bockemühls' wedding.

The interview took place in Frau Bockemühl's home in Wuppertal, 13 February 1990. Also present for the audio-recorded conversation was Pastorin Leni Immer.

Pastor Hans-Gerhard Böttcher

Pastor Böttcher is the son of Pastor Johannes Böttcher, who "ordained" Aenne Kaufmann in Essen in 1935. He granted an interview in his schoolrooms in Neukirchen-Vluyn on 5 February 1990.

Ruth Eissen

Frau Eissen is the widow of Pastor Anton Eissen, who served Confessing parishes in the Saarland and Wuppertal.

Frau Eissen participated in an interview in the home of Lydia Heiermann, Wuppertal, together with Frau Heiermann, Frauke Heiermann, and Pastorin Leni Immer on 13 February 1990.

Edith Feldmann

Frau Feldmann is the widow of Confessing pastor Winfreid Feldman who fell in Russia in December 1942. Pastorin Ilse Härter is her sister. Interviews which included Frau Feldmann took place on 20-21 January 1990, primarily in the Pastorin's home.

Lieselotte Fendler

Frau Fendler is the daughter of Pastor Martin Vedder and Felicitas Vedder. She experienced the Church Struggle as a girl in Pomerania, including the horrors of evacuation, and her mother's arrest and imprisonment.

Frau Fendler participated in interviews of her mother in Frau Vedder's home in Oldenburg 27-28 January 1990.

Pastorin Ilse Härter

Pastorin Härter was one of the first two women to be fully ordained to ministry in Germany; she served in three of the Confessing *Landeskirchen*: Berlin-Brandenburg, the Rhineland, and Wurttemberg. She is the sister of Edith Feldmann.

Interviews with Pastorin Härter were conducted 20-21 January 1990 in her home in Goch, Germany.

Lydia Heiermann

Frau Lydia Heiermann was engaged to, and later married to, Vikar Bernhard Heiermann during the years of the Church Struggle in the Rhineland. She also worked as his unpaid secretary in his leadership role with the Brotherhood of Assistant Preachers and Vikare of the Rhineland.

Frau Heiermann hosted Ruth Eissen, Frauke Heiermann, Pastorin Leni Immer and the author for an audio-recorded interview in her Wuppertal home over *Kaffeee und Kuchen* on 13 February 1990.

Pastorin Leni Immer

Pastorin Immer is the eldest daughter of Pastor Karl and Tabea Immer of Wuppertal. As a teenager and young woman, Leni Immer had personal contact with virtually all the national leaders of the Confessing Church. She studied at the Burckhardthaus in Berlin during the height of the Church Struggle.

Pastorin Immer granted an interview in her Wuppertal home on Stahlstrasse (more recently renamed "Karl-Immer-Strasse") in June 1987, and again on 12 and 13 February 1990 in her home and throughout the city of Wuppertal. She actively participated in the interviews with Ruth Bockemühl, Ruth Eissen, and Lydia Heiermann.

Pastorin Sieghild Jungklaus

Pastorin Jungklaus grew up in a Confessing Church in Pankow, Berlin, where her father pastored. She was ordained in 1944, and continued to serve in Pankow until her retirement.

Pastorin Jungklaus gave an interview in her home in Berlin on 15 January 1990, and has been generous with correspondence and documents since.

Pastorin Aenne Kaufmann

Pastorin Kaufmann, the first woman to be "ordained" in the Confessing Church of the Rhineland, served in churches in Essen until her retirement. She granted an interview on 4 February 1990 in her home in Essen-Stadtwald.

Mechthild Kehr

Mechthild Kehr is the widow of Pastor Rudolf Kehr, the daughter of Confessing pastor Ferdinand Vogel, and the sister of Heinrich Vogel. In her husband's imprisonment and absence, she pastored the church in Seelow, east of Berlin in Brandenburg.

The interview with Frau Kehr was conducted in her home in Berlin on 16 January 1990.

Senta Maria Klatt

Frau Klatt, a "non-Aryan" Christian kindergarten teacher, served as secretary to both Superintendent (later Bishop) Otto Dibelius and Pastor (later *Präses* and Bishop) Kurt Scharf.

The second of Frau Klatt's two interviews was video-recorded in her hospital room in Berlin. Interviews took place on 12 and 13 January 1990.

Pastorin Elisabeth Charlotte Lawerenz

Pastorin Lawerenz spent the Church Struggle in the service of the Confessing

Church of Berlin-Brandenburg. She traveled widely within the territory, and became familiar with the interiors of churches as well as prisons during those years.

Pastorin Lawerenz agreed to an interview in her home in Detmold on 8 February 1990, and has been instrumental in putting the author in contact with other participants in the Church Struggle.

Ingeborg von Mackensen

The daughter of Stephanie von Mackensen, Ingeborg von Mackensen experienced the Church Struggle as a teenager in Pomerania, where her mother was a member of the brotherhood council and served for awhile as the sole administrator of the Confessing Church.

Frau von Mackensen granted two interviews, one in July 1987 in her home in Iserlohn, and again in Minden 16-18 February 1990 on the occasion of the Konvent Evangelischer Gemeinden aus Pommern.

Pastorin Ruth Mielke

Pastorin Mielke was a student of Karl Barth in Bonn. A Westphalian Theologin who was ordained during the Church Struggle, Pastorin Mielke granted an interview in her home in Minden on 16 February 1990.

Dora von Öttingen

Frau von Öttingen was a congregational assistant (*Gemeindehelferin*) in Frankfurt where she endured imprisonment because she had distributed a document purporting to be a government plan for overhauling the Christian Churches after the war. A close friend of the Immer family, she provided information about a wide range of topics, particularly life in the Immer parsonage in Barmen, and her experiences as a prisoner of the Third Reich.

Frau von Öttingen's interview was conducted in her apartment in Frankfurt am Main on 20 February 1990.

Irmgard Reger

Frau Reger talked freely about Minna Reger, her husband's first wife, and about her own experiences as a young girl in the Third Reich and the Confessing Church. Pastor Christian Reger served a church in Stieglitz, but was imprisoned in Dachau. Irmgard Reger grew up under the influence of the older Pfarrfrau, Minna Reger.

The author and his wife conducted the audio-recorded interview with Frau Reger over parts of two days in July 1987 in Frau Reger's home in Lorch (Württemberg).

Bishop Emeritus Kurt Scharf and Renate Scharf

Renate Scharf married her widowed cousin, Pastor Kurt Scharf, and raised his children during the Third Reich. Her husband was Martin Niemöller's personal representative during the eight years of Niemöller's Moabit, Sachsenhausen, and Dachau imprisonments.

The Scharfs granted an interview on 18 January 1990 in their home in Berlin.

Margarete Schneider and Evamarie Vorster

Frau Schneider is the widow of Pastor Paul Schneider, the "Preacher of Buchenwald," whom concentration camp officials evidently murdered with injections of digitalis in 1939. Her daughter Evamarie Vorster contributed substantially to the interview.

Also present during the audio-recorded 19 February 1990 interview in the Vorsters' home in Liederbach were Reinhold and Käthe Haag, together with Pastor Johannes Vorster, and Angelika Vorster.

Bishop Emeritus Albrecht Schönherr

A student of Dietrich Bonhoeffer, Bishop Schönherr's interview covered Stephanie von Mackensen, Dietrich Bonhoeffer, and Schönherr's late first wife, Hilde Enterlein Schönherr.

Bishop Schönherr granted an interview in an ice cream cafe in East Berlin-Köpeneck in July 1987, and again in Seattle, Washington in March 1992.

Elisabeth Stein and Superintendent Joachim Stein

Frau Stein is the daughter of Pastor Bruno and Louise Tecklenburg. Both Superintendent Stein and his wife participated in the Church Struggle in their youth.

The Steins participated in the interview of Louise Tecklenburg in the Tecklenburg home in Berlin-Lichterfelde in the evening of 16 January 1990.

Louise Tecklenburg

Frau Louise Tecklenburg's husband, Pastor Bruno Tecklenburg, served as pastor in Brandenburg and Berlin-Lichterfelde. When he was drafted into the army, his wife represented him on the elders' board of the Lichterfelde congregation.

Frau Tecklenburg granted an interview over *Kaffee and Kuchen* on 16 January 1990 in her Berlin-Lichterfelde home.

Annemarie Tiedtke

Frau Tiedtke is the daughter of Confessing Pastor Karl Buth and Bertha Buth, and the widow of Pastor Helmut Tiedtke, who served as an illegal Vikar during the Church Struggle.

Frau Tiedtke offered information about her parents during an interview in Haus Salem in Minden on 17 February 1990.

Felicitas Vedder

The widow of Pastor Martin Vedder of Gross Poplow, Pomerania, Felicitas

Vedder performed, during her husband's wartime absence, every sacerdotal service of her church except the administration of Holy Communion.

Video-tape captured part of the interviews with Frau Vedder in her home in Oldenburg 27-28 January 1990.

Dr. Christa Vogel, Pastor Konrad Vogel, Maria Vogel
These grown children of Pastor Heinrich and Frau Irmgard Vogel discussed their parents' role in the Church Struggle and their parents' complicity in the July 1944 assassination attempt on Hitler. The interview, held in Dr. Christa Vogel's home in Berlin, took place Sunday evening, 14 January 1990.

Pastor Egbert Zieger, Gerda Zieger
The Ziegers served a church in Arnhausen, Pomerania, until Pastor Zieger was sent to Greece as a soldier. Leadership of the church and community of Arnhausen fell to Frau Zieger.

The Ziegers granted an interview over two days 30-31 January in their home in Winsen-Aller. Herr Pastor Zieger was available for conversation again in Minden 16-18 February 1990.

THE THEOLOGICAL DEBATE
OVER THE ORDINATION OF WOMEN IN GERMANY, 1931-1945

Here follows an annotated list of books, articles, papers, and speeches that informed the debate over the ordination of women in the Protestant Church of the Old Prussian Union (APU) from 1931 to 1942. The documents are arranged in order of their chronological appearance.

Käthe Gombert, "The Woman Question and the New Testament" (Die Frauenfrage und das Neue Testament). Speech delivered at the Sixth Meeting of the Verband evangelischer Theologinnen Deutschlands (Union of Protestant *Theologinnen* of Germany) in Bethel, 21-26 October, 1931. A detailed report of the content of the speech is preserved in *Mitteilungen des Verbandes evangelischer Theologinnen Deutschlands*, 1 (fourth quarter 1931) under the title, "Bericht über die 6. Tagung des Verbandes evangelischer Theologinnen Deutschlands in Bethel und Bielefeld," unsigned, but probably written by Marianne Schleypen, the periodical's editor. Although Gombert's speech predates the Confessing Church, among the thirty members of her audience in 1931 were a significant number of women who were later active Confessors. My copy of *Mitteilungen* is from the Landeskirchliches Archiv Stuttgart, Bestand 356aI.

Anna Paulsen, *Mutter und Magd: Das Biblische Wort über die Frau* (Mother and Maid: The biblical word on woman). Berlin: Furche Verlag, 1935. Paulsen taught at the Burkhardthaus in Berlin where pastoral assistants and other church servants were trained. She had earned the academic title *"Lic.,"* equivalent to a doctorate. According to Pastorin Sieghild Jungklaus, she was a cousin of Hans Asmussen, but they stood on opposite sides of the question regarding ordination of women.

"Theological Reflection on the Question of an Office for Female Curates" (Zur theologischen Besinnung über die Frage des Vikarinnenamtes). 1 July 1938. This document, according to a letter of 10 August 1940 from Klara Hunsche, is the work of a circle of Vikarinnen in the Rhineland. Zentralarchiv der Evangelischen Kirche, Berlin, Bestand 611/15, 13.

Vikarinnen of Prussia. "Petition (Eingabe)."Draft" (Entwurf). [The two words are handwritten additions to the document]. 2 November 1939. This four-page, typewritten document addressed to the superintendent from Berlin is unsigned. It appears to speak for the Prussian Vikarinnen and asks for clarification of their ministries. It makes reference to the fact that many of the Vikarinnen are already in Emergency Pastorates and are currently preaching. It asks that their consecrations be recognized as ordinations and that the Church officially call them to preach, regulate their financial status, and so forth. Evangelisches Zentralarchiv in Berlin. Bestand 611/15, 12.

Hans Asmussen. Untitled essay beginning with the words, "In every way, woman in the New Testament takes a secondary place." (In jeder Weise tritt die Frau im N.T. zurück.) September 1940. Zentralarchiv der Evangelischen Kirche, Berlin, Bestand 611/15, 17. Evidently, Klara Hunsche wrote Asmussen's name on the document. Her accompanying letter in the archive collection identified the document and helps date it before 27 September 1940.

Peter Brunner. The so-called "Brunner Gutachten": "Discussion of the Question, Whether a Vikarin Can be Called to Preach and be Ordained" (Gutachten über die Frage, ob die Vikarin in das Predigtamt berufen und ordiniert werden kann,) Wuppertal, November 1940. The copy of this document in my collection contains this handwritten note on the last page: "Signed (first draft) in Wuppertal in November 1940: Lic. Dr. Joachim Beckmann, Pastor; D. Peter Brunner, Pastor; Lic. Martin Graeber, Pastor; Stud[ien] Dir[ektor] D. Hermann Hesse, Pastor; Hermannus Obendieck, Pastor; Lic. Heinrich Schlier, Pastor; Johannes Schlingensiepen; Prof. D. Otto Schmitz; For the reliability [of the copy], signed, D. Peter Brunner."

Brunner opposed the ordination of women. A contemporary précis of the "Brunner Gutachten" is afforded in the "Report on the Meeting of Rhenish Theologinnen in the AVH in Barmen on 20 April 1941" (Bericht über das Treffen der rheinischen Theologinnen im AVH in Barmen am 20. April 1941) from the papers of Aenne Kaufmann. Archiv der Evangelischen Kirche des Rheinlands, Düsseldorf, Akte 27.

The following documents are reactions to the first six:

Martin Albertz. "May One Allow a Theologically Trained Woman the Right to Preach the Word and Administer the Sacraments?" ("Darf der theologisch vorgebildeten Frau die Verkündigung des Wortes und die Verwaltung der Sakramente gestattet werden? Gutachten von Martin Albertz.") Undated. Zentralarchiv der Evangelischen Kirche, Berlin, Bestand 50/514/10, 12 [page 11 is missing]; the document is a carbon copy. Ilse Härter, "Persönliche", dates it December 1940, directly following the "Brunner Gutachten." Albertz's position is that women may be called to both preach and fill pastorates.

Hermann Diem. "Critical Comments on the Paper by D. P. Brunner Concerning the Question, Whether the Vikarin Can be Called to Preach and Be Ordained" (Kritische Bemerkungen zu dem Gutachten von D.P. Brunner über die Frage, ob die Vikarin in das Predigtamt berufen und ordiniert werden kann). Dated Ebersbach/Fils 19 March 1941. Diem's paper, which is in support of the ordination of women, was written at the request of the Brotherhood of Rhenish Assistant Preachers and Curates (Bruderschaft rheinischer Hilfsprediger und Vikare), which contained a number of women in its membership. The document is preserved in the Zentralarchiv der Evangelischen Kirche in Hessen und Nassau, Darmstadt, Bestand 35/432.

Lic. E. Käsemann. "The Participation of Woman in the Proclamation of the Word According to the New Testament," ("Der Anteil der Frau an der Wortverkündigung nach dem NT"). Twenty-one single-spaced typewritten pages, followed by three pages of "Discussion Questions Suggested by Hermann Diem." Undated, but a date of 29-30 November 1941 is suggested by E. Wolf, "Critical Comments." Härter, "Persönliche," dated the Käsemann document as being delivered 24-25 January 1942. Zentralarchiv der Evangelischen Kirche, Berlin, Bestand 6ll/15,16, pp. 1-24.

In this document opposing the ordination of women, Käsemann provides footnotes offering a glimpse into the bibliography from which he prepared his judgment. He cites Adolf von Harnack, *Die Mission und Ausbreitung des Christentums in den ersten drei Jahrhunderten* (Leipzig: J. C. Henrich'sche Buchhandlung, 1902), where there is a substantial discussion (on pp. 395-407) on which he seems to rely, and he acknowledges the use of Leopold Zscharnack, *Der Dienst der Frau in den ersten Jahrhunderten der christlichen Kirche* (Göttingen: Vandenhoeck and Ruprecht, 1902). He references a "Weiss" without noting the title, but it is probable that the reference was to Johannes Weiss, *Der erste Korintherbrief* (Göttingen: Vandenhoeck and Ruprecht, 1910) where, on pp. 342-343, the discussion "Über die Frauen" suggests that the offending passage about women maintaining silence is unauthentic. Weiss was also the author of *Das Urchristentum* (1914), available in English as *Earliest Christianity: A History of the Period A.D. 30—150* (New York: Harper, 1959), in which pp. 584—585 deal with Paul's view of emancipation and women. Similarly, Käsemann acknowledges "Schmiedel," most probably Paul Wilhelm Schmiedel (1851-1935) whose *Die Briefe an die Thessalonicher und die Korinther* (Freiburg: J. C. B. Mohr, 1891) mentions the speculation that the 1 Corinthians 14:35 passage stems from a hand other than St. Paul's. Käsemann also cites Lydia Stoecker, *Die Frau in der alten Kirche* (Tübingen: Mohr, 1907). The author's attempts to identify another Käsemann source, "Bonsett," have proven unfruitful.

Lic. O. Michel (*sic*: the spelling of the name also appears as Michael). "Diakonia and Diakonia Tou Logou. On Ministry and Ministry of the Word. Charismen and Office" (Diakonia und Diakonia Tou Logou. Vom Dienst und Dienst am Wort, Gnadengabe und Amt). Twenty-two page, typed document followed by a three-page "Diskussion" signed by E. Wolf. Undated, but with a date of 29-30 November 1941 suggested by E. Wolf, "Critical Commentary." Evangelisches Zentralarchiv in Berlin, 611/15, 16.

"Reaction of the Vikarinnen to the Papers" ("Äusserung der Vikarinnen auf die Gutachten.") No signatures. Undated. Zentralarchiv der Evangelischen Kirche, Berlin, Bestand 50/615b, pp. 336-43 and Bestand 6ll/15, 17. An unsigned argumentation for the right of women to preach. There are three parts: "Biblical/Theological," "Church Historical," and "Practical/Theological." Ilse Härter described this as "the hurried work of three Vikarinnen at Berlin. Unfortunately so far we do not know yet the names." Ilse Härter's letter to the author, 3.11.90, p. 3.

"Memorandum." A report of the subcommittee to the Synod of the Old Prussian Union, which met in October 1942. The memorandum is signed by I. [Julius] Schniewind, P[eter] Brunner, E[rnst]. Käsemann, A[nna] Paulsen, E. Schlink, and A[enne] Schümer, and dated 14 September

1942. It concludes that the ministry of the Vikarin is the proclamation of the Word to women, youths, and children, whereby the possibility of preaching to the entire congregation is not legally precluded. If, in emergencies, the Vikarin preaches, this does not indicate that she is exercising the role of pastor. Zentralarchiv der Evangelischen Kirche in Hessen und Nassau, Darmstadt, Bestand 35/432.

"Extract from the Minutes of the Eleventh Confessional Synod of the Protestant Church of the Old Prussian Union of October 1942." Contains Resolutions IV and V and rules for implementation of Resolution V. My copies are not stamped with archival information.

D. E. Wolf. "Critical Comments to the Resolutions Concerning the Office and Ministry of the Vikarin" (Kritische Bemerkungen zu den Beschlüssen über das Amt bzw. den Dienst der Vikarin"). 10 January 1943. The document refers to presentations made by Lic. E. Käsemann and Lic. O. Michel, which it dated 29-30 November 1941.

Liselotte Berli, Ilse Fredrichsdorff, Ilse Härter, Liselotte Lawerenz, Erika Lenz, and Hannelotte Reiffen. "Position on the Rules of Implementation of Decision IV: The Ministry of the Vikarin ("Stellungnahme zu den Ausführungsbestimmungen zu Beschluß IV: Der Dienst der Vikarin") The document contains seven objections to decisions made at the October 1942 synodical meeting of the Confessing Synod of the Protestant Church of the Old Prussian Union. The primary authors were Ilse Härter and Hannelotte Reiffen. Copies exist in two forms: (1) Zentralarchiv der Evangelischen Kirche, Berlin, Bestand 611/15, 17; and (2) Zentralarchiv der Evangelischen Kirche in Hessen und Nassau, Darmstadt, Bestand 35/432. The Darmstadt document cites a still earlier source: Kirchenkampfarchiv der kirchlichen Hochschule West Berlin, KKA 615b 479 + 514. The Darmstadt document also records signatures of the Vikarinnen. Ilse Härter wrote, on 3 November 1990, "H[annelotte] Reiffen and I signed on the 11th of January 1943, nearly three months after the synod of Hamburg." Härter's letter to the author, March 1990, p. 3.

Heinrich Held. "Proposals for Additions to the Law Regarding Vikarinnen" (Anträge zum Vikarinnengesetz) 4 February 1944. Provenance unstated, signed by Held, a Rhineland Präses. The proposals are that the office of Vikarin be lifelong, that a Sisterhood be established to which all Vikarinnen of the Confessing Synod of the Old Prussian Union would belong, and that in every provincial church a committee oversee the activities of the Vikarinnen. There follows a suggestion for the installation of a Vikarin, called an "Ordination," by which is expressly stated that the Vikarin will not preach at the ordination service and in which she is reminded that her ministry is to women, youth, and children.

BIBLIOGRAPHY

PRIMARY SOURCES

Unpublished Articles

Unless otherwise indicated, these unpublished items are in the author's files.

Arndt, Gertrud. "Als Pfarrfrau zur Zeit des National-sozialismus." Undated. Frau Arndt, who was living in Oldenburg at the time, supplied the author with this four-page typed document describing life in Sodehnen, East Prussia.

Dany, Henny. "Blutbefleckter Rösch." Undated. Entered into a short story writing competition, according to information supplied by Pastorin Lieselotte Lawerenz.

Derschau, Irmgard von. "Die Arbeit in Kirchengemeinden der Synode Stolp-Land 1945-1946." Undated. The document, in Frau von Derschau's own hand, was evidently in her home in Asslar.

———. "Vom 'Jungfrauenverein' zur Mädchenarbeit." Undated. Frau von Derschau wrote the two-and-a-half page typewritten document at her home in Asslar.

Fischer, Ella. "Bericht von Frau Ella Fischer." Undated. Frau Martha Link supplied a copy of the document (two and a half single-spaced typewritten pages), representing pages 130-134 of the unpublished memoirs of Ella and Rudolf Fischer.

Fischer, Rudolf. "Pfarrer Rudolf Fischer in Saalfeld." Undated. Frau Martha Link supplied copies of pages 8-12 of a manuscript of the unpublished memoirs of Pastor Fischer.

Gadow, Hartmut, and Herta Gadow-Meyer. *Geflüchtet—Gejagt—Bewahrt: Brandenburg-Pommersche Erinnerungen 1944-1945.* The manuscript was written in the spring of 1991 for "das Archiv des ehemaligen Kreises Arnswalde/Neumark," Alfeld, Germany.

Tettenborn, Helga. "Jugendarbeit im 3. Reich in Pommern." Undated (possibly late 1989). Frau Tettenborn recorded this one-and-a-half page essay for the Konvent Evangelischer Gemeinden aus Pommern, e.V., Hannover, meeting in Minden in February 1990.

Vedder, Felicitas. "Erinnerungen aus der Zeit des Kirchenkampfes." Undated.

The one-page manuscript was probably written in Frau Vedder's home in Oldenburg for publication in *Pommersche Heimatskirche*.

————. "Der Sonntag Reminiscere 1935." Undated. Probably written at Frau Vedder's home in Oldenburg.

Zieger, Egbert. "Beitrag des Zeitzeugen, Pastor Egbert Zieger, Inhaber der Pfarre Arnhausen, Kreis Belgard in Ost-Pommern, zur Beantwortung der zu recht auftretenden Frage, `Warum haben die Pfarrer der Bekennenden Kirche in Pommern in den Jahren der nationalsozialistischen Herrschaft nicht stärkeren Widerstand geleistet'?" [sic]. Autumn 1989. From Pastor Zieger's home in Winsen/Aller.

Zieger, Gerda. "Erlebte 'Kirchengeschichte' der Pfarrfrau in Arnhausen Kr. Belgard/Pom. vom September 1939-September 1945." Undated. Mimeographed by the Konvent evangelischer Gemeinden aus Pommern e.V., Hannover.

————. "Das Gemeindeleben im Kirchspiel Arnhausen Kr. Belgard/Pommern nach dem Einmarsch der russischen Armee am Samstag, den 3. März, 1945 und unter der polnischen Besatzung." Undated. From Frau Zieger's home in Winsen/Aller.

————. "Von der Kriegswalze überrollt in Arnhausen Kr. Belgard/Pommern. Nach Kalendernotizen von Januar bis Ende September 1945." Undated. From Frau Zieger's home in Winsen/Aller.

Excerpts from Unpublished Diaries

Hesse, H. Klugkist. Diary. Ruth Bockemühl and Pastorin Leni Immer supplied a manuscript entitled, "Peter Bockemühl im Tagebuch H. Klugkist Hesses 1936-August 1939," consisting of excerpts from Pastor Hesse's diary that deal with Pastor Peter Bockemühl.

Link, Martha. "Tagebuchaufzeichnungen 1932-1935." Frau Link typed these excerpts from her personal diary to present to her sister Lydia Heiermann on the occasion of the latter's fiftieth wedding anniversary, 26 October 1985. The manuscript begins with an entry dated 21 November 1932 and concludes with words written on 11 November 1935.

Texts of Unpublished Speeches

Härter, Ilse. "Die Kölner 'konzertierter Aktion' 1928/1929 zur Abänderung des Vikarinnengesetzes vom 9.5.1927." Text of a speech. Undated.

Vedder, Felicitas. "Die kleinen Wunder." Undated. Audio tape with autobiographical information.

Books

Aden, Christel. *"Vikare beisst man nicht:"* Kinderjahre einer pommerschen *Pastorentochter.* Privately published in Neuenkirchen-Vörden, n.d.
Asmussen, Hans. *Die Offenbarung und das Amt.* München: Christian Kaiser Verlag, 1937.
Beckmann, Joachim, ed. *Briefe zur Lage der Evangelischen Bekenntnissynode im Rheinland, Dezember 1933 bis Februar 1939.* Neukirchen-Vluyn: Neukirchener Verlag, 1977. These "Letters on the Situation of the Protestant Confessing Synod" appeared in the Rhineland to keep Confessing pastors apprised of unfolding events.
Brauer-Dede, Helene. *Frau Pastor.* Oldenburg: Verlag Klaus Dede, 1986. In spite of the recent publication date, material in the book was written as early as 1943.
Delitzsch, Friedrich. *Die grosse Täuschung: Kritische Betrachtungen zu den alttestamentlichen Berichten über Israels Eindringen in Kanaan, die Gottesoffenbarung vom Sinai, und die Wirksamkeit der Propheten.* Stuttgart: Deutsche Verlags-Anstalt, 1920.
Dibelius, Otto. *In the Service of the Lord.* New York: Holt, Rinehart and Winston, 1964. Partial translation of *Ein Christ ist immer im Dienst.* Stuttgart: Kreuz Verlag, 1961.
Eckart, Dietrich. *Der Bolschewismus von Moses bis Lenin: Zwiegespräch zwischen Adolf Hitler und mir.* München: Hoheneichen Verlag, 1925.
———. *Das ist der Jude! Laienpredigt über Juden- und Christentum.* München: Hoheneichenverlag, [192-?].
Fleisch-Thebesius, Marlies. *Hauptsache Schweigen: Ein Leben unterm Hakenkreuz.* Frankfurt: Radius Verlag, 1988.
Gollwitzer, Helmut, and Käthe Kuhn, eds. *Dying We Live: The Final Messages and Records of the Resistance.* New York: Pantheon, 1956. The original appeared as *Du hast mich heimgesucht bei Nacht: Abschiedsbriefe und Aufzeichnungen des Widerstandes 1933-1945* (München: Christian Kaiser Verlag, 1955, 1954).
Gröber, Conrad. *Christus und die Frauen: Alte Wahrheiten für die neue Zeit.* Freiburg: Herder, 1935.
Hahn, Hugo. *Kämpfer wider Willen: Erinnerungen des Landesbischofs von Sachsen D. Hugo Hahn aus dem Kirchenkampf 1933-1945.* Metzingen: Brunnquell Verlag, 1969.
Hübner, Anneliese. *Wenn Stürme toben: Mutmachende Lebenserinnerungen einer Pfarrfrau.* Neuhausen-Stuttgart: Hänssler Verlag, 1984.
Immer, Leni. *Aus dem Leben eines Glaubenszeugen: Karl Immer. [E]rzählt von Leni Immer.* Mönchengladbach: Friedenskirchengemeinde, 1984.
Kirschbaum, Charlotte von. *Die wirkliche Frau.* Zollikon Zürich: Evangelischer Verlag, 1949. Though the publication postdates the discussion in this work, von Kirschbaum's book is included under primary sources on the

assumption that her arguments were current in Karl Barth's immediate circle during the Church Struggle.

Lilje, Hans. *Memorabilia: Schwerpunkt eines Lebens.* Nürnberg: Laetare, 1973.

Mielke, Ruth. *Lebensbild einer westfälischen Pfarrerin: Erfahrungen mit Theologinnengesetzen von 1927 bis 1974.* Minden: Privately printed, 1991.

Paulsen, Anna. *Mutter und Magd: Gottes Wort über die Frau.* Berlin: Im Furche Verlag, n.d. The penciled date "1935" was supplied by the librarian of the Kartäuser Kirche in Köln.

Querverain, Alfred de. *Volk und Obrigkeit eine Gabe Gottes.* Elberfeld: Selbstverlag des Bruderrats der Evangelischen Kirche der Altpreußischen Union, 1937.

Rosenberg, Alfred. *An die Dunkelmänner unserer Zeit: Eine Antwort auf die Angriffe gegen den "Mythus des 20. Jahrhunderts."* München: Hoheneichenverlag, 1935.

———. *Der Mythus des 20. Jahrhunderts.* München: Hoheneichen Verlag, 1930.

Seyler, Gertrud. *Aus meinem Leben.* Minden: Privately printed, n.d. The text reveals it to have been written after 1978. Obtained from Frau Seyler's daughter, Frau Gertrud Simon of Wiefelstede.

Staritz, Katharina. *Des grossen Lichtes Widerschein: Berichte und Verse aus der Gefangenschaft.* Münster in Westfalen: Evangelische Frauenhilfe in Deutschland e.V., n.d. Probably published 1952.

Steiner, Robert. *Die Anfänge des Kirchenkampfes in der Synode Braunfels: Aufzeichnungen aus dem Jahr 1936.* Köln: Rheinland Verlag, 1979. No. 57 in the series, Schriftenreihe für rheinische Kirchengeschichte.

Stoltenhoff, Ernst. *Die gute Hand Gottes: Lebenserinnerungen des letzten rheinischen Generalsuperintendenten (1879-1953).* Köln: Rheinland Verlag, 1990. No. 85 in the series, Schriftenreihe des Vereins für rheinische Kirchengeschichte.

Thadden, Reinold von. *Auf verlorenem Posten? Ein Laie erlebt den evangelischen Kirchenkampf.* Tübingen: Furche Verlag, 1948.

Thomas, Edith. *Edith Thomas: 1923-1934, 1935, 1943, Hildesheim.* Hildesheim [?]: privately printed (mimeograph), n.d.

Walter, Konrad. *Der Kampf um die Kanzeln. Erinnerungen und Dokumente aus der Hitlerzeit.* Alfred Toepelmann, 1957.

Wartenburg, Marion Gräfin York von. *Die Stärke der Stille: Erzählungen eines Lebens aus dem deutschen Widerstand.* Köln: Eugen Diederichs Verlag, 1984.

Wurm, Theophil. *Erinnerungen aus Meinem Leben.* Stuttgart: Quell-Verlag, 1953.

———. *Fünfzig Jahre im Dienste der Kirche: Predigten und Reden.* Stuttgart: Evangelisches Verlagswerk, 1950.

Articles

Bennigsen, Adelheid von. "Noch ein Wort zur christlichen Frauenbewegung."
  Die Frauenbewegung (Berlin: Ferdinand Dümmlers Verlagsbuchhand-
  lung) 7 (1901):116.
Casparin, Graf Agenor von. "Was die Frauen wollen." *Der Frauen-Anwalt*
  (Berlin), 4 (1873-1874):149-153.
Fahrenholz, Luise. "Bericht der Pfarrfrau Luise Fahrenholz (Eschbruch)." In E.
  Schendel and Hans Schauer, eds., *Erinnerungen an Stadt und Land
  Friedberg Nm.* Berlin: Selbstverlag des kirchlichen Betreuungsdienstes
  für Friedberg in Berlin, 1974, pp. 311-13.
Gnauck-Kühne, Elisabeth. "Vorkämpfer der christlichen Frauenbewegung." *Die
  Frauenbewegung* (Berlin: Ferdinand Dümmlers Verlagsbuch-handlung)
  7 (1901):99.
Gollwitzer, Helmut. "1937—Erinnerungen an den 1. Juli 1937." *Gemeinde-
  nachrichten aus Dahlem* (Berlin-Dahlem, Thielallee 1+3), (June-July
  1977):1-4.
Grimme, Gerturd. "Von der Vikarin zur Oberkirchenrätin—Der Weg einer
  engagierten Theologin." In Hans Martin Linnemann, ed., *Theologinnen
  in der Evangelischen Kirche von Westfalen. Drei Erfahrungsberichte.*
  Bielefeld: Luther-Verlag, 1990, pp. 9-43.
Gschlössl, Ina, and Annemarie Rübens. "Ein notwendiges Wort in Sachen der
  Theologinnen." *Die Christliche Welt*, 44, No. 5 (March 1930):cols.
  216-20.
Härter, Ilse. "Einführung bei der Eröffnung der Ausstellung 'Das Weib schweigt
  nicht mehr' in der Kirchlichen Hochschule in Wuppertal am
  17.1.1991." *Reformierte Kirchenzeitung*, (Neukirchen-Vluyn:
  Neukirchener Verlag, 1991) 132, No. 4:128-31.
———. "Ina Gschlößl wird 90 Jahre." *BRU: Magazin für die Arbeit mit Berufs-
  schülern* (Schwerte: Gesellschaft für Religionspädagogik e.V. Villigst),
  9 (1988):38-40.
———. "Der Weg der Frauen zu Ordination und Pfarramt." *Schlangebrut:
  Zeitschrift für feministisch und religiös interessierte Frauen* (München:
  Schlangebrut e.V.), No. 22 (August 1988):4-7.
Härter, Ilse and Günther van Norden. "Persönliche Erfahrungen mit der
  Ordination von Theologinnen in der Bekennenden Kirche des
  Rheinlands und in Berlin-Brandenburg." In Günther van Norden, ed.,
  *Zwischen Bekenntnis und Anpassung, Aufsätze zum Kirchenkampf in
  rheinischen Gemeinden, in Kirche und Gesellschaft.* No. 84 in the
  series Schriftenreihe des Vereins für rheinische Kirchengeschichte."
  Köln: Rheinlandverlag, 1985.
Immer, Leni. "Ein Pfarrhaus im Kirchenkampf." Mimeographed manuscript
  supplied by the author, which is substantially reproduced in Leni
  Immer, *Aus dem Leben eines Glaubenszeugen. Karl Immer. [E]rzählt*

von Leni Immer Mönchengladbach: Friedenskirchengemeinde, 1984.

———. "Zwischen Zivilkourage und Widerstand." Article published in the Sunday handout of 29 January 1990 in the Evangelische Akadamie Mühlheim/Ruhr. It stemmed from the 26-28 January 1990 meeting entitled "Zwischen Zivilkourage und Widerstand—Karl Immer im Kirchenkampf."

Keller, Gerda. "Inmitten einer Kirche von Männern-Eine Frau entscheidet sich für die Theologie." In Hans Martin Linnemann, ed., *Theologinnen in der Evangelischen Kirche von Westfalen. Drei Erfahrungsberichte.* Bielefeld: Luther-Verlag, 1990, pp. 44-66.

Lüders, Else. "Die 4. Generalversammlung des Deutsch-Evangelischen Frauenbundes in Bonn (24. -25. September)." *Die Frauenbewegung* (Berlin: Ferdinand Dümmlers Verlagsbuchhandlung), 9 (1903):157.

Lutschewitz, Gisela. "Trotz vieler Schwierigkeiten trafen wir uns." *Pommersche Heimatskirche. Evangelische Kirchenblatt der Vertriebenen Pommerns* (Hannover: Konvent evangelischer Gemeinden aus Pommern, e.V.), 12 (1989):1.

"Niemöller: Der mit Benzin löscht." *Der Spiegel* (Berlin), 17 January 1951, pp. 9-14 and cover.

"Reich Clergy Warn Hitler He Does Not Outrank God—Text of Confessional Protest Reveals Bold Stand Against Drive to 'Ban Christianity' in Germany—'Blood, Race, Soil' Theory Assailed—4,000 Word Blast at Nazi Methods Gets No Reply, but Repercussions Are Regarded as Inevitable." New York *Herald Tribune*, 28 July 1936:1,4.

Sauer, Minna. "Der deutsch-evangelische Frauentag in Cassel am 5. und 6. Juni." *Die Frauenbewegung* (Berlin: Ferdinand Dümmlers Verlagsbuchhandlung), 5 (1899):115-116.

———. "Die Frauenfrage auf der Hauptversammlung der freien kirchlich-sozialen Konferenz vom 14.-16. April zu Berlin." *Die Frauenbewegung* (Berlin: Ferdinand Dümmlers Verlagsbuchhandlung) 9 (1903):74-75.

———. "Die Haltung der kirchlichen Kreise zur Frauenbewegung." *Die Frauenbewegung*, (Berlin: Ferdinand Dümmlers Verlagsbuchhandlung) 6 (1900):89-90.

———. "Zum Stimmrecht der Frau bei Kirchenwahlen." *Die Frauenbewegung* (Berlin: Ferdinand Dümmlers Verlagsbuchhandlung) 9 (1903):91-92.

Stritt, Marie. "Frauenfrage auf dem evangelischen-sozialen Kongress." *Die Frauenbewegung* (Berlin: Ferdinand Dümmlers Verlagsbuchhandlung) 3 (1897):133-36.

Vedder, Felicitas. "Begegnung in Potsdam. Unerwartete Freude im Altersheim." *Die Schwester* (Oldenburgisches Diakonissenhaus Elisabethstift), Freundesbrief No. 4 (Weihnachten 1989).

———. "Ein Handvoll Schnee gegen den Durst." [Kolberg?], [February 1964?] The copy in the author's collection does not reveal the name of the publication.

————. "Kriegserlebnisse eines Abendmahlkelches." *Pommersche Heimatskirche* (Hannover: Konvent ev. Gemeinden aus Pommern e.V.) 25, no. 13 (March 1975):10.

————. "Nur 10 Nächte. Tagebuchaufzeichnungen von Frau Pastor Vedder— Gr. Poplow." In Kolberger Zeitung, *Mitteilungsblatt der Heimatkreisarbeiter Kolberg-Stadt, Kolberg-Land*. Leichlingen/Rheinland: Ostesee Verlag, [n.d.]. The article in the author's collection is a photocopy of the original. The photocopy contains no dates, no page numbers.

————. "Russische Panzer in Sicht!" March, 1964. The copy of the published article in the author's files does not reveal the name or city of the publication.

————. "Vor 40 Jahren im Kreis Belgard: Harmonium gegen Kopfschmerzpulver." The photocopied article which Frau Vedder gave the author offers no indication from which journal it was clipped.

Wegele, Agnes. "Der christliche Standpunkt in der Frauenfrage." *Die Frauenbewegung* (Berlin: Ferdinand Dümmlers Verlagsbuchhandlung), 2 (1896):1.

Wetzel, Cläre. "Bericht von Frau Cläre Wetzel (ehemals Büssow)." In E. Schendel and Hans Schauer, eds., *Erinnerungen an Stadt und Land Friedberg Nm.* Berlin: Selbstverlag des kirchlichen Betreuungsdienstes für Friedberg in Berlin, 1974, pp. 314-18.

Published Speeches

Kaufmann, Aenne. "Erlebnisse und Erfahrungen aus der Zeit der Bekennenden Kirche in Essen. Ein persönlicher Bericht. Vorgetragen auf der Kreissynodaltagung des Kirchenkreises Essen-Nord am 15. November 1980 im Haus der evangelischen Kirche." The speaker published the text privately.

Sass, Gerhard. "Der Kirchenkampf in Pommern 1933-1945: Eine Zwischenbilanz." Text of a speech that Pastor Sass gave at the Convention of Protestant Pomeranian Congregations on 10 October 1982 in Minden.

Journals

Hirsch, Jenny, ed. *Der Frauen-Anwalt.* Berlin: Wedekind and Schwieger, 1870-1881.

Mitteilungen des Verbandes evangelischer Theologinnen Deutschlands. Ostheim v.d. Rhön: Buchdruckerei R. Werner, 1928-1942.

Sauer, Minna, ed. *Die Frauenbewegung*, 9 volumes. Berlin: Ferdinand Dümmlers Verlagsbuchhandlung, 1895-1903.

SECONDARY SOURCES

Books

Anderson, Bonnie S., and Judith P. Zinsser. *A History of Their Own: Women in Europe From Prehistory to the Present*. Vols. 1, 2. New York: Harper and Row, 1988.

Bainton, Roland H. *Women of the Reformation in France and England*. Boston: Beacon Press, 1973.

———. *Women of the Reformation in Germany and Italy*. Boston: Beacon Press, 1971.

Baranowski, Shelley. *The Confessing Church, Conservative Elites, and the Nazi State*. Lewiston, NY: Mellon Press, 1986.

Barth, Karl. *The German Church Conflict*. Richmond, Va: John Knox Press, 1965. Trans. P. T. A. Parker. First published as *Karl Barth zum Kirchenkampf*. Ed. E. Wolf. No. 49 of Theologische Existenz heute, Neue Folge. München: Christian Kaiser Verlag, 1956.

Bäumer, Gertrud. *Die Frau im neuen Lebensraum*. Berlin: F. A. Herbig, 1931.

———. *Die Frau in der Volkswirtschaft und Staatsleben der Gegenwart*. Vol. 5 of *Das Weltbild der Gegenwart—Ein Überblick über das Schaffen und Wissen unserer Zeit in Einzeldarstellungen*. Eds. Karl Lamprecht and Hans F. Helmholt. Stuttgart: Deutsche Verlags-Anstalt, 1914.

———. *Gestalt und Wandel: Frauenbildnisse*. Berlin: F. A. Herbig, [ca. 1939].

———. *Im Lichte der Erinnerungen*. Tübingen: R. Wunderlich, 1953.

———. *Der neue Weg der deutschen Frau*. Stuttgart: Deutsche Verlags-Anstalt, 1946.

———. *Studien über Frauen*. Berlin: F. A. Herbig, 1921.

Bauer, K. A., ed. *Predigtamt ohne Pfarramt?* Neukirchen-Vluyn: Neukirchener Verlag, 1992.

Baumgärtel, Friedrich. *Wider die Kirchenkampf-Legenden*. Freimund: Verlag Neuendettelsau Mfr., 1958.

Beckmann, Joachim, and Hans Prolingheuer. *Zur Geschichte der Bekennenden Kirche im Rheinland*. Köln: Rheinlandverlag Bonn: In Kommission bei Habelt, 1981. No. 63 in the series, Schriftenreihe des Vereins für rheinische Kirchengeschichte.

Bentley, James. *Martin Niemöller, 1892-1984*. New York: Free Press, 1984.

Bertinetti, Ilse. *Frauen im geistlichen Amt. Die theologische Probelmatik in Evangelisch-Lutherischer Sicht*. Berlin: Evangelische Verlags-anstalt, 1965.

Beste, Niklot. *Der Kirchenkampf in Mecklenburg 1933-1945*. Göttingen: Van den Hoeck and Ruprecht, 1975.

Bethge, Eberhard. *Dietrich Bonhoeffer: Man of Vision, Man of Courage*. New York: Harper and Row, 1970. Partial translation of *Dietrich Bonhoeffer: Theologie [sic]. Christ. Zeitgenosse*. München: Christian

Kaiser Verlag, 1970.

Blau, Bruno. *Das Ausnahmerecht für die Juden in Deutschland 1933-1945*. Düsseldorf: Verlag Allgemeine Wochenzeitung der Juden in Deutschland, 1965.

Bleuel, Peter. *Sex and Society in Nazi Germany*. Trans. J. Maxwell Brownjohn. New York: Bantam Books, 1974. Previously published in German as *Das saubere Reich*. Bern and München: Scherz Verlag, 1972; and in English as *Strength through Joy* (Lippencott, 1973).

Boberach, Heinz. *Berichte des SD und der Gestapo über Kirchen und Kirchenvolk in Deutschland 1934-1944*. Mainz: Matthias Grünewald, 1971.

Borg, Daniel R. *The Old Prussian Church and the Weimar Republic: A Study in Political Adjustment, 1917-1927*. Hanover, N.H.: University Press of New England, 1984.

Brebeck, H. S. *Martin Niemöller: Bekenner, Politiker oder Demagoge?* Henef: H. E. Schneider, [1959?].

Bridenthal, Renate, Atine Grossmann, and Marion Kaplan, eds. *When Biology Became Destiny: Women in Weimar and Nazi Germany*. New York: Monthly Review Press, 1984.

Brunotte, Heinz. *Die evangelische Kirche in Deutschland: Geschichte, Organisation, und Gestalt der EKD*. Gütersloher Verlagshaus Gerd Mohn, 1964.

Buchheim, Hans. *Glaubenskrise im Dritten reich: Drei Kapitel nationalsozialistischer Religionspolitik*. Stuttgart: Deutsche Verlags-Anstalt, 1953.

Bullock, Alan. *Hitler, a Study in Tyranny*. New York: Harper Torchbooks, 1962.

Burgsmüller, Alfred, and Rudolf Weth, eds. *Die Barmer theologische Erklärung. Einführung und Dokumentation*. Neukirchen-Vluyn: Neukirchener Verlag, 1984.

Busch, Eberhard. *Karl Barth: His Life from Letters and Autobiographical Texts*. Trans. John Bowden. Philadelphia: Fortress Press, 1976. Original title: *Karl Barths Lebenslauf, Nach seinen Briefen und autobiographischen Texten*. München: Christian Kaiser Verlag, 1975.

Bushnell, Katherine C. *God's Word to Women. One Hundred Bible Studies on Woman's Place in the Divine Economy*. A reprint of the original, which was published in Berkeley, Calif., 1927. Reprint [n.d.]. Eds. Phil and Joyce French, Testimony Books, Gaithersburg, Md.

Clausen, Regina, and Siegfried Schwarz. *Vom Widerstand lernen: Von der Bekennenden Kirche bis zum 20. Juli 1944*. Bonn: Bouvier Verlag Herbert Grundmann, 1986.

Cochrane, Arthur C. *The Church's Confession under Hitler*. Pittsburgh: Pickwick Press, 1976.

Conway, John S. *The Nazi Persecution of the Churches 1933-1945*. New York:

Basic Books, 1968.

Craig, Gordon A. *Germany 1866-1945*. New York: Oxford University Press, 1978.

Denzler, Georg, and Volker Fabricius. *Die Kirchen im Dritten Reich. Band 1: Darstellungen. Band 2: Dokumente.* Frankfurt am Main: Fischer Taschenbuchverlag, 1984.

Diehl, Guida. *Christsein heisst Kämpfer sein: Die Führung meines Lebens.* Giessen: Brunnen, 1960.

Douglass, Paul F. *God among the Germans.* Philadelphia: University of Pennsylvania Press, 1935.

Duncan-Jones, Arthur Stuart. *The Crooked Cross.* London: Macmillan and Co., 1940.

Ehrenforth, Gerhard. *Die schlesische Kirche im Kirchenkampf 1932-1945.* Göttingen: Van den Hoeck and Ruprecht, 1968.

Elisabeth-von-Thadden Schule Heidelberg-Wieblingen: Annäherung an eine 60-jährige Schulgeschichte. Heidelberg-Wieblingen, 1987.

Ericksen, Robert P. *Theologians under Hitler: Gerhard Kittel—Paul Althaus—Emanuel Hirsch.* New Haven, Conn.: Yale University Press, 1985.

Evangelische Kirche im Rheinland. *Der Christuszeuge Paul Schneider: Gedenkschrift anlässlich des 50. Todestages.* Düsseldorf, 1989.

Forck, Bernhard Heinrich. *". . . und folget ihrem Glauben nach": Gedenkbuch für die Blutzeugen der Bekennenden Kirche.* Stuttgart: Evangelisches Verlagswerk, 1949.

Franz, Helmut. *Kurt Gerstein, Aussenseiter des Widerstandes der Kirche gegen Hitler.* Zürich: EVZ Verlag, 1964.

Frevert, Ute. *Women in German History: From Bourgeois Emancipation to Sexual Liberation.* New York: Berg Publishers, 1989. The book is translated from the 1986 Suhrkamp publication of *Frauen-Geschichte zwischen Bürgerlicher Verbesserung und Neuer Weiblichkeit.*

Friedlander, Saul. *Kurt Gerstein, the Ambiguity of Good.* New York: Alfred A. Knopf, 1969.

Gauger, Joseph. *Gotthard Brief: Chronik der Kirchenwirren.* Elberfeld, 1934-35.

Geiger, Max. *Der Deutsche Kirchenkampf 1933-1945.* Zürich: EVZ Verlag, 1965.

Gerlach, Wolfgang. *Als die Zeugen schwiegen: Bekennende Kirche und die Juden.* Berlin: Wichern Verlag, 1987.

Goldschmidt, Arthur. *Geschichte der evangelischen Gemeinde Theresienstadt 1942-1945.* Tübingen: Furche Verlag, 1948. No. 7 in the series Das christliche Deutschland 1933 bis 1945.

Goltz, Eduard Alexander Freiherr von. *Dienst der Frau in der christlichen Kirche.* Potsdam: Stiftungsverlag, 1914.

[Grüber, Heinrich]. *An der Stechbahn. Erlebnisse und Berichte aus dem Büro Grüber in den Jahren der Verfolgung.* Berlin: Evangelische

Verlagsanstalt, 1951.

Grüber, Heinrich. *Erinnerungen an sieben Jahrzehnten.* Köln: Kiepenheuer and Witsch, 1968.

Gurian, Waldemar. *Der Kampf um die Kirche im dritten Reich.* Luzern: Vita Nova Verlag, 1936.

Heine, Ludwig. *Geschichte des Kirchenkampfes in der Grenzmark Posen-Westpreussen 1930-1940.* Göttingen: Vandenhoeck and Ruprecht, 1961. Vol. 9 in the series, "Arbeiten zur Geschichte des Kirchenkampfes."

Hellmann, Manfred. *Friedrich von Bodelschwingh d.J. Widerstand für das Kreuz Christi.* Wuppertal: Brockhaus Verlag, 1988.

Helmreich, Ernst Christian. *The German Churches under Hitler—Background, Struggle, and Epilogue.* Detroit, Mich.: Wayne State University Press, 1979.

Herbert, Karl. *Der evangelische Kirchenkampf: Kirchengeschichte oder bleibendes Erbe?* Frankfurt am Main: Evangelisches Verlagswerk, 1985.

Herman, Stewart W. *The Rebirth of the German Church.* New York: Harper and Brothers, 1946.

Hermelinck, Heinrich. *Kirche im Kampf: Dokumente des Widerstands und des Aufbaus in der bekennenden Kirche in Deutschland 1933-1945.* Tübingen: R. Wunderlich, 1950.

Hoffmann, Konrad, ed. *Sieger in Fesseln: Christuszeugnisse aus Lagern und Gefängnissen.* Freiberg i.B.: Verlag Herder, 1947.

Hornig, Ernst. *Die Bekennende Kirche in Schlesien 1933-1945: Geschichte und Dokumente.* Göttingen: Vandenhoeck and Ruprecht, 1977.

Hübner, Paul-Gerhard. *Pommerscher Kirchenkampf 1933-1945.* Stettiner historischer Skizzen 3. Datteln: Zwolle-Druck Schübel and Hellweg, 1983.

Joffroy, Pierre. *A Spy for God: The Ordeal of Kurt Gerstein.* London: Collins, 1971.

Kaiser, Jochen-Christof. *Frauen in der Kirche: Evangelische Frauenverbände im Spannungfeld von Kirche und Gesellschaft 1890-1945. Quellen und Materialien.* Düsseldorf: Schwann, 1985.

Kater, Horst. *Die Deutsche Evangelische Kirche in den Jahren 1933 und 1944. Eine rechts- und verfassungsgeschichtliche Untersuchung zu Gründung und Zerfall einer Kirche im nationalsozialistischen Staat.* Göttingen: Vandenhoeck and Ruprecht, 1970.

Kaufmann, Doris. *Frauen zwischen Aufbruch und Reaktion: Protestantische Frauenbewegung in der ersten Hälfte des 20. Jahrhunderts.* München: Piper, 1988.

Kerschbäumer, Marie Therese. *Der weibliche Name des Widerstands: Sieben Berichte.* München: Deutsches Taschenbuch. 1982.

Kirchenkanzlei der Evangelischen Kirche in Deutschland. *Die Evangelische*

Kirche in Deutschland: Ihre Organe, Amtsstellen und Einricht-ungen (nach dem Stand vom 1. Februar 1969). Hannover: Kirchenkanzlei der Evangelischen Kirche in Deutschland, 1969.

Klappert, Bertold, and Günther van Norden, eds. *Tut um Gottes willen etwas Tapferes! Karl Immer im Kirchenkampf*. Neukirchen-Vluyn: Neukirchenerverlag, 1989.

Köbler, Renate. *Schattenarbeit: Charlotte von Kirschbaum—Die Theologin an der Seite Karl Barths*. Köln: Pahl-Rugenstein, 1987.

Konvent evangelischer Gemeinden aus Pommern, pub. *Die pommersche Heimatkirche in Vergangenheit und Gegenwart*. Hannover: Konvent evangelischer Gemeinden aus Pommern, e.V. Advent, 1989.

Konvent evangelischer Theologinnen in der Bundesrepublik und Berlin (West). *Das Weib schweigt nicht mehr: Wie das Amt der Theologin Wirklichkeit wird. Katalog zur Ausstellung*. Lilienthal: Dietlinde Cunow, 1990.

Koonz, Claudia. *Mothers in the Fatherland: Women, the Family and Nazi Politics*. New York: St. Martin's Press, 1987.

Korth, Hermann, ed. *Gemeinde Aachen im Dritten Reich: Sitzungsprotokolle der kirchlichen Körperschaften von 1933 bis 1943*. Köln: Rheinland Verlag, 1980. No. 58 in the series, Schriftenreihe des Vereins für rheinische Kirchengeschichte.

Kuessner, Dietrich. *Materialsammlung zur Ausstellung: Die evangelisch-lutherische Landeskirche in Braunschweig und der Nationalsozialismus*. Braunschweig: Döring-Druckerei und Verlag, 1982.

Kuhn, Annette. *Frauen in der Kirche*. Düsseldorf: Schwann-Verlag, 1985.

Leber, Annedore, and Freya Gräfin von Moltke. *Für und Wider: Entscheid-ungen in Deutschland 1933-1945*. Berlin: Mosaik Verlag, 1962.

———, ed. *Das Gewissen Steht auf: 64 Lebensbilder aus dem deutschen Wider-stand 1933-1945*. Berlin: Mosaik Verlag, 1957.

Legters, Lyman. *Western Society after the Holocaust*. Boulder, Colo.: Westview Press, 1983.

Linnemann, Hans-Martin, ed. *Theologinnen in der Evangelischen Kirche von Westfalen: Drei Erfahrungsberichte*. Bielefeld: Luther-Verlag, 1990.

Littell, Franklin Hamlin. *The German Phoenix: How the German Church's Resistance to Hitler Gave Birth to the Massive Lay Movements of the Kirchentag and the Academies*. New York: Doubleday, 1960.

Locke, Hubert G., ed. *The Church Confronts the Nazis: Barmen Then and Now*. New York: Edward Mellen Press, 1984.

———. *Exile in the Fatherland. Martin Niemöller's Letters from the Moabit Prison*. Grand Rapids, Mich.: William B. Eerdmans Publishing Company, 1986.

Ludecke, Kurt G. W. *I Knew Hitler: The Story of a Nazi Who Escaped the Blood Purge*. New York: Charles Scribner's Sons, 1937.

Lühe, Irmgard von der. *Elisabeth von Thadden: Ein Schicksal unserer Zeit*. Köln: Eugen Diedrichs Verlag, 1966.

Maas, Hermann, Gustav Radbruch, and Lambert Schneider, eds. *Den unvergessenen Opfern des Wahns 1933 bis 1945*. Heidelberg: Verlag Lambert Schneider, 1952.

Maser, Peter, ed. *Der Kirchenkampf im deutschen Osten und in den deutschsprachigen Kirchen Osteuropas*. Göttingen: Vandenhoeck und Ruprecht, 1992. The book is a Festschrift: "Peter Hauptmann zur Vollendung des 65. Lebensjahres am 25. März 1993.

Massner, Hans-Joachim. *Aus Vergangenheit und Gegenwart unserer Kirche in Essen (Kleine Essendische Kirchengeschichte)*. Köln: Rheinlandverlag, 1978. No. 54 in the series, Schriftenreihe des Vereins für rheinische Kirchengeschichte.

Meier, Kurt. *Der evangelische Kirchenkampf*. Göttingen: Vandenhoek and Ruprecht, 1976.

Meseberg-Haubold, Ilse. *Widerspruch und Widerstand christlicher Frauen im Dritten Reich*. Unpublished, 1989. Oldenburg.

Mueller, David L. *Karl Barth*. Waco, TX: Word Books, 1972.

Mybes, Fritz. *Agnes von Grone und das Frauenwerk der Deutschen Evangelischen Kirche*. Düsseldorf: Presseverband der Evangelischen Kirche im Rheinland e.V., n.d.

———. *Geschichte der evangelischen Frauenhilfe in Bildern*. Gladbeck: Schriftenmissions-Verlag, 1975.

———. *Geschichte der evangelischen Frauenhilfe in Quellen*. Gladbeck: Schriftenmissions-Verlag, 1975.

Neumann, Peter. *Die Jungreformatorische Bewegung*. Göttingen: Vandenhoeck and Ruprecht, 1971. No. 25 in the series, "Arbeiten zur Geschichte des Kirchenkampfes."

Niemöller, Gerhard. *Die erste Bekenntnissynode der Deutschen Evangelischen Kirche zu Barmen I und II. Geschichte, Kritik, und Bedeutung der Synode und ihrer Theologischen Erklärung*. Göttingen: Vandenhoeck and Ruprecht, 1959. Vol. 5 in the series, "Arbeiten zur Geschichte des Kirchenkampfes."

Niemöller, Wilhelm. *Bekennende Kirche in Westfalen*. Bielefeld: Ludwig Bechauf Verlag, 1952.

———. *Die evangelische Kirche im Dritten Reich: Handbuch des Kirchenkampfes*. Bielefeld: Ludwig Bechauf Verlag, 1956.

———. *Kampf und Zeugnis der Bekennenden Kirche*. Bielefeld: Ludwig Bechauf Verlag, 1948.

Niesel, Wilhelm. *Kirche unter dem Wort: der Kampf der bekennenden Kirche in der Altpreussischen Union 1933-1945*. Göttingen: Vandenhoeck and Ruprecht, 1978.

Norden, Günther van, and Fritz Mybes. *Evangelische Frauen im Dritten Reich*. Düsseldorf: Verlag Presseverband der Evangelischen Kirche im Rheinland, 1979.

Norden, Günther van, Paul Schönborn, and Volkmar Wittmütz. *1934 Barmen*

1984: Ausstellung der Evangelischen Kirche im Rheinland zur Barmer Theologischen Erklärung und zum Kirchenkampf. Wuppertal-Barmen: Jugenddienst Verlag, 1984.

Obendieck, Hermannus. *D. Paul Humburg: Der Zeuge—Die Botschaft.* Wuppertal: Emil Müller, Evangelischer Verlag, 1949.

Öhme, Werner. *Märtyrer der evangelischen Christenheit 1933-1945: Neunundzwanzig Lebensbilder.* Berlin: Evangelisches Verlagsanstalt, 1980.

Paassen, Pierre van, and James Waterman Wise, eds. *Nazism: An Assault on Civilization.* New York: Harrison Smith and Robert Haas, 1934.

Pechel, Rudolf. *Deutscher Widerstand.* Erlenbach-Zürich: E. Rentsch, 1947.

Pejsa, Jane. *Matriarch of Conspiracy: Ruth von Kleist 1867-1945.* Minneapolis, Minn: Kenwood Publishing, 1991.

Phayer, Michael J. *Protestant and Catholic Women in Nazi Germany.* Detroit, Mich.: Wayne State University Press, 1990.

Prittie, Terrence Cornelius Farmer. *Germans against Hitler.* Boston: Little, Brown and Company, 1964.

Prolingheuer, Hans. *Ausgetan aus dem Land der Lebendigen: Leidensgeschichten unter Kreuz und Hakenkreuz.* Neukirchen-Vluyn: Neukirchener Verlag, 1983.

———. *Der Fall Karl Barth. 1934-1935. Chronographie einer Vertreibung.* Neukirchen-Vluyn: Neukirchener Verlag, 1977.

———. *Kleine politische Kirchengeschichte: 50 Jahre evangelischer Kirchenkampf von 1919 bis 1969.* Köln: Pahl-Rugenstein, 1984-1985.

———. *Wir sind in die Irre gegangen: Die Schuld der Kirche unterm Hakenkreuz.* Köln: Pahl-Rugenstein, 1984-1985.

Rauschning, Hermann. *Voice of Destruction.* New York: G. P. Putnam's Sons, 1940.

Reichle, Erika. *Die Theologin in Württemberg—Geschichte, Bild, und Wirklichkeit eines neuen Frauenberufes.* Bern: Herbert Lang, 1975.

Remak, Joachim, ed. *The Nazi Years: A Documentary History.* New York: Simon and Schuster, 1969.

Ritter, Gerhard. *The German Resistance: Karl Goerdeler's Struggle against Tyranny.* Trans. R. T. Clark. New York: Frederick A. Praeger, 1958.

Roark, Dallas M. *Dietrich Bonhoeffer.* Waco, Tex: Word Books, 1972.

Robertson, E. H. *Paul Schneider: The Pastor of Buchenwald.* London: SCM Press, 1956. Original German title: *Der Prediger von Buchenwald: Das Märtyrium Paul Schneiders.* Berlin: Lettner Verlag. See also the entries in this section under Margarete Schneider und Heinrich Vogel.

Röhm, Eberhard, and Jörg Thierfelder, eds. *Evangelische Kirche zwischen Kreuz und Hakenkreuz: Bilder und Texte einer Ausstellung.* Stuttgart: Calwer Verlag, 1981.

Röhrbein, Waldemar R. *Reformation und Kirchentag: Kirche und Laienbewegung in Hannover. Handbuch zur Ausstellung.* Hannover:

Historisches Museum am Hohen Ufer, 1983.

Ruhm von Oppen, Beate. *Religion and Resistance to Nazism.* Research Monograph no. 35, Center of International Studies, Woodrow Wilson School of Public and International Affairs, Princeton University, March 1971.

Sautter, Reinhold. *Theophil Wurm: Sein Leben und Sein Kampf.* Stuttgart: Calwer Verlag, 1960.

Scharf, Kurt. *Widerstehen und Versöhnen: Rückblicke und Ausblicke.* Stuttgart: Radius Verlag, 1987.

Scherffig, Wolfgang. *Junge Theologen im "Dritten Reich." Dokumente, Briefe, Erfahrungen. Band I, 1933-1935. Es begann mit einem Nein!* Neukirchen-Vluyn: Neukirchener Verlag, 1989.

Schmidt, Kurt Dietrich. *Dokumente des Kirchenkampfes II. Die Zeit des Reichskirchenausschusses 1935-1937.* Göttingen: Vandenhoeck and Ruprecht, 1964. Volume 13 of the series, Arbeiten zur Geschichte des Kirchenkampfes.

Schneider, Margarete. *Der Prediger von Buchenwald: Das Märtyrium Paul Schneiders.* Neuhausen-Stuttgart: Hänssler Verlag, 1985.

Scholder, Klaus. *The Churches and the Third Reich. Volume One: 1918-1934. Volume Two: The Year of Disillusionment, 1934: Barmen and Rome.* Philadelphia: Fortress Press, 1988. First pubished in German in 1977.

Schreiber, Matthias. *Friedrich Justus Perels: Ein Weg vom Rechtskampf der Bekennenden Kirche in den politischen Widerstand.* München: Christian Kaiser Verlag, 1989.

See, Wolfgang, and Rudolf Weckerling. *Frauen im Kirchenkampf: Beispiele aus der Bekennenden Kirche Berlin-Brandenburg 1933 bis 1945.* Berlin: Wichern Verlag, 1986.

Seraphim, Hans-Günther. *Das politische Tagebuch Alfred Rosenbergs aus den Jahren 1934-35 und 1939-40.* Göttingen: Musterschmidt-Verlag, 1956.

Solberg, Richard. *God and Caesar in East Germany: The Conflicts of Church and State in East Germany Since 1945.* New York: Macmillan Co., 1961.

Sonne, Hans-Joachim. *Die politische Theologie der Deutschen Christen.* Göttingen: Vandenhoeck and Ruprecht, 1982.

Spotts, Frederic. *The Churches and Politics in Germany.* Middletown, Conn: Wesleyan University Press, 1973.

Stegmann, Erich. *Der Kirchenkampf in der Thüringer Evangelischen Kirche 1933-1945: Ein Kapitel Thüringer Kirchengeschichte.* Berlin: Evangelische Verlagsanstalt, 1984.

Stein, Leo. *I was in Hell with Niemöller.* London: Stanley Paul and Co., 1942. The book's contention that the author was a fellow inmate with Pastor Martin Niemöller has been judged a fraud (see *The Christian Century,* December 17, 1941, pp. 1568-70). For that very reason the volume is an example of the hagiographic approach to the Church Struggle.

Stephan, Hanns-Ulrich, ed. *Das eine Wort für alle: Barmen 1934-1984. Eine Dokumentation.* Neukirchen-Vluyn: Neukirchener Verlag, 1986.

Sterik, Edita, ed. *Else Niemoeller: Die Frau eines bedeutenden Mannes.* Darmstadt: Zentralarchiv der Evangelischen Kirche in Hessen und Nassau, July 1990.

Szepansky, Gerda. *"Blitzmädel," "Heldenmutter," "Kriegerwitwe": Frauenleben im Zweiten Weltkrieg.* Frankfurt am Main: Fischer Taschenbuchverlag, 1986.

Thalmann, Rita. *Frausein im Dritten Reich.* Frankfurt am Main: Ullstein, 1987.

Thomas, Katherine. *Women in Nazi Germany.* London: Victor Gollancz, 1943.

Tucker, Ruth A., and Walter Liefeld. *Daughters of the Church. Women and Ministry from New Testament Times to the Present.* Grand Rapids, Mich.: Zondervan, 1987.

Vogel, Heinrich. *Der Prediger von Buchenwald: Das Märtyrium Paul Schneiders.* Berlin: Lettner Verlag, 1953.

Wagner, Heintz. *Reinold von Thadden-Trieglaff: Ein Edelmann nach dem Herzen Gottes.* Giessen: Brunnen Verlag, 1969.

Waite, Robert G. L. *The Psychopathic God: Adolf Hitler.* New York: Basic Books, 1977.

Walsdorf, Hartmut, ed. *Warum ich Pfarrer wurde: Männer und Frauen erzählen von ihrem Weg ins Pfarramt.* Berlin: Wichern Verlag, 1988.

Wentorf, Rudolf. *Der Fall des Pfarrers Paul Schneider: Eine biographische Dokumentation.* Neukirchen-Vluyn: Neukirchener Verlag, 1989.

Wentscher Else. *Die Frau im Urteil grosser Männer.* Berlin-Tempelhof: Hans Bott Verlag, 1937.

Wiggershaus, Renate. *Frauen unterm Nationalsozialismus.* Wuppertal: Peter Hammer Verlag, 1984.

Williams, Wythe, with Albert Parry. *Riddle of the Reich.* New York: Prentice-Hall, 1941.

Wise, Robert. *The Pastors' Barracks.* Wheaton, Ill: Victor Books, 1986.

Zerbst, Fritz. *The Office of Woman in the Church—a Study in Practical Theology.* Trans. Albert G. Merkens. St. Louis, Mo.: Concordia, 1955.

Articles

"Als erste Frau im Rheinland ordiniert." *Der Weg* (Düsseldorf), 50, no. 85 (8 December 1985).

"Bekenntnisbewegung in Niedersachsen: Kritik an Frauenordination; Gegen eine falsche Religionstoleranz." *idea-spektrum* [sic]: *Nachrichten und Meinungen aus der evangelischen Welt* (Wetzlar: Informationsdienst der Evangelischen Allianz) no. 25 (1987):10.

Deutsch, Bernard S. "The Disenfranchisement of the Jew." In Pierre van

Paassen and James Waterman Wise, eds., *Nazism: An Assault on Civilization.* New York: Harrison Smith and Robert Haas, 1934, pp. 39-58.

"Dora von Öttingen." *Taunus Kurier* (Bad Homburg) 25 June, 1987.

"German Woman Slated to Give Trinity Sermon." *St. Petersburg Times* (Florida), 10 February 1951.

Hamilton, Alice. "The Enslavement of Women." In Pierre van Paassen and James Waterman Wise, eds., *Nazism: An Assault on Civilization.* New York: Harrison Smith and Robert Haas, 1934, pp. 76-87.

Henze, Dagmar. "Die Geschichte der evangelischen Theologin—Ein Überblick." In *Reformierte Kirchenzeitung,* March 1991, p. 98.

"'Herr, du weisst, dass ich dich liebhabe.' Abschied von Frau Ella Fischer (Saalfeld)." *Glaube und Heimat* (Jena) no. 41 (1978).

High, Stanley. "The War on Religious Freedom." In Pierre van Paassen and James Waterman Wise, eds., *Nazism: An Assault on Civilization.* New York: Harrison Smith and Robert Haas, 1934, pp. 25-38.

"Hört Vormarsch der Pfarrerinnen auf?" *idea-spektrum* [*sic*]: *Nachrichten und Meinungen aus der evangelischen Welt* (Wetzlar: Informations-dienst der Evangelischen Allianz) no. 25 (1985):p. 8.

"Immer mehr Frauen im evangelischen Pfarramt." *idea-spektrum* [*sic*]: *Nachrichten und Meinungen aus der evangelischen Welt* (Wetzlar: Informationsdienst der Evangelischen Allianz) no. 38 (1986):3.

"Junger Pfarrer legt Amt nieder. Viele Amtsbrüder haben resigniert." *idea-spektrum* [*sic*]: *Nachrichten und Meinungen aus der evangelischen Welt* (Wetzlar: Informationsdienst der Evangelischen Allianz) no. 9 (1986):11.

Leicher, Herbert. "Paul Schneider bleibt unvergessen. Der 'Prediger von Buchenwald' wäre heute 90 Jahre alt—Ein Hunsrück Pfarrer wird zum Bekenner. Die Witwe des Märtyrers ruft Jugend zum Glauben." *Rhein Zeitung* (Koblenz) no. 199 (29-30 August 1987).

Maser, Peter. "Vom Kampf der Bekennenden Kirche in den Ostgebieten." In Peter Hauptmann, ed., *Kirche im Osten. Studien zur osteuropäischen Kirchengeschichte und Kirchenkunde.* Göttingen: Vandenhoeck and Ruprecht, 1980.

Meseberg-Haubold, Ilse. "Frauenbiographien als Quelle zur Kirchengeschichte in der Zeit des Nationalsozialismus." In Wilhelm-Ludwig Federlin and Edmund Weber, eds., *Unterwegs für die Volkskirche. Festschrift für Dieter Stoodt zum 60. Geburtstag.* Frankfurt am Main: Verlag Peter Lang.

"Mission Services Open. Packed House Greets Corp. Hitler's Prisoner." *St. Petersburg Times* (Florida), 12 February 1951.

"Nein zur Frauenordination." *idea-spektrum* [*sic*]: *Nachrichten und Meinungen aus der evangelischen Welt* (Wetzlar: Informationsdienst der Evangelischen Allianz) no. 17 (1986):8.

"Niemöllers here: German Pastor Will Address Church Assembly." *St. Petersburg Times* (Florida), 8 February 1951.

"Niemoeller's Wife Speaks Tomorrow. *St. Petersburg Times* (Florida), 3 February 1951.

Öhme, Werner. "Frauen als Märtyrer der Bekennenden Kirche." *Standpunkt* no. 5 (May, 1985):16-17. Provenance of the journal is unknown, but was somewhere in what was then the German Democratic Republic.

Orlt, Gudrun. "Das Verbot eines bösen Menschen brachte erste Frau in die Gemeinde. Vor 50 Jahren wurde Pastorin Aenne Kaufmann ordiniert." *Der Weg* (Düsseldorf) no. 50 (December 89, 1985).

Pfisterer, Rudolf. "Ist das Alte Testament überflüssig? Die Deutschen Christen und die feministische Theologie." *idea spektrum* [*sic*]: *Nachrichten und Meinungen aus der evangelischen Welt* (Wetzlar: Informationsdienst der Evangelischen Allianz) no. 18 (1987).

Piotrowski, Christa. "Die Frage nach dem 'echten Christentum:' Die Kirchen und ihr Verhältnis zur Macht—Streitgespräch zwischen Altbischof Scharf und Kirchenkritiker Deschner." *Der Tagesspiegel* (Berlin), 14 January 1990, 14.

Quer, Gudrun. "Dietrich Bonhoeffer und die theologische Kandidatenausbildung der Bekennenden Kirche in Hinterpommern." In Manfred Vollack, ed., *Der Kreis Schlawe: Ein pommersches Heimatbuch.* Husum, 1986.

Rupp, Leila J. "Mother of the *Volk*: The Image of Women in Nazi Ideology." *Signs* (Chicago: University of Chicago Press), Winter 1977:362-79.

Sass, Gerhard, and Wolfgang Marzahn. "Kirchenkampf in Pommern." In *Pommersche Heimatkirche* (Hannover: Konvent Evangelischer Gemeinden aus Pommern, e.V.) 32, no 11 (1982):1.

Schileker, Anita. "'. . . and dat hett se nich secht!' Wahrenholzer Pastorenfrau sass 1943 in Wolfsburg im KZ." *Evangelische Zeitung* (Hannover), 13 March 1987, 6.

Thiel-Kaiser, Gerda, and Bettine von Clausewitz-Zwick, "Interview mit Aenne Kaufmann." *unterwegs* [*sic*], (Essen), January 1985. Based on an interview conducted in November 1984.

Radio/Television Scripts and Video

See, Wolfgang. "Schwestern im Bruderrat: Frauen der Bekennenden Kirche von Berlin-Brandenburg." Radio program. Edited by Manfred Rexin, broadcast 7 April 1984 as a part of RIAS Bildungsprogramm.

Sender Freies Berlin. "Frauen die nicht vergassen." Transcript of a six-part radio series (16 March-27 April 1989) on women in the Third Reich. Berlin: Freies Berlin, Haus des Rundfunks, Masurenallee 8-14.

Weber, Hartmut, and Leni Immer. "Und Sara zog mit." Bayrischer Rundfunk—Kirchenfunk—6 April 1986. Transcript of a radio program dealing with

the role of pastors' wives during the Hitler period.
Wheeler, Jake. "Jake Wheeler's Nightline," WBRA-TV (Channel 15),
    Lynchburg, Va., 28 Nov 1989. Lynchburg, Va: The Bagby Archive.

Index

About the Author

THEODORE N. THOMAS is Minister of the Silver Spring Church of Christ in Silver Spring, Maryland. He is a frequent university lecturer on the German Church Struggle.

ISBN 0-275-94619-3

HARDCOVER BAR CODE